'A ton of people have been waiting for this book ...' ow it! Brian has given us a clear and con path together, around the table, in the l and growing. This book is going to hel
  — Rob Bell, author of *What We* God

'This is one of the most remarkabl ..... in recent Christian writings . . . There is no evangelizing here, and no preaching, only a sinewy, but orderly and open, presentation of the faith that holds. The result is as startling as it is beautiful.'
  — Phyllis Tickle, author of *The Age of the Spirit*

'It is at once inspiring and challenging, ancient and contemporary, intellectually rigorous and profoundly practical. It changed the way I engage Scripture, the way I pray, the way I experience communion, and the way I interact with my neighbours.'
  — Rachel Held Evans, author of *A Year of Biblical Womanhood*

'This is Brian McLaren at his best, and I think this is what so many readers want from him: Deeply rooted in scripture, yet offering fresh, even radical, readings. *We Make the Road by Walking* will surely be a benefit and blessing to many.'
  — Tony Jones, theologian-in-residence at Solomon's Porch, author of *The Church Is Flat*

'I love this book, because through each page you will hear the whisper of Jesus echo in your heart. You will find yourself taken on a journey that will make you more alive, more loving, and with a bigger vision for changing the world. I'm buying copies for all my friends!'
  — Canon Mark Russell, CEO, Church Army UK and Ireland

'We've used this deep and thought-provoking book in our church plant in Washington DC, and each week we are invited to consider long-familiar biblical texts in a new light. Perfect for individual or group use.'
  — Bryan Berghoef, author of *Pub Theology* and pastor of Roots DC, an urban faith community in Washington, DC

'Around the table in my home, our small, diverse faith community used this book as our guide back to connection, to hope, to aliveness and ultimately to a way forward in our spiritual journeys, both individually and corporately.'
  — Sarah Dammann Thomas, leader of a faith community in her home in Santa Barbara, CA

Also by Brian D. McLaren

WE MAKE THE ROAD BY WALKING

A Year-Long Quest for Spiritual Formation, Reorientation and Activation

BRIAN D. MCLAREN

HODDER &
STOUGHTON

First published in Great Britain in 2014 by Hodder & Stoughton
An Hachette UK company

3

Copyright © Brian D. McLaren, 2014

The right of Brian D. McLaren to be identified as the Author of the Work has been asserted
by him in accordance with the Copyright, Designs and Patents Act 1988.

A CIP catalogue record for this title is available from the British Library

ISBN 978 1 444 70370 2
eBook ISBN 978 1 444 78594 4

Typeset in Sabon by Hewer Text UK Ltd, Edinburgh
Printed and bound in the UK by CPI Group (UK) Ltd, Croydon CR0 4YY

Hodder & Stoughton policy is to use papers that are natural, renewable and recyclable products
and made from wood grown in sustainable forests. The logging and manufacturing processes
are expected to conform to the environmental regulations of the country of origin.

Hodder & Stoughton Ltd
338 Euston Road
London NW1 3BH

www.hodderfaith.com

Contents

FOUR: **Alive in the Spirit of God**

What this Book Is About and How to Use It

You are not finished yet. You are 'in the making'. You have the capacity to learn, mature, think, change and grow. You also have the freedom to stagnate, regress, constrict and lose your way. Which road will you take?

What's true of you is also true for every community of people, including our spiritual communities. Like the individuals who constitute them, they are unfinished and 'in the making'. They have the capacity to move forward if they choose . . . and the freedom to stagnate and regress. Which road will they follow in the years ahead? Does their future depend solely on the action or inaction of officials in the headquarters of religious bureaucracies? Do the rest of us have to wait until somebody somewhere figures things out and tells the rest of us what to do?

I believe that all of us play a role in choosing and creating our futures – as individuals and as communities. We don't need to wait passively for history to happen to us. We can become protagonists in our own story. We can make the road by walking.

Growing numbers of us believe that we are in the early stages of a new moment of emergence, pulsing with danger and promise. In this catalytic period, all our spiritual traditions will be challenged and all will change – some negatively and reactively, tightening like angry fists, and others positively and constructively, opening like extended arms.[1] More and more of us want to participate in that positive and constructive opening. We want to explore new possibilities, to develop unfulfilled potential, to discover new resources to bless, inspire and enliven. We don't shrink back from this moment; we feel God is calling us to walk into it with faith, hope and love.

I've written *We Make the Road by Walking* to help individuals and groups seize this moment and walk wisely and joyfully into the future together. It is a work of Christian theology, but people of any faith tradition will find seeds of meaning they can let take root in their own spiritual soil. It is a work of *constructive* theology – offering a positive, practical, open, faithful, improvable and fresh articulation of Christian faith suitable for people in our dynamic times. It is also a work of *public* and *practical* theology – theology that is worked out by 'normal' people in daily life.

The title suggests that faith was never intended to be a destination, a status, a holding tank or a warehouse.[2] Instead, it was

---

1 For a variety of perspectives on this pivotal moment, see relevant works by Ewert Cousins, Phyllis Tickle, Diana Butler Bass, Philip Clayton, Leonardo Boff, Doug Pagitt, Soong-Chan Rah, Tony Jones, Harvey Cox, Robin Meyers, Marcus Borg, David Felten, Jeff Procter-Murphy, Jack Spong, Richard Rohr, Rob Bell, Lillian Daniel, Elaine Heath and Joan Chittister.

2 I originally heard 'We make the road by walking' as a quote from one of my heroes, Brazilian educator/activist Paulo Freire. I later learned that it became the title of a book that was a dialogue between Freire and another seminal educator/activist, Myles Horton, who was an important

to be a road, a path, a way out of old and destructive patterns into new and creative ones. As a road or way, it is always being extended into the future. If a spiritual community only points back to where it has been or if it only digs in its heels where it is now, it is a dead end or a car park, not a way. To be a living tradition, a living way, it must forever open itself forward and forever remain unfinished – even as it forever cherishes and learns from the growing treasury of its past.

The simplest way for you to use this book is to read it as you would any other. At the beginning of each chapter, you'll find a few Bible passages that you can read in any responsible translation such as the New Revised Standard Version or the Common English Bible. Your enjoyment of the chapter will be enriched if you take the time to read those passages. The chapter itself offers a response to those passages. Of course, the line of interpretation and application I have chosen is one of many possible responses to each text. At times, it may differ from the interpretation you have heard in the past; you are asked only to give it an honest and open hearing, and you should feel free to prefer another interpretation. At the end of each chapter you'll find some 'Engage' questions that you can either skip, ponder for a few minutes on your own, or perhaps respond to in a private journal or public blog.

After reading a few chapters, you may decide to recommend the book to a few friends. Then you could invite your circle of friends to gather in your living room or around your kitchen table.[3] Guided by the liturgical resources in Appendix I, your

---

figure in the civil rights movement in the United States. Freire may have derived the quote from the great Spanish poet Antonio Machado (1875–1939): '*Caminante, son tus huellas / el camino, y nada más; / caminante, no hay camino, / se hace camino al andar. / Al andar se hace camino, / y al volver la vista atrás / se ve la senda que nunca / se ha de volver a pisar. / Caminante, no hay camino, / sino estelas en la mar.*'

3   I could imagine learning circles using this book in a college hall of residence or church basement, in a prison or residential care home, in a school

learning circle could pray together, then read the Bible passages and the chapter, then enjoy conversation using the 'Engage' questions, and then conclude with more resources from Appendix I, including the simplified eucharistic liturgy if appropriate.[4]

Denominational leaders could encourage pastors under their care to take a year or season out of their normal church rhythms and use this book in public worship.[5] Or they could use it in adult education classes or in small groups in homes. Four or five churches from different ethnic groups, denominational backgrounds and social classes could send two or three people from each church to form a combined multichurch learning circle. Their learning would be enriched by a diversity their home churches may not have. They would bring this enrichment back to their home congregations, while strengthening ties among the participating congregations.

The fifty-two-plus chapters are organised in four seasonal quarters, following a simplified version of the traditional church year that is built around Advent, Epiphany, Lent, Holy Week, Easter and Pentecost. I've chosen to begin in September with a pre-Advent overview of the Hebrew Scriptures. But a year-long

cafeteria or coffee shop, at a retreat centre or summer camp, on a hiking trail or before a yoga class, on a beach or in a video chat.

4 By *liturgy* I mean a format of a gathering – written or unwritten – that orders a series of practices, like prayer, thanksgiving, silent meditation, a sermon and singing. By *Eucharist* I mean the Christian practice of using bread and wine to remember Jesus.

5 Many churches already use the Revised Common Lectionary (RCL), a plan that assigns certain Bible passages to be read each Sunday over a four-year cycle. I appreciate and enjoy the RCL. However, it assumes significant familiarity with the Bible and with a generous Christian vision that many do not yet have. Other churches have no intentional plan for introducing people to the Bible or a generous Christian faith. For both groups of churches, *We Make the Road by Walking* offers a comprehensive orientation (or reorientation) to Christian living – a kind of on-ramp, if you will, for both 'new' and 'used' Christians.

group could start at any appropriate point in the church year and work its way around the cycle. Several groups have already field-tested the book in a variety of ways, and their responses have been highly enthusiastic. You can make this book work for you by adapting it as needed.

The road of faith is not finished. There is beautiful land ahead, *terra nova* waiting to be explored. It will take a lot of us, journeying together, to make the road. I hope you'll be part of the adventure. The Christian faith is still learning, growing and changing, and so are we.

Note: In addition to the resources included here in Appendices I and II, you will find a variety of resources and links at my website (www.brianmclaren.net), including commentary on each chapter, Scripture references, suggestions for using the book in weekend and week-long formats, suggestions for daily times of prayer and reflection, and more.[6]

---

6 Most Bible passages quoted in the text are from the New Revised Standard Version. Some are the author's paraphrase. The Contemporary English Bible (CEB) and New American Standard Bible (NASB) are cited when quoted.

Seeking Aliveness

Philippians 3:12–14

Not that I have already obtained this or have already reached the goal; but I press on . . . this one thing I do: forgetting what lies behind and straining forward to what lies ahead, I press on . . .

What we all want is pretty simple, really. We want to be alive. To feel alive. Not just to exist but to thrive, to live out loud, walk tall, breathe free. We want to be less lonely, less exhausted, less conflicted or afraid . . . more awake, more grateful, more energised and purposeful. We capture this kind of mindful, overbrimming life in terms like *well-being, shalom, blessedness, wholeness, harmony, life to the full* and *aliveness*.[7]

---

7 *Zoein aionian*, a Greek term in the New Testament, is often translated to English as 'eternal life'. Sadly, that translation suggests 'life after death' to most people and is equated with going to heaven rather than hell. The term means, literally, 'life of the ages' (*zoe*, as in *zoology*; *aionian*, of the *aeons*). It should be understood in contrast to 'life in this present age', which could in turn be rendered 'life in this economy' or 'life in contemporary culture' or 'life under the current regime'. My suspicion is that 'true aliveness' is a good contemporary translation of the term. Luke (18:18–24) uses *zoein aionian* as a synonym for *kingdom of God*, and in the Gospel of John, *kingdom of God* seems to be rendered as *life, eternal life*

The quest for aliveness explains so much of what we do. It's why readers read and travellers travel. It's why lovers love and thinkers think, why dancers dance and filmgoers watch. In the quest for aliveness, chefs cook, foodies eat, farmers plough, drummers riff, fly-fishers cast, runners run and photographers shoot.

The quest for aliveness is the best thing about religion, I think. It's what we're hoping for when we pray. It's why we gather, celebrate, eat, abstain, attend, practise, sing and contemplate. When people say, 'I'm spiritual,' what they mean, I think, is simple: 'I'm seeking aliveness.'

Many older religious people – Christians, Muslims, Jews and others – are paralysed by sadness that their children and grandchildren are far from faith, religion and God as they understand them. But on some level, they realise that religion too often shrinks, starves, cages and freezes aliveness rather than fostering it. They are beginning to see that the only viable future for religion is to become a friend of aliveness again.

Meanwhile, aliveness itself is under threat at every turn. We have created an economic system that is not only too big to fail, it is too big to control – and perhaps too big to understand as well. This system disproportionately benefits the most powerful and privileged 1 per cent of the human species, bestowing upon them unprecedented comfort, security and luxury. To do so, it destabilises the climate, plunders the planet and kills off other forms of life at unprecedented rates.

The rest, especially the poorest third at the bottom, gain little and lose much as this economic pyramid grows taller and taller. One of their greatest losses is democracy, as those at the top find

---

and *life to the full*. In Paul's writings, terms like *fullness*, *freedom*, *new life*, *life in the Spirit* and *life in Christ* seem closely related if not synonymous. All point to an excelling quality, intensity, expansiveness, meaningfulness, fruitfulness and depth of life.

clever ways to buy votes, turning elected governments into their puppets. Under these circumstances, you would think that at least those at the top would experience aliveness. But they don't. They bend under constant anxiety and pressure to produce, earn, compete, maintain, protect, hoard and consume more and more, faster and faster. They lose the connection and well-being that come from seeking the common good. This is not an economy of aliveness for anyone.

As these tensions mount, we wake up every morning wondering what fool or fiend will be the next to throw a lit match – or assault, nuclear, chemical or biological weapon – onto the dry tinder of resentment and fear. Again, this is a formula for death, not a recipe for life.

So our world truly needs a global spiritual movement dedicated to aliveness. This movement must be *global*, because the threats we face cannot be contained by national borders. It must be *spiritual*, because the threats we face go deeper than brain-level politics and economics to the heart level of value and meaning. It must be *social*, because it can't be imposed from above; it can only spread from person to person, friend to friend, family to family, network to network. And it must be a *movement*, because by definition, movements stir and focus grass-roots human desire to bring change to institutions and the societies those institutions are intended to serve.

I believe that the Spirit of God works everywhere to bring and restore aliveness – through individuals, communities, institutions and movements. Movements play a special role. In the biblical story, for example, Moses led a movement of liberation among oppressed slaves. They left an oppressive economy, journeyed through the wilderness and entered a promised land where they hoped to pursue aliveness in freedom and peace. Centuries after that, the Hebrew prophets launched a series of movements based on a dream of a promised time . . . a time of justice when swords and spears, instruments of death, would be turned into ploughshares and pruning hooks, instruments of aliveness. Then came John the Baptist, a bold and non-violent movement leader who dared to challenge the establishment of his day and call people to a movement of radical social and spiritual rethinking.

John told people he was not the leader they had been waiting for; he was simply preparing the way for someone greater than himself. When a young man named Jesus came to affiliate with John's movement through baptism, John said, 'There he is! He is the one!' Under Jesus' leadership, the movement grew and expanded in unprecedented ways. When Jesus was murdered by the powers that profited from the status quo, the movement didn't die. It rose again through a new generation of leaders like James, Peter, John and Paul, who were full of the Spirit of Jesus. They created learning circles in which activists were trained to extend the movement locally, regionally and globally. Wherever activists in this movement went, the Spirit of Jesus was alive in them, fomenting change and inspiring true aliveness.

Sometimes institutions welcomed this non-violent spiritual movement and were strengthened by it. Sometimes they co-opted, smothered, squelched, frustrated, corrupted or betrayed it. If the movement slowed, receded or weakened for a while in one place, eventually it resurged again in some new form. For example, there were the monastic movements led by the desert mothers and fathers, the Celtic movement led by St Patrick, St Brigid and others, and the beautiful movements of St Francis and St Clare. Later reform movements grew up around people like Menno Simons, Martin Luther, John Wesley and Walter Rauschenbusch. Over the last century, we've seen new movements being born through people like Dorothy Day, Ella Baker, Martin Luther King, Desmond Tutu, Wangari Maathai, Óscar Romero, Rene Padilla, Richard Twiss, Joan Chittister, Jim Wallis, Tony

Campolo, Richard Rohr, Phyllis Tickle, William Barber, John Dear, Steve Chalke and Shane Claiborne.

And of course, just as the Spirit has moved among Christians, the Spirit has been at work in other communities, too. Too seldom have these diverse movements recognised their common inspiration, and too seldom have they collaborated as they should. It's surely time for that to change.

This book is a resource for this emerging spiritual movement in service of aliveness. It is written primarily for use in Christian communities, but it excludes no one. (I can imagine parallel books being written primarily for Jews, Muslims and others.) As I explained in the Preface, you can read it as you are reading now, a personal resource for your own thinking and rethinking. But you can also use the book to form a learning circle, as Appendix I explains, creating a community for spiritual formation, reorientation and activation.

There's an old religious word for this kind of learning experience: *catechesis* (cat-uh-*key*-sis). At first glance, catechesis hardly seems like a resource for aliveness and movement building. To most people, it evokes either nothing at all or the unpleasant aroma of dust and mould. For those of us raised in highly religious households, it may bring to mind boring classes taught by stern nuns or lay teachers where we memorised answers we didn't understand to questions we didn't care about for reasons we never knew. It suggests pacifying, indoctrinating and domesticating people for institutional conformity.

But before Christianity was a rich and powerful religion, before it was associated with buildings, budgets, crusades, colonialism or televangelism, it began as a revolutionary non-violent movement promoting a new kind of aliveness on the margins of society. It dared to honour women, children and unmarried adults in a world ruled by married men. It dared to elevate slaves to equality with those who gave them orders. It challenged slave masters to free their slaves and see them as peers. It defied religious taboos that divided people into us and them, in and out, good and evil, clean and unclean.

It claimed that everyone, not just an elite few, had God-given gifts to use for the common good. It exposed a system based on domination, privilege and violence and proclaimed in its place a vision of mutual service, mutual responsibility and peaceable neighbourliness. It put people above profit, and made the audacious claim that the Earth belonged not to rich tycoons or powerful politicians, but to the Creator who loves every sparrow in the trees and every wildflower in the field. It was a peace movement, a love movement, a joy movement, a justice movement, an integrity movement, an aliveness movement.

It had no bank accounts, but was rich in relationships and joy. It had no elaborate hierarchy and organisation, but spread like wildfire through simple practices of empowerment and self-organisation. It had no colleges, but it was constantly training new waves of courageous and committed leaders through the 'each one teach one' strategy of catechesis. It had lots of problems, too, but it grappled with those problems courageously.

In this light, catechesis was a subversive practice of movement building. It was a 'people's college', transforming any room, campfire or shady spot beneath a tree into a movement school. It equipped the oppressed and oppressors to become partners and protagonists in their mutual liberation. Mentors (or *catechists*) would invite a student or students (*catechumens*) to meet regularly. They used a simple curriculum (or *catechesis*) of meaningful stories, healing teachings and transformative practices. Their course of preparation traditionally culminated in a kind of oral examination based on a series of predetermined questions (a *catechism*). Those who had been mentored through this process would then be ready to pass on what they had learned. In so doing, they would learn the catechism more deeply, since teaching is surely the best way to learn.

The subversive nature of catechesis was all the more remarkable because many of the teachers and students were illiterate. It was through the personal give-and-take of face-to-face conversation and interaction that people were formed and transformed, equipped and deployed as non-violent activists in the movement of the Spirit.

In the second century, catechesis became more formalised as a preparation for baptism. Through a rigorous and long process, catechists helped catechumens understand core teachings and adopt virtuous behaviour. Catechumens would be examined and passed on from one stage, or level, of discipleship to the next before they would be accepted for baptism and full participation in the Christian community. Catechesis became less an orientation to participate in a movement and more a requirement for membership in an institution.

As churches began baptising infants, and as persecution gave way to political and social privilege for baptised Christians, catechesis became less important. From time to time it was reinvigorated to counter spiritual lukewarmness and ignorance. During regular church services, priests would teach or remind parishioners about the basics of the faith – often centred on the Lord's Prayer, the Apostles' Creed and the Ten Commandments. For a time in the Middle Ages, communities even developed summer drama festivals during which they acted out stories from the Bible in their historical sequence – an especially helpful practice when most people were illiterate and confused by a complex church calendar over-full of saints' days. As early as the ninth century, question-and-answer formats came into use to prepare children for their first communion.

Catechesis had a resurgence about five hundred years ago. Martin Luther designed a catechism to help a head of household train or retrain family members in the emerging Protestant faith using simple questions and answers.[8] A young leader named John Calvin also published a catechism that served as a foyer or an entryway into an intricate doctrinal system he was constructing.[9] John Wesley came along two centuries later. In many ways, he rediscovered the original power of catechesis as a movement school. He encouraged people to self-organise into small learning cohorts called classes and bands that gathered for spiritual formation, reorientation and activation. He published his sermons to help resource these groups. And to make his movement's essential vision available to children, he published a catechism-like book called *Instructions for Children*.[10]

---

8   The preface to Luther's *Small Catechism* begins with Luther's characteristic rhetorical energy:

'Martin Luther to All Faithful and Godly Pastors and Preachers: Grace, Mercy, and Peace in Jesus Christ, our Lord. The deplorable, miserable condition which I discovered lately when I, too, was a visitor, has forced and urged me to prepare [publish] this Catechism, or Christian doctrine, in this small, plain, simple form. Mercy! Good God! what manifold misery I beheld! The common people, especially in the villages, have no knowledge whatever of Christian doctrine, and, alas! many pastors are altogether incapable and incompetent to teach [so much so, that one is ashamed to speak of it]. Nevertheless, all maintain that they are Christians, have been baptized and receive the [common] holy Sacraments. Yet they [*do not* understand and] cannot [*even*] recite either the Lord's Prayer, or the Creed, or the Ten Commandments; they live like dumb brutes and irrational hogs; and yet, now that the Gospel has come, they have nicely learned to abuse all liberty like experts.' (http://bookofconcord.org/smallcatechism. php#preface)

9   Calvin's first version was published in 1537, was revised in the mid-1540s, and was revised again in 1560.

10   *Instructions for Children* was first published in 1745. Wesley also wrote a revision of the Westminster Shorter Catechism. The Shorter Catechism had been adopted by the Church of England in 1648. It was strongly Calvinistic, or deterministic, in its tone, and Wesley's revisions just over a century later (1753) show where his vision of the faith differed from the Calvinistic vision of his forebears.

These examples from history have helped give shape to the fifty-two (plus a few) chapters that follow.

Based on their format, some might wonder if I'm recommending learning circles gathered around *We Make the Road by Walking* as an alternative to traditional churches.

My first answer is a firm no. Wherever possible, I would hope that these simple learning circles would be supplemental to participation in a traditional congregation and denomination (as were the early monastic and Methodist movements within Catholicism and Anglicanism). In fact, I would be thrilled for pastors in traditional congregations to use these fifty-two-plus sermons, along with the accompanying simple liturgy and Bible reading plan, as a year-long template for spiritual formation, reorientation and activation in traditional church settings.[11]

But this won't always be possible, so my second answer is maybe yes. I hope that *We Make the Road by Walking* will facilitate the spontaneous formation of grass-roots learning circles that can bring together people who don't feel welcome or wanted in conventional churches. I would discourage these self-organising groups from using the word *church* to describe what they're doing – at least initially. A lot of unintended pressure, baggage, expectation, criticism and complications can come along with that word.[12] Eventually, spontaneously formed learning circles

---

11 Having spent over twenty years as a pastor, I think it's good for pastors to prepare original sermons each week. But I also know that periodically, it can be good for a pastor to use prepared sermons like the ones in this book, either for a season or a whole year. During that time, a pastor could take the time and energy normally invested in sermon preparation and use it for some other generative purpose – physical recreation, engagement with the poor, a writing project, an artistic pursuit, outreach to the community, civic engagement, interfaith work, marriage enrichment, parenting time, or good, old-fashioned fun and rest.

12 For example, a 'church' that does enormous good for five years and then shuts down is seen as a failure, whereas many congregations survive

may find existing congregations or denominations that will welcome them. Maybe they will eventually choose to use the word *church* to name what they have become. In the spiritual life, as in all of life, it's better to have the substance without the label than the label without the substance.[13]

If you're a seeker exploring Christian faith, or if you're new to the faith and seeking a good orientation, here you'll find the introduction I wish I had been given. If you're a long-term Christian whose current form of Christianity has stopped working and may even be causing you and others harm, here you'll find a reorientation from a fresh and healthy perspective.[14] If your faith seems to be a lot of talk without much practice, I hope this book will help you translate your faith to action. And if you're a parent trying to figure out what you should teach your children and grandchildren – knowing you want to introduce them to a kind of Christian faith, but not exactly the version you were given – I hope this book will fit the need.[15]

Right now I'm imagining a couple of each of you, gathered around a table filled with brimming glasses and plates of flavourful foods. You're all engaged in animated conversation, telling jokes, sharing stories about your experiences since you last

for decades while actually accomplishing little. For some reason, longevity becomes a requirement for many people when the word *church* is applied.

13 It is my hope that denominations will create special protected zones for learning circles and other innovative faith communities, zones where fresh expressions of Christian spirituality, community and mission can experiment and flourish without being subjected to normal protocols and expectations. In a sense, denominations can understand themselves to be entering into 'new lines of business' by fostering new faith communities in this experimental space.

14 For the theologically informed, I've created a resource that provides commentary on each chapter, explaining what I did and why. You can learn more about it at www.brianmclaren.net.

15 The 'Engage' questions and liturgical resources in Appendix I encourage adults to include children in learning circles whenever possible.

gathered. Partway through your meal, someone says, 'The Living God is with us!' and everyone else responds, 'And with all creation!' And then someone begins to read.

PART 1

ALIVE IN THE STORY OF CREATION

You are entering a story already in process. All around you, things are happening, unfolding, ending, beginning, dying, being born. Our ancient ancestors tried to discern what was going on. They conveyed their best wisdom to future generations through stories that answered certain key questions:

Why are we here?

What's wrong with the world?

What's our role, our task, our purpose?

What is a good life?

Is there meaning and hope?

What dangers should we guard against?

What treasures should we seek?

From the Hopi to the Babylonians, from Aztecs to Australian Aboriginals, from the Vikings in Europe to the Han in China to the Yoruba in Africa to the ancient Hebrews of the Middle East – human tribes have developed, adapted and told powerful creation narratives to convey their best answers to key questions like these. Of course, their language often sounds strange to us, their assumptions foreign, the details of their culture odd or alien. But if we listen carefully, mixing their ancient wisdom with our own, we can let their stories live on in us. We can learn to be more fully alive in our time, just as they learned in theirs. In that spirit, we turn to the creation narratives of the ancient Hebrews.

For learning circles, Part 1 would most naturally be used during the thirteen weeks before Advent. In the traditional church calendar, this is during Ordinary Time, the season after Pentecost. For many, it coincides with the beginning of the school year in late August or early September. Be sure to review the Five Guidelines for Learning Circles in Appendix II at your first few gatherings.

CHAPTER 1

Awe and Wonder

Genesis 1:1 – 2:3
Psalm 19

The heavens are telling the glory of God.

Matthew 6:25–34

Big bangs aren't boring. Dinosaurs aren't boring. Coral reefs aren't boring. Elephants aren't boring. Hummingbirds aren't boring. And neither are little children. Evolution isn't boring. Magnetism and electricity aren't boring. $E=MC^2$ might be hard to understand, but it certainly isn't boring. And even glaciers aren't boring, although their dramatic pace is at first quite hard for us to perceive. And God, whatever God is, must not be boring either, because God's creation is so amazingly, wonderfully, surprisingly fascinating.

The first and greatest surprise – a miracle, really – is this: that anything exists at all, and that we get to be part of it. Ripe peach, crisp apple, tall mountain, bright leaves, sparkling water, flying flock, flickering flame, and you and me . . . here, now!

On this, the first pages of the Bible and the best thinking of today's scientists are in full agreement: it all began in the beginning, when space and time, energy and matter, gravity and light, burst or bloomed or banged into being. In light of the Genesis story, we would say that the possibility of this universe overflowed into actuality as God, the Creative Spirit, uttered the original joyful invitation: *Let it be!* And in response, what happened? Light. Time. Space. Matter. Motion. Sea. Stone. Fish. Sparrow. You. Me. Enjoying the unspeakable gift and privilege of being here, being alive.

Imagine how uncountable nucleii and electrons and sister particles danced and whirled. Imagine how space dust coalesced into clouds, and how clouds coalesced into galaxies, and how galaxies began to spin, sail and dance through space. Imagine how in galaxy after galaxy, suns blazed, solar systems twirled and worlds formed. Around some of those worlds, moons spun, and upon some of those worlds, storms swirled, seas formed and waves rolled. And somewhere in between the smallest particles and the largest cosmic structures, here we are, in this galaxy, in this solar system, on this planet, in this story, around this table, at this moment – with this chance for us to breathe, think, dream, speak and be alive together.

The Creator brought it all into being and now, some 14 billion years later, here we find ourselves: dancers in this beautiful, mysterious choreography that expands and evolves and includes us all. We're farmers and engineers, parents and students, theologians and scientists, teachers and shopkeepers, builders and fixers, drivers and doctors, dads and mums, wise grandparents and wide-eyed infants.

Don't we all feel like poets when we try to speak of the beauty and wonder of this creation? Don't we share a common amazement about our cosmic neighbourhood when we wake up to the fact that we're actually here, actually alive, right now?

Some theologians and mystics speak of the Creator withdrawing or contracting to make space for the universe to be . . . on its own, so to speak, so that it has its own life, its own being and history. Others imagine God creating the universe within God's self, so the universe in some way is contained 'in' God, within God's presence, part of God's own life and story. Still others imagine God creating an 'out there' of space and time, and then filling it with galaxies, and then inhabiting it like a song fills a forest or light fills a room or love fills a heart. Interestingly, some scholars believe the Genesis story echoes ancient Middle Eastern temple dedication texts. But in this story, the whole universe is the temple, and the Creator chooses to be represented by human beings, not a stone idol.

The romance of Creator and creation is far more wonderful and profound than anyone can ever capture in words. And yet we try, for how could we be silent in the presence of such beauty, glory, wonder and mystery? How can we not celebrate this great gift – to be alive?

To be alive is to look up at the stars on a dark night and to feel the beyond-words awe of space in its vastness. To be alive is to look down from a mountaintop on a bright, clear day and to feel the wonder that can only be expressed in 'Oh!' or 'Wow!' or maybe 'Hallelujah!' To be alive is to look out from the beach towards the horizon at sunrise or sunset and to savour the joy of it all in pregnant, saturated silence. To be alive is to gaze in delight at a single bird, tree, leaf or friend, and to feel that they whisper of a creator or source we all share.

Genesis means 'beginnings'. It speaks through deep, multilayered poetry and wild, ancient stories. The poetry and stories of Genesis reveal deep truths that can help us be more fully alive today. They dare to proclaim that the universe is God's self-expression, God's speech act. That means that everything every-where is always essentially holy, spiritual, valuable, meaningful. All matter matters.

If you ask what language the Creator speaks, the best answer is this: God's first language is full-spectrum light, clear water, deep sky, red squirrel, blue whale, grey parrot, green lizard, golden aspen, orange mango, yellow warbler, laughing child, rolling river, serene forest, churning storm, spinning planet.

A psalmist said the same thing in another way – the universe is God's work of art, God's handiwork. All created things speak or sing of the God who made them. If you want to know what the Original Artist is like, a smart place to start would be to enjoy the art of creation.

Genesis tells us that the universe is good – a truth so important it gets repeated like the theme of a song. Rocks are good. Clouds are good. Sweet corn is good. Every river or hill or valley or forest is good. Skin? Good. Bone? Good. Mating and eating and breathing and giving birth and growing old? Good, good, good. All are good. Life is good.

The best thing in Genesis is not simply human beings, but the whole creation considered and enjoyed together, as a beautiful, integrated whole, and us a part. The poetry of Genesis describes the 'very goodness' that comes at the end of a long process of creation ... when all the parts, including us, are working together as one whole. That harmonious whole is so good that the Creator takes a day off, as it were, just to enjoy it. That day of restful enjoyment tells us that the purpose of existence isn't money or power or fame or security or anything less than this: to participate in the goodness and beauty and aliveness of creation. And so we join the Creator in good and fruitful work ... and in delightful enjoyment, play and rest as well.

So here we are, friends. Here we are. Alive!

And this is why we walk this road: to behold the wonder and savour this aliveness. To remind ourselves who we are, where we are, what's going on here, and how beautiful, precious, holy and meaningful it all is. It's why we pause along the journey for a simple meal, with hearts full of thankfulness, rejoicing to be part of this beautiful and good creation. This is what it means to be alive. Amen.

Engage

1. What one thought or idea from today's lesson especially intrigued, provoked, disturbed, challenged, encouraged, warmed, warned, helped or surprised you?

2. Share a story about a time when you most felt the humble awe and joyful wonder described in this chapter.

3. What is the most beautiful place you have ever seen? What was so special about it?

4. For children: What is your favourite animal? Why do you like it so much?

5. Activate: This week, choose one facet of creation that you love – birds, trees, weather, soil, water, light, children, sex, ageing, sleep. Observe it, think about it, learn about it at every chance you can, with this question in mind: If that element of creation were your only Bible, what would it tell you about God?

6. Meditate: Observe a few moments of silence. Let a silent prayer of gratitude arise from within you.

CHAPTER 2

Being Human

Genesis 2:4–25

Psalm 8

When I look at your heavens, the work of your fingers, . . . what are human beings that you are mindful of them?

Mark 3:1–6

Two eyes are better than one, because they make depth perception possible. The same goes with ears. Two ears make it possible to locate the direction of a sound. And we often say that two heads are better than one, because we know that insight from multiple perspectives adds wisdom.

The same is true with stories. We can best think of the Bible not as one tidy story with many chapters, but as a wild and fascinating library with many stories told from many perspectives. On any given subject, these multiple stories challenge us to see life from a variety of angles – adding depth, a sense of direction and wisdom. So, we're given four Gospels to introduce us to Jesus. We're given dozens of parables to illustrate Jesus' message. We're given two sections or Testaments in which the story of God unfolds. And right at the beginning, we're given two different creation stories to help us know who we are, where we came from and why we're here.

According to the first creation story, you are part of creation. You are made from common soil . . . *dust*, Genesis says; *stardust*, astronomers tell us . . . soil that becomes watermelons and grain and apples and peanuts, and then they become food, and then that food becomes you. As highly organised dust, you are closely related to frogs and tortoises, lions and fieldmice, bison and elephants and gorillas. Together with all living things, you share the breath of life, participating in the same cycles of birth and death, reproduction and recycling and renewal. You, with them, are part of the story of creation – different branches on the tree of life. In that story, you are connected and related to everything everywhere. In fact, that is a good partial definition of God: *God is the one through whom we are related and connected to everything.*

In the first creation story, we learn two essential truths about ourselves as human beings. First, *we are good*. Along with all our fellow creatures, we were created with a primal, essential goodness that our Creator appreciates and celebrates. And second, *we all bear God's image*. Women and men, girls and boys, toddlers, the elderly and teenagers, rich or poor, popular or misunderstood, powerful or vulnerable, whatever our religion or race or marital status, whatever our nationality or culture . . . we *all* bear God's image, no exceptions.

What is the image of God? An image is a small imitation or echo, like a reflection in a mirror. So if we bear the image of God, then like God, we experience life through relationships. Like God, we experience love through our complementary differences. Like God, we notice and enjoy and name things – starting with the animals, our companions on the Earth. Like God, we are caretakers of the garden of the Earth. And like God, we are 'naked and not ashamed', meaning we can be who we are without fear.

Back in ancient times, this was a surprising message. Yes,

kings and other powerful men were seen as image-bearers of God. After all, since they were powerful, rich, sophisticated and 'civilised', they could reflect God's power and glory. But in Genesis, the term is applied to a couple of naked and 'uncivilised' hunter-gatherers, a simple woman and man living in a garden with no pyramids or skyscrapers or economies or religions or technological inventions or even clothing to their credit! Centuries later, Jesus said something similar: the Creator loves every sparrow and every wildflower, and so how much more precious is every person – no matter how small, frail or seemingly insignificant? Every woman, man and child is good! Every person in every culture has value! Every person bears the image of God! It's all good!

But that's not the only story. The second creation account, which many scholars think is a much older one, describes another dimension to our identity. In that account, the possibility of 'not good' also exists. God puts the first couple in a garden that contains two special trees. The Tree of Life is theirs to enjoy, but not the Tree of the Knowledge of Good and Evil. The Tree of Life is a beautiful image – suggesting health, strength, thriving, fruitfulness, growth, vigour and all we mean by *aliveness*. What might that second tree signify?

There are many answers, no doubt. But consider this possibility: the second tree could represent the desire to play God and judge parts of God's creation – all of which God considers good – as evil. Do you see the danger? God's judging is always wise, fair, true, merciful and restorative. But our judging is frequently ignorant, biased, retaliatory and devaluing. So when we judge, we inevitably *mis*judge.

If we humans start playing God and judging good and evil, how long will it take before we say this person or tribe is good and deserves to live, but that person or tribe is evil and deserves to die, or become our slaves? How long will it take before we judge that this species of animal is good and deserves to survive, but that one is worthless and can be driven to extinction? How long until we judge that this land is good and deserves to be preserved, but that river is without value and can be plundered, polluted or poisoned?

If we eat from the second tree, we will soon become violent, hateful and destructive. We will turn our blessing to name and know into a licence to kill, to exploit and to destroy both the Earth and other people. God sees everything as good, but we will accuse more and more things of being evil. In so doing, we will create in ourselves the very evil we claim to detect in others. In other words, the more we judge and accuse, the less we will reflect God . . . and the less we will fulfil our potential as image-bearers of God.

So the second creation story presents us with our challenge as human beings. We constantly make a crucial choice: Do we eat from the Tree of Aliveness – so that we continue to see and value the goodness of creation and so reflect the image of the living God? Or do we eat from the Tree of the Knowledge of Good and Evil – constantly misjudging and playing God and as a result mistreating our fellow creatures?

It's a good and beautiful thing to be an image-bearer of God. *But it's also a big responsibility.*

We can use our intelligence to be creative and generous, or to be selfish and destructive.

We can use our physical strength to be creative and generous, or to be selfish and destructive.

We can use our sexuality to be creative and generous, or to be selfish and destructive.

We can use our work, our money, our time and our other assets to be creative and generous, or to be selfish and destructive.

Think of your hand. It can make a fist or it can extend in peace. It can wield a weapon or it can play a violin. It can point in derision or it can reach out in compassion. It can steal or it can serve. If the first creation story is about the gift of being human, the second story is about the choice all humans live with, day after day. To be alive means to bear responsibly the image of God. It means to stretch out your hand to take from the Tree of Aliveness – and to join in God's creative, healing work.

Engage

1. What one thought or idea from today's lesson especially intrigued, provoked, disturbed, challenged, encouraged, warmed, warned, helped or surprised you?

2. Share a story about a time when someone played God and judged you, or a time when you played God and judged someone else.

3. Tell us about a person who has reflected God to you in some special way.

4. For children: Think about your hands. What is something kind and creative you can do with your hands? What is something mean or harmful you can do with your hands? How can the same hands do both kind and mean things?

5. Activate: If part of being image-bearers of God means that we represent God in caring for the Earth, it's important to learn about your corner of the Earth. You know your postal address (road, city, county, postcode). What is your environmental address? Learn about your watershed, what makes it special, and the environmental issues it faces.

6. Meditate: Observe a few moments of silence. Let a silent prayer rise from within you.

A World of Meaning

Psalm 145:1–16
Proverbs 8:1–36
John 1:1–17

What has come into being in him was life, and the life was the light of all people. The light shines in the darkness . . .

OK. Pay attention. (Feel free to take a few minutes to discuss your answers.)

1, 6, 11, 16, 21, 26, 31 . . . What comes next?
1, 4, 2, 5, 3, 6, 4, 7 . . . What comes next?
1, 2, 3, 5, 8, 13, 21, 34 . . . What comes next?
I, space, L, O, V, E, space, Y, O . . . What comes next?

You know the answers because you are paying attention to the pattern.

It becomes more obvious the longer you live that all life is full of patterns. Reality is trying to tell us something. Life is speaking to us. There's lots of mystery out there, to be sure, and no shortage of chaos and unpredictability. But there's also lots of meaning . . . messages trying to find expression, music inviting us to listen and sing, patterns attracting our attention and interpretation. The chaos becomes a backdrop for the patterns, and the mysteries seem to beckon us to try to understand.

Sometimes the universe feels like this:

71, 6, 2, -48, -213, 9 . . . random numbers with no pattern. Or . . .
G, M, B, O, I, space, Q, H, Z, space, P . . . random letters with no meaning. Or . . .
1,1,1,1,1,1,1,1 . . . sameness or repetition going nowhere.

But above and behind and beyond the sometimes confusing randomness of life, something is going on here. From a single molecule to a strand of DNA, from a bird in flight to an ocean current to a dancing galaxy, there's a logic, a meaning, an unfolding pattern to it all.

Like wood, reality has a grain. Like a river, it has a current. Like a story, it has characters and setting and conflict and resolution. Like poetry, it has syntax and structure, so letters are taken up in words, and words are taken up in phrases and sentences, and they're all taken up in a magnificent pattern of beauty and meaning that we can glimpse and savour, even if it's too big and deep to comprehend fully. Creation reveals wisdom through its patterns. It reveals wisdom about its source and purpose, and about our quest to be alive . . . if we are paying attention.

Of course, we often struggle to know how to interpret those patterns. For example, if a tornado destroys our house, an enemy army drops bombs on our village, a disease takes away someone we love, we lose our job, someone we love breaks our heart, or our best friends betray us, what does that mean? Is the logic of the universe chaos or cruelty? Does might make right? Do violence and chaos rule? Is the Creator capricious, heartless and evil? If we had only our worst experiences in life to guide us, that might be our conclusion.

This is where the Gospel of John adds its insight to the

creation stories we find in the book of Genesis. John had a special term for the pattern of meaning God has spoken or written into the universe. He called it *Logos*, which is often translated in English as 'Word'. We find *logos* in words like biology, anthropology and psychology – the logic of life, human development or the human personality.

This Word or *Logos*, he said, was 'made flesh' in a man named Jesus. In other words, if we want to know what God is like and what the universe is about, we should pay attention to the logic, meaning, wisdom and patterns found in the life of Jesus. He communicated the *logos*, or logic, of God in his teachings. He lived the *logos*, or pattern, of God in his life. He showed the *logos*, or essence, of God in the way he treated others. From his birth to his death and beyond, John believes, Jesus translates the logic or meaning or pattern or heart of God into terms we humans can understand: skin and bone, muscle and breath, nerve and action.

So, inspired by Genesis, we are guided to look for the pattern, meaning, wisdom and logic of God woven into galaxies, planets, forests, fields, plants, animals, you and me. In John's Gospel, we are inspired to look for the pattern in a poor man travelling across the land with a band of students and friends, telling stories, confronting injustice, helping people in need. If we learn and trust the wisdom that comes in creation and in Jesus, we will live our lives in a new way, John says. We will discover God as our loving parent, and we will encounter all other creatures as our relations, our relatives, in one family of creation.

Of course, we have other options. For example, many of us live by the logic of rivalry. Under this logic, the cosmos is a huge battlefield or coliseum in which participants can survive only by competing, defeating, deceiving, displacing or killing their rivals. In this universe, the strongest survive, the ruthless are rewarded, the kind are killed and the meek are crushed. You'd better fight, or you'll be trampled.

Others of us live by the logic of compliance. Under this logic, the cosmos is a big organisation ruled by powerful bosses, and your job is to learn the rules and comply. Stay in your allotted place, do what you're told, curry favour in the 'inner circle' of power, and the logic of compliance will work in your favour. You'd better play it safe, or you'll get into a lot of trouble.

Still others of us think of the universe as a giant machine, and live by the logic of mechanism – action, reaction; cause, effect; stimulus, response. You can use the mechanisms of the universe to seek whatever pleasure, power and security you can during your short lives. But in the end, there is no meaning to the machine, so you'd better grab whatever moments of fleeting pleasure you can. That's all there is or ever will be.

Clearly, the creation stories of Genesis and John offer us a powerful alternative to the logic of rivalry, the logic of compliance and the logic of meaningless mechanism.

They dare us to believe that the universe runs by the logic of creativity, goodness and love. The universe is God's creative project, filled with beauty, opportunity, challenge and meaning. It runs on the meaning or pattern we see embodied in the life of Jesus. In this story, pregnancy abounds. Newness multiplies. Freedom grows. Meaning expands. Wisdom flows. Healing happens. Goodness runs wild.

So here we are, alive and paying attention. We discern patterns in life. We interpret those patterns and we open ourselves to the possibility of a creative *logos* of love and wisdom that runs through the universe like a current and can play in our lives like a song.

Engage

1. What one thought or idea from today's lesson especially intrigued, provoked, disturbed, challenged, encouraged, warmed, warned, helped or surprised you?

2. Share a story about a time when you lived by the logic of rivalry, compliance or meaningless mechanism. How did that work out for you?

3. Imagine and describe what your life would be like if you chose to live more by the *logos* of love than you do now.

4. For children: Is there one cartoon or film that you like to watch again and again? What about it makes you want to keep enjoying it again and again?

5. Activate: Share with someone this week – a family member, a friend, a co-worker or an acquaintance – the idea that we all live by a certain *logos* or logic. Ask them which *logos* they see to be most powerful in today's world – rivalry, compliance, meaningless mechanism or love.

6. Meditate: Observe a few moments of silence to imagine yourself living more fully in the *logos* of love.

CHAPTER 4

The Drama of Desire

Genesis 3:1–13

...man and his wife hid themselves from the presence of the LORD God among the trees of the garden. But the LORD God called to the man, and said to him, 'Where are you?'

Psalm 32
Philippians 2:3–11

In the ancient wisdom of storytelling, Genesis tells us that we are part of God's good creation. It then tells us we have a special responsibility as God's reflections or image-bearers. It tells us that in order to reflect God's image, we have to desire the Tree of Life, not the tree that feeds our pride so that we think we can play God and judge between good and evil.

Of course, we know what happened. The story of Adam and Eve doesn't need to be about literal historical figures in the past to tell us something very true about us, our history and our world today. We humans have consistently chosen the wrong tree. Instead of imitating and reflecting God as good image-bearers should do, we start competing with God, edging God out, playing God ourselves. We reject the Creator and choose another model instead: a snake (the story says), who seems to represent a subtle and dangerous desire to choose rivalry and violence over harmony and well-being.

In Genesis, after feeding on the Tree of the Knowledge of Good and Evil, Adam and Eve suddenly feel a change come over them. Perhaps they each fear that the other will judge them for being different, so they fashion crude clothing to hide their sexual differences. When God approaches, they no longer see God as a friend, but as a rival and threat. So they hide from God in fear. When God asks what has happened, they blame one another and refuse to admit their mistake. Soon they face a harder life of pain, competition, sweat, labour, frustration and death – east of Eden, outside the beautiful garden that was their home.

Later, their two sons repeat the pattern. The older brother – we might say he is 'more advanced' – becomes an agriculturalist. His life is wrapped up in fields, fences, ownership, barns and accumulated wealth, with all the moral complexity they bring. The younger brother – we might say he is 'more vulnerable' or 'less developed' – is a nomadic herdsman. He can't own land or accumulate wealth, because he moves constantly with his herds to wherever the fresh grass is growing. Their different ways of life are expressed in different forms of religious sacrifice. They soon become religious rivals, competing for a higher degree of God's favour. The perceived loser in the competition, Cain, envies and resents his brother.

Sometime later, we can imagine Abel leading his flocks into his brother's field. At that moment Cain, his resentment simmering, no longer sees a brother: he sees a trespasser, an enemy. He plays God and judges his brother as evil and therefore worthy of death. Abel soon becomes the first victim of violence, and Cain the first murderer. So we humans quickly turn from reflecting the image of a creative, generous, life-giving God. With Adam and Eve we become graspers, hiders, blamers and shamers. With Cain and Abel we become rivals, resenters, murderers and destroyers – the very opposite of God's image.

What do these ancient stories mean for us today?

They help us know what's broken with our world: something in us human beings.

And they help us know what's broken in human beings: something in our desires.

And they help us know what's broken with our desires: we have stopped imitating God's good desires to create and bless and give life. Instead we've started imitating the prideful, competitive, fearful and harmful desires we see in one another . . . the desire to acquire what someone else has, the desire to compete and consume, the desire to judge as evil those who get in our way, even the desire to harm or kill those who are obstacles to our desires.

Think about how much imitation runs our lives.

Somebody hits or criticises you and what do you want to do? Hit them back! Criticise them back!

Somebody buys a new shirt or a new TV, and what do you want to do? Buy an even better shirt or bigger TV!

Somebody moves to a bigger house in a different neighbourhood, and what do you desire? To get an even bigger house in an even better neighbourhood!

And what happens if you can't get what you desire? You'll be tempted to cheat, steal, lie, harm or maybe even kill to get what you desire.

Now there's nothing wrong with desire. The question is, whose desires are you imitating? To be alive is to imitate God's generous desires . . . to create, to bless, to help, to serve, to care for, to save, to enjoy. To make the opposite choice – to imitate one another's desires and become one another's rivals – is to choose a path of death.

If we imitate our way into that rat race, we will compete rather than create, impress rather than bless, defeat rather than protect, dominate rather than serve, and exploit rather than respect. As a result, we will turn our neighbour first into a rival, and then an enemy, and then a victim.

We all live in this drama – the drama of desire. We have the opportunity to imitate God's generous and good desires on the one hand – and we have the temptation to imitate selfish, fearful, envious human desires on the other hand.

Think of all the advertisers who are trying to influence our desires. Think of all the politicians who are eager to mould our desires so they can manipulate us for their advantage. Think of all the potential rivals who are glad to engage us in competition – their desires against ours. What's true of us as individuals can also be true of us as groups – both personally and socially, we are caught in the drama of desire.

That's another reason Jesus is so important to us: because he modelled a different way of life. He gave us a down-to-Earth example of God's creative self-giving. True, Adam and Eve grabbed for the chance to be like gods – judging others as good or evil, exploiting rather than preserving the Earth, competing with one another rather than loving and serving one another. But Jesus didn't grasp at god-like status. He humbly poured himself out for others – in service, in suffering, even to the point of death. He even gave us a way of remembering his attitude of self-giving: he said that his life was like food, like bread and wine, and he freely gave himself for us. His constant invitation – 'Follow me' – could also be expressed as 'Imitate me'.

To be alive is to be mindful that we live in the drama of desire. We can imitate one another's competitive desires, and so be driven to fear, rivalry, judging, conflict and killing. Or we can imitate God's generous desires . . . to create, bless, help, serve, care for, save and enjoy. At this moment, let us turn towards God, not as rivals who want to play God, but as image-bearers who want to imitate and reflect God. Let us humbly and fervently desire the right kind of desire.

Engage

1. What one thought or idea from today's lesson especially intrigued, provoked, disturbed, challenged, encouraged, warmed, warned, helped or surprised you?

2. Share a story about your interaction with someone you were jealous of or considered a rival. What did they have or desire that you desired? How did your relationship play out?

3. How do you respond to reading the Philippians 2 passage as a reversal of the Genesis 3 passage?

4. For children: How do you feel when you win or lose in a game? How do you feel when you do better or worse at something than someone else? Tell us a story about it.

5. Activate: Be especially sensitive to rivalry this week. When you feel it, ask what 'desire to acquire' is driving you. And ask whom you are imitating in this 'desire to acquire'. In this way, seek to become more aware of the Cain and Abel struggling in your own life and heart.

6. Meditate: After a few moments of silence, let one emotion rise to the surface and express that emotion to God – and, if you'd like, to your companions, with a brief explanation.

CHAPTER 5

In Over Our Heads

Genesis 4:1–17; 6:5–8; 7:1–5; 8:1; 9:7–17
Psalm 51
James 4:1–8

Those conflicts and disputes among you, where do they come from? Do they not come from your cravings that are at war within you?

In the ancient Genesis stories, our species was created in the image of God – to reflect God's character faithfully in the world, both to our fellow creatures and to one another. Soon, though, we wanted to be little gods ourselves. We wanted to judge good and evil for ourselves, to decide who would live and who would die, who would rule and who would be enslaved. Consumed by the desire to grasp what others had, we became rivals of God and our neighbours. That crisis of desire has led to great shame, pain, suffering, violence, counterviolence and fear . . . in our lives, our communities and our world. Today's headlines tell the same story in a hundred different ways.

In the Genesis story, the descendants of Cain, the first murderer, started building cities, and those cities reflected the violence of Cain. As city-states competed with each other and defeated one another, the winners created growing empires that elevated a few to god-like status and reduced most to oppression and slavery. The situation became so unbearable that in the story of Noah and the flood, God felt sorry for making the world in the first place. Eventually God decided to wipe the whole slate clean and start again. Maybe Noah's descendants would do better than Adam's had.

Although many people think of this as a cute story about animals and a boat ride, those who think more deeply find it deeply disturbing. The image of violent oppressors and innocent victims drowning together seems only to make a bad situation worse. At the very least, one would think God would have more creativity, moral finesse and foresight than to create a good world only to destroy it because it went so bad so (relatively) quickly. Shouldn't God be better than this?

To understand this story – and others like it – properly, we need to remember that ancient cultures were oral cultures. Few people were literate, and oral storytelling was to them what reading books, using the internet, going to concerts and watching films and TV shows are to us today. Ancient stories had a long life as oral compositions before they were ever written down. As oral compositions, stories could evolve over time. In a sense, writing them down ended their evolution.

For ancient people in oral cultures, a story was like a hypothesis. A good and helpful story, like a tested hypothesis, would be repeated and improved and enhanced from place to place and generation to generation. Less helpful stories would be forgotten like a failed theory, or adjusted and revised until they became more helpful. Sometimes, competing stories would stand side by side like competing theories, awaiting a time when one would prevail – or both would fail, and a new story would arise with more explanatory power. In all these ways, storytelling was, like the scientific method, a way of seeking the truth, a way of grappling with profound questions, a way of passing on hard-won insights. As our ancestors deepened their understanding, their stories changed – just as our theories change.

In this light, we can reconsider the story of Noah as an adaptation of even older stories from the Middle East. In one of those earlier versions, a gang of gods unleashed a catastrophic flood as a personal vendetta against some noisy people who kept the gods awake at night. Ancient Jewish storytellers would have found that story repulsive. So they adapted it to reveal more of God's true character, replacing many vindictive gods who were irritable from lack of sleep with one Creator who unleashes a flood to flush out human violence.

That's certainly a step in the right direction, but the process doesn't need to end with the Noah story. After all, God's violence doesn't really solve anything in the Noah story, since Noah's family quickly starts cooking up more trouble so that soon things are just as bad as they were before the flood. Again, we can't help but wonder, shouldn't God be better than that? To answer that question, we need to bring in another story. Later in Genesis, in the story of Joseph, God responds to violence in a very different way – not with more violence, but with kindness. Another big step in the right direction!

We see the same pattern in the story of the Tower of Babel. The ancient world was filled with huge structures – towers and pyramids and temples and the like – that were built with slave labour. Just about everyone in those days assumed that the gods chose a few high-echelon people to sit pretty at the top of the pyramid. The masses were destined to be slaves at the bottom, sweating to make bricks or haul stones or irrigate fields so that the elite could have a nice day. Everyone assumed that the gods supported these slave-based economies of empire, and everyone understood that the towers, pyramids and temples both pleased and honoured the gods of the status quo.

But in the Tower of Babel story, the storytellers realise that the living God must be better than that. So in their story, tower-building is exposed as another form of rivalry with God. God opposes their soaring ambition of assimilation and domination. God diversifies the languages of the Babylonian Empire so that its ambition of global empire fails, memorialised for ever in an unfinished tower. This new version of an old story is a big step in the right direction. Later, when we come to the story of Pentecost in the Acts of the Apostles, we'll see another giant step forward, revealing God even more beautifully and fully.

As we progress through the biblical library, these stories interact with one another again and again. Together they reveal an ever fuller and deeper vision of God. We come to know a God who consistently refuses to support a pyramid economy with a few at the top and the masses at the bottom. We come to trust a God who consistently opposes the oppressors and consistently takes the side of the humble, the vulnerable and the poor. We eventually come to understand God as one who consistently prefers non-violence over violence, equality over dominance and justice over injustice. Taken together, these stories make one of the most audacious claims in all of history: the living God doesn't uphold the status quo . . . but repeatedly disrupts it and breaks it open so that something better can emerge and evolve.

Do you see what's happening? Generation after generation, people are telling stories that improve upon previous stories and prepare the way for even better stories to emerge. The process leaps forward in the story of Jesus. He comes proclaiming the message of the commonwealth – or kingdom, or alternative economy – of God. He shows how in God's way of arranging things, the last are first and the first are last. Leaders serve, and the humble – not the arrogant – inherit the Earth. In word and deed, in parable and miracle, Jesus shows that God is at work in history to heal what is broken – on the personal level of individual lives, and on the societal level of economics and government too. And he proclaims God not as a reactive avenger who sweeps away the innocent with the guilty, but as a forgiving, merciful, gracious parent who loves all creation with a perfect, holy, faithful, compassionate love.

No wonder he told people to 'repent' – which means to 'rethink everything'. No wonder he was known as a brilliantly creative and original storyteller.

As with the parables of Jesus, the Adam and Eve, Cain and Abel, flood and tower stories in Genesis don't need to be *factually* true to tell an *actual* truth about us and our civilisation. Those ancient stories courageously expose how all civilisations were founded on violence and oppression, producing luxury and ease for a few but exhaustion and degradation for the many. They warn us that unjust structures are unsustainable. They advise that floods of change will sweep injustice away and internal conflicts will thwart arrogant ambitions. They promise that in the long run, justice and reconciliation will prevail over injustice and rivalry.

If we aren't careful, we can grow comfortable and complacent with a status quo of injustice, oppression and violence. That's why we are wise to gather often and retell these ancient stories. Rather than being conformed to this world and its mixed-up priorities, we can seek together to be transformed by a different and better story so we can join with God in the healing of our world.

To be alive is to join God in caring about the oppressed, the needy, the powerless, the victims and the vulnerable. To be alive is to believe that injustice is not sustainable and to share God's desire for a better world. To be alive is to look at our world and say, 'God is better than that!' – and know that our world can be better too. *And so can we.*

Engage

1. What one thought or idea from today's lesson especially intrigued, provoked, disturbed, challenged, encouraged, warmed, warned, helped or surprised you?

2. Share a story where you felt like someone at the top of the pyramid, or like someone at the bottom.

3. How do you respond to the comparison between stories and scientific theories, or to the distinction between factual and actual truth?

4. For children: Have you ever known a bully, or have you ever been a bully, or have you ever been bullied? Tell us about it.

5. Activate: Look for moments this week when it might be appropriate for you to say, 'God must be better than that.' And look for examples this week of the powerful exploiting the vulnerable when it might be appropriate for you to say, 'We can be better than that.'

6. Meditate: Ask yourself, in God's presence, 'What *desire to acquire* may be driving me into trouble?' After a few moments of silence, acknowledge the desires that come to mind. Then ask for other, better desires to replace the *desire to acquire*.

CHAPTER 6

Plotting Goodness

Genesis 12:1–9

I will make of you a great nation, and I will bless you, and make your name great, so that you will be a blessing . . .

Galatians 3:6–9
Mark 11:15–19

According to the ancient stories of Genesis, God is up to something surprising and amazing in our world. While we're busy plotting evil, God is plotting goodness.

Yes, sometimes we humans try to rope God into our dark plots and use God to help us scramble to the top of the pyramid, where we can dominate over others. Yes, we sometimes try to enlist God to condemn those we want to condemn, deprive those we want to deprive, even kill those we want to kill. But God isn't willing to be domesticated into our little tribal deity on a leash who will attack our enemies on our command. While we plot ways to use God to get blessings for ourselves, God stays focused on the big picture of blessing the world – which includes blessing us in the process.

You see this pattern unfold when God chooses a man named Abram and a woman named Sarai. They are from a prominent family in a great ancient city-state known as Ur, one of the first ancient Middle Eastern civilisations. Like all civilisations, Ur has a dirty little secret: its affluence is built on violence, oppression and exploitation. Behind its beautiful facade, its upper classes live each day in luxury, while its masses slave away in squalor.

God tells this couple to leave their life of privilege in this great civilisation. He sends them out into the unknown as wanderers and adventurers. No longer will Abram and Sarai have the armies and wealth and comforts of Ur at their disposal. All they will have is a promise – that God will be with them and show them a better way. From now on, they will make a new road by walking.

God's promise comes in two parts. In the first part, Abram and Sarai will be blessed. They will become a great nation, and God will bless those who bless them and curse those who curse them. That's the kind of promise we might expect. It's the second part that's surprising.

Not only will they be blessed, but they will be a blessing. Not only will their family become a great nation, but all the families on Earth will be blessed through them.

This is a unique identity indeed. It means the children of Abram and Sarai will be a unique *us* in relation to all the other *thems* of the world. No, their identity will not be *us at the top* of the pyramid and *them at the bottom*, or vice versa. Nor will their identity be *us assimilated into them*, or *us assimilating them* into us. Nor will it be *us against them*, *us apart from them*, or *us in spite of them*. No, Abram and Sarai's unique identity will be *us for them*, *us with them*, *us for the benefit and blessing of all*.

That 'otherly' identity – *us for the common good* – wasn't intended only for Abram's and Sarai's clan. It is the kind of identity that is best for every individual, every culture, every nation, every religion. It says, 'We're special!' But it also says, 'They're special, too.' It says, 'God has a place for us and a plan for us.' But it also says, 'God has a place and plan for others, too.' When we drift from that high calling and start thinking only of *me*, only of *our* clan or *our* nation or *our* religion, our sense of identity begins to go stale and sour, even toxic.

So the story of Abram's and Sarai's unique identity tells us something powerful about God's identity, too: God is not the tribal deity of one group of 'chosen' people. God is not for us and against all others. God is for *us* and for *them*, too. God loves everyone everywhere, no exceptions.

And this story also tells us something about true faith. Faith is stepping off the map of what's known and making a new road by walking into the unknown. It's responding to God's call to adventure, stepping out on a quest for goodness, trusting that the status quo isn't as good as it gets, believing a promise that a better life is possible.

True faith isn't a deal where we use God to get the inside track or a special advantage or a secret magic formula for success. It isn't a mark of superiority or exclusion. True faith is about joining God in God's love for everyone. It's about seeking goodness with others, not at the expense of others. True faith is seeing a bigger circle in which we are all connected, all included, all loved, all blessed. True faith reverses the choice that is pictured in the story of Adam and Eve. In that story, Adam and Eve want to set themselves above everyone and everything else. True faith brings us back down to Earth, into solidarity with others and with all creation.

Sadly, for many people, faith has been reduced to a list. For some, it's a list of beliefs: ideas or statements that we have to memorise and assent to if we want to be blessed. For others, it's a list of dos and don'ts: rituals or rules that we have to perform to earn the status of being blessed. But Abram didn't have much in the way of beliefs, rules or rituals. He had no Bibles, doctrines, temples, commandments or ceremonies. For him, true faith was simply trusting a promise of being blessed to be a blessing. It wasn't a way of being religious: it was a way of being alive.

And so this story not only tells us something about God's true identity and about the true nature of faith, it also tells us about true aliveness. If you scramble over others to achieve your goal, that's not true aliveness. If you harm others to acquire your desire, that's not true aliveness. If you hoard your blessings while others suffer in need, that's not true aliveness. True aliveness comes when we receive blessings and become a blessing to others. It's not a blessing racket – figuring out how to plot prosperity for me and my tribe. It's a blessing economy where God plots goodness for all.

Like all of us, Abram and Sarai will lose sight of this vision of aliveness sometimes. But even when they lose faith, God will remain faithful. Through their mistakes and failures, they will keep learning and growing, discovering more and more of God's desire to overflow with abundant blessing for all.

Are you ready to step out on the same journey of faith with Sarai and Abram? Will you join them in the adventure of being blessed to be a blessing? Are you ready to make the road by walking?

Engage

1. What one thought or idea from today's lesson especially intrigued, provoked, disturbed, challenged, encouraged, warmed, warned, helped or surprised you?

2. Share a story about a time when you observed or participated in a group that saw itself as blessed *to the exclusion of others* rather than *for the blessing of others*.

3. Where in today's world do you see people practising the kind of 'otherly' identity to which God called Abram – 'us for the sake of others'?

4. For children: Tell us about a grown-up or another child who often asks you to help him or her. How does helping someone make you feel?

5. Activate: Look for opportunities to 'be a blessing' to others this week. Come back with some stories to share.

6. Meditate: In silence, hold this truth in God's presence: *I am blessed to be a blessing.*

CHAPTER 7

It's Not Too Late

Genesis 18:9–33; 22:1–14

Micah 6:6–8

. . . what does the Lord require of you but to do justice, and to love kindness, and to walk humbly with your God?

Acts 17:19–34

Have you ever felt that it was too late? That things were so awful they could never get better, that you had failed so horribly and so often you could never, ever recover, that the situation was too far gone ever to be salvageable?

That was how Abram and Sarai felt at one point in their lives. Like many couples, they had dreamed all their lives of having children. But the years passed and no children came. They had received a promise from God that they would become a great family and that all people everywhere would be blessed through their descendants. But there was one problem: they had no descendants. When they were far too old to have children, you can imagine how they felt: it was just too late.

Then they received reassurance from God that they would have a child. No wonder, according to the book of Genesis, that Sarai laughed when she first heard the promise!

However they felt at first, over time Abram and Sarai came to believe that what seemed impossible was possible after all. When that impossible baby was born, guess what they named him? They named him Isaac, which means 'laughter'. And their names were changed, too, reflecting their new status as parents – from Abram and Sarai to Abraham and Sarah.

You might expect a happy ending at this point, but it was not that simple. Even after embarking on the adventure of faith, and even after becoming parents when it seemed too late, Abraham and Sarah faced another huge challenge.

Put yourself in their sandals. Imagine that you and everyone you know believes that God is a severe and demanding deity who can bestow forgiveness and other blessings only after human blood has been shed. Imagine how that belief in human sacrifice will affect the way you live, the way you worship and the way you treat others. Now imagine how hard it would be to be the first person in your society to question such a belief. Imagine how much courage it would take, especially because your blood might be the next to be sacrificed!

Questioning widely held assumptions about God can be a dangerous venture indeed. But if our assumptions aren't sometimes questioned, belief in God becomes less and less plausible. For example, biblical writers used the imagery of God sitting on a throne to express their belief that God was powerful and glorious, like an ancient king. Even though we may agree that God is powerful and glorious, does that mean we must believe that God's power and glory are exactly like those of ancient kings – who could often be insecure, capricious, vain or vicious? Does it mean we must conclude that God has a literal gluteus maximus that rests on a really big chair floating up in the sky somewhere? Are we allowed to question or point out problems with these images and understandings that are widely held and emotionally comforting for many?

Perhaps we can agree that whoever and whatever God is, our best imagery can only point towards God like a finger. We can never capture God in our concepts like a fist. In fact, the more we know about God, the more we have to acknowledge we don't know. The bigger our understanding about God, the bigger the mystery that we must acknowledge. Our faith must always be open to correction, enhancement and new insight. That's why humility is so essential for all who speak of God.

Science faces a similar problem, by the way. Scientists have names for gravity and light and electricity and magnetism. But even though they have names for these realities, and even though they can create models and formulas to predict how they will work, what these forces really are remains a mystery. It's pretty humbling when you think about it. That's why, in the world of science, people are constantly questioning old assumptions and creating new theories or models. Scientists test and argue about those new theories and models until they are either confirmed or replaced with something even better.

The dominant theory of God in Abraham's and Sarah's day taught that the gracious God who gives human life would also demand human life as a sacrifice. So when Abraham believed God was commanding him to kill Isaac, he was being faithful to a traditional model of how God and life worked. We might wish that Abraham had argued over this theory, just as he did when he believed God was about to destroy the cities of Sodom and Gomorrah. But strangely, what Abraham did for two cities he refrained from doing for his own son.

So, one day Abraham led Isaac up a mountain. He piled stones into an altar, tied up his son and placed him on the stones. He raised the knife, and once again it seemed too late. But at that last possible instant, Abraham saw a ram nearby, its horns stuck in a thicket. Suddenly he realised that God had provided a ram to sacrifice in place of Isaac, his son. What a powerful new insight! Animal blood could please or appease their God as a substitute for human blood!

It was commonplace in the ancient world for a man to lead his son up a mountain to be sacrificed to his deity. It was extraordinary for a man to come down the mountain with his son still alive. Through that ancient story, Abraham's descendants explained why they had changed their theory or model of God, and why they dared to be different from their neighbours who still practised human sacrifice. It wasn't too late to challenge widely held assumptions and change their theory of God!

But they still weren't finished. Many generations after ritualised human sacrifice was left behind for ever, prophets and poets arose among Abraham's descendants who made the shocking claim that God doesn't need animal sacrifices either. They realised that God could never need anything *from* us, since God provides everything *for* us. Not only that, but they realised God isn't the one who is angry and hostile and needs appeasement. We humans are the angry ones! Our hostile, bloodthirsty hearts are the ones that need to be changed!

So over many centuries, led along by many teachers and prophets, Abraham's descendants came to believe that God wanted one thing from humanity . . . not sacrifice, whether human or animal, but this: to do justice, to love kindness and to walk humbly with God. The only sacrifice that mattered to God was the holy gift of humble hearts and lives dedicated to his way of love.

So with faith, it's not too late. It's not too late for a dream to come true, and it's not too late to learn something new.

That's true for us today as we follow in the footsteps of Abraham and Sarah, walking this road together. We're still learning, rethinking, growing, discovering. In spite of long delays and many disappointments, will we dare to keep dreaming impossible dreams? In spite of the assumptions that everyone around us holds to be true, will we dare to ask new questions and make new discoveries – including lessons about God and what God really desires? It may seem as if it's too late to keep hoping, to keep trying, to keep learning, to keep growing. But to be alive in the story of creation means daring to believe it's not too late.

Engage

1. What one thought or idea from today's lesson especially intrigued, provoked, disturbed, challenged, encouraged, warmed, warned, helped or surprised you?

2. Share a story about a time when you almost gave up, but are glad you didn't.

3. What are some critical issues in today's world – or in our personal lives – where we might say 'It's too late' or 'It's impossible'?

4. For children: What makes you laugh? Why do you think Sarah laughed in this story?

5. Activate: This week, try saying 'It's not too late' when you're tempted to be cynical or give up. Or practise the art of 'the second laugh'. The first laugh comes as a reflex when we think something is impossible. The second laugh comes as a choice when we laugh at our lack of faith.

6. Meditate: After a few moments of silence, complete this sentence as your prayer: 'Living God, it's not too late to change my mind about . . .'

CHAPTER 8

Rivalry or Reconciliation?

Genesis 32:22 – 33:11; 50:15–21
Matthew 25:31–40
Luke 10:25–37

You shall love the Lord your God with all your heart, and with all your soul, and with all your strength, and with all your mind; and your neighbour as yourself.

If you had siblings, how did you get along? The book of Genesis is full of stories of brothers and sisters in competition and conflict. After the tragic story of Cain and Abel, we come to the story of Ishmael and Isaac. Ishmael was Abraham's first son, born not to his wife Sarah but to her Egyptian slave Hagar. According to Genesis, there was a bitter rivalry between the two mothers and their two sons. Hagar and Ishmael were treated terribly, while Sarah and Isaac were given every advantage. God intervened and made it clear that even if Abraham and Sarah failed to love Hagar and Ishmael, God cared for them deeply.

Years later, Abraham's grandson Jacob was caught up in bitter sibling rivalry with his older twin brother, Esau. At the heart of their conflict was the belief that God loved Jacob and hated Esau. Based on this belief that he was uniquely favoured, Jacob felt entitled to take advantage of everyone around him, especially his disfavoured brother Esau. He seemed to get away with his trickery again and again until, eventually, Esau grew so angry at Jacob that Jacob had to flee for his life. For many years, the two brothers lived far apart, maturing, but still alienated from each other. During this time, Jacob married two sisters – a favoured one named Rachel and a disfavoured one named Leah. Leah became the mother of six of Jacob's twelve sons, so her story had a happier ending than anyone expected.

After he became a rich and successful man, Jacob began a homeward journey. He learned that the next day he would be forced to encounter the brother he had wronged in so many ways so many years before. You can imagine how afraid he was. He had lived his whole life by trickery. Now his old tricks weren't working any more. So all that night, he felt like he was in a wrestling match with God.

His sleepless night of inner wrestling seems like an image for the human struggle common to us all. Like Jacob, we wrestle to get our own way by trying to cheat or defeat anyone who has something we desire – including God. Like Jacob, we grapple with changing old habits, even when those habits aren't working for us any more. Like Jacob, we agonise through the long night, held in a headlock by despair, fearing that it's too late for us to hope for a new beginning.

So hour after hour through the night, Jacob wrestled. When the new day dawned, he rose from the struggle with two signs of his emergence into maturity as a human being. First, he received the blessing of a new name, Israel, which means 'God-wrestler'. And he received a hip injury that required him to walk with a limp, a lifelong memento of his long night of struggle.

Jacob was now ready – limping – to face his brother. Instead of trying to trick Esau as the old Jacob would have done, he sent Esau a huge array of gifts to honour him. When Jacob finally met Esau face to face, Esau had his chance. Now the older twin could finally get revenge on his upstart younger twin for all Jacob's dirty tricks in the past. Esau could treat Jacob to a taste of the disdain and contempt Jacob had repeatedly poured upon him.

But Esau surprised everyone. He made it clear that he wasn't holding a grudge. He desired no revenge, nor did he require any gifts or appeasement. He simply wanted to be reconciled.

Jacob was so touched that he said these beautiful words: 'Truly, to see your face is like seeing the face of God, since you have received me with such grace.' The upstart trickster had finally learned to see the face of God in the face of the one he formerly tricked and despised. He discovered God's grace in the one he had always considered disgraced. In the face of the other, he rediscovered a brother. In the face of the one everyone assumed God hated . . . God had been revealed. What a story!

Even though Jacob learned an important lesson that day, sibling rivalry had a resurgence in the next generation. Jacob had twelve sons. One son, Joseph, was resented by his eleven brothers, because – as with Abel over Cain, Sarah over Hagar, Isaac over Ishmael, Jacob over Esau, and Rachel over Leah before him – Joseph was favoured over them. In fact, Joseph dreamed that one day his brothers would grovel before him. Eventually, driven by the resentment of the disfavoured, they plotted to kill him. At the last minute, however, they decided to sell him as a slave to some Egyptian traders instead. Through a dramatic series of temptations, delays, setbacks and recoveries, Joseph rose from slavery to a place of honour in the court of the Egyptian Pharaoh.

Many years later, when a famine sent the brothers to Egypt as refugees, Joseph had his chance, just as Esau did: he could get revenge on those miserable brothers who had treated him so badly. He could do to them what they had done to him. But Joseph, like Esau, made a different choice – not for revenge, but for forgiveness. When his brothers grovelled before him, as Joseph had dreamed they would when he was a boy, and when they offered to be treated as slaves rather than brothers, Joseph didn't gloat. He refused to play God, judge them evil and sentence them to death or enslavement. Instead, he reinterpreted the whole story of their relationship. Their evil intent had been overshadowed by God's good intent, so that Joseph could save their lives. He had suffered and he had been blessed, he realised, for their benefit. So instead of imitating their resentful and violent example, he imitated the gracious heart of God. By refusing to play God in judging them, he imaged God in showing kindness to them.

In this way, Joseph – the victim of mistreatment by his brothers – became the hero. The one everyone cruelly rejected was the one whose kindness everyone needed. The one who was considered favoured wasn't made superior so others could grovel before him; he was made strong so he could serve them.

In both of these stories of sibling rivalry, the rejected brother, the 'other brother', is the one in whose face the grace of God brightly shines.

These stories pulsate with some of the most powerful and radical themes of the Bible. Blessing, power or favour is not given for privilege over others, but for service for the benefit of others. The weaker brother or sister, the one who is deemed ugly or dull or disfavoured or illegitimate, is always beloved by God. From Abel to Ishmael to Hagar to Esau to Leah to Joseph, God keeps showing up, not in the victors who have defeated or exploited or rejected a weaker rival, but in the weaker ones who have been defeated or rejected.

These same themes are the heartbeat of two of Jesus' greatest parables. In the parable of the prodigal son, the father who runs out to welcome his runaway younger son behaves exactly as Esau did – running to him, embracing him, kissing him, showing grace rather than retaliation. And he acts just as Joseph did, as well, not making the runaway grovel as a slave, but welcoming him as a beloved member of the family. And in the parable of the good Samaritan, it is the disfavoured Samaritan, not the high-status priest or Levite, who models the love of God.

As in Genesis, life today is full of rivalries and conflicts. We all experience wrongs, hurts and injustices through the actions of others – and we all inflict wrongs, hurts and injustices upon others. If we want to reflect the image of God, we will choose grace over hostility, reconciliation over revenge, equality over rivalry. When we make that choice, we encounter God in the face of our former rivals and enemies. And as we are humbled, surrendering to God and seeking to be reconciled with others, our faces too reflect the face of God. We come alive as God's image-bearers indeed.

Engage

1. What one thought or idea from today's lesson especially intrigued, provoked, disturbed, challenged, encouraged, warmed, warned, helped or surprised you?

2. Share a story about how a conflict or rivalry with a family member, friend or colleague challenged you to face yourself . . . and God.

3. Respond to the idea that in revenge, we seek to imitate the person who has wronged us, and that in reconciliation, we imitate and reflect God.

4. For children: Tell us about someone you had a chance to forgive.

5. Activate: This week, look for opportunities for others to 'see the face of God' in your face, and seek the face of God in their faces, too – especially those you may see as rivals or outcasts.

6. Meditate: In silence, ponder forgiveness, and thank God for the joy of being forgiven – and for the release of forgiving others.

CHAPTER 9

Freedom!

Exodus 1:1–14; 3:1–15

I have observed the misery of my people who are in Egypt; I have heard their cry on account of their taskmasters. Indeed, I know their sufferings . . .

John 8:1–11
Galatians 5:1, 13–15

Slavery was a sad and common reality in the ancient world. There were at least four ways that people became slaves. First, when people suffered a terrible misfortune like sickness, accident, flood, debt, theft or famine, they could quickly find themselves in danger of death by starvation or homelessness. In that desperate situation, they might be forced to sell themselves into slavery, under the simple reasoning that being a live slave was better than being a dead non-slave. Second, when nations won a war, they often killed off all their vanquished enemies. But some nations decided to keep their defeated foes alive as slaves instead of killing them. Third, refugees or other vulnerable minorities might be enslaved by the dominant majority. Finally, babies born to slaves were destined to be slaves.

That was what happened to the descendants of Abraham between the end of Genesis and the beginning of Exodus in the Bible. As Genesis ended, Joseph had welcomed his brothers into

Egypt as refugees to escape a famine in their land to the north. Finding refuge solved the famine problem, but refugee and minority status made them vulnerable to enslavement.

As Exodus begins, the Hebrews, as Abraham's descendants were then called, have been enslaved. And they have also grown in numbers, so much so that the Egyptians have begun to fear that they might rebel. In response, the Egyptian ruler, the Pharaoh, calls for a gradual genocide by decreeing that all the male babies born to the Israelite slaves be thrown into the River Nile to drown. You can see how this strategy would leave the next generation of Hebrew women either barren or vulnerable to sexual enslavement by Egyptian men. After one generation, no more 'pure' Hebrews would be born.

Often in the Bible, when there is a big problem God prepares a person or people to act as God's partners or agents in solving it. In other words, God gets involved by challenging us to get involved. In this case, God prepared a man named Moses.

Moses was one of the babies whom the Pharaoh required to be drowned in the Nile. His mother came up with a creative way to save his life. She placed him in the Nile as required, but first she put baby Moses in a little raft of reeds. His raft floated downstream, where it was found by one of Pharaoh's daughters. She felt sorry for the little baby and decided to raise him as her own. So this vulnerable slave boy was adopted into the privileged household of Pharaoh – and to top it off, Moses' own mother was hired to be the wet nurse. Quite a turn of events! Now Moses could live happily ever after, right?

Not quite. The good news was that Moses survived. The bad news? Moses grew up with an identity crisis. He was an Israelite by birth but an Egyptian by culture. So a huge question was hanging over him as he matured: on whose side would he stand when he came of age? As a young man, his moment of decision came when he saw an Egyptian beating up an Israelite. He stood up for the Israelite and killed the Egyptian oppressor. Now he had made his choice. But to his surprise, his kinfolk didn't welcome him as a hero. Instead, when he tried to intervene in a quarrel between two Israelites, they distrusted him. So he went from belonging to both sides to being considered an outsider by both sides.

In disgrace, he ran away from Egypt and came to an oasis in the desert. There, he saw a group of male shepherds drive away some girls from a well. Now, sensitised to the victims of oppression, he stood up for the girls. Their father was so grateful that he welcomed Moses into his family, and Moses married one of the daughters he had helped protect.

Finally Moses had a place to belong, right? Now he could settle down and be happy, right? They lived happily ever after, right? Not quite.

Imagine the scene: Moses is out tending sheep one day and something strange catches his attention: a bush is on fire, but it's not burning up. When Moses comes closer to check it out, he hears a voice calling his name. It's God – and God is telling him to go back to Egypt, confront Pharaoh about his exploitation of the Israelites, and lead them on a long road to freedom.

Moses feels he has already failed at helping the Israelites, so it takes some persuasion for him to agree to accept this mission. But finally he goes, supported by his older brother, Aaron. They confront Pharaoh with the message: 'God says, "Let my people go!"' Predictably, Pharaoh refuses. So God sends plagues as pressure on Pharaoh, as if to say, 'Oppressing others may seem like the easy road to riches, power and comfort, but there are high costs to following that road.' After that cost is dramatised ten times through ten plagues, Pharaoh relents and tells the people they can leave. Now everything will be fine, right? Happily ever after, right?

Not quite. Soon after saying 'yes' to Moses, Pharaoh has

second thoughts and sends his army to pursue the Israelites and bring them back into slavery.

So Moses and the Israelites find themselves trapped between the Egyptian army and a huge body of water. At the last minute, God opens up a path through the water and the Israelites escape. When Pharaoh's army follows, the path closes and they all drown. The fate they had planned for the Israelite babies now becomes their own fate.

Surely now there will be a happy ending for the former slaves, right? Not quite.

If you're looking for a thirty-minute story with a happy ending every time, it's hard to find in the Bible – just as it is in real life. Instead, we discover the presence of God with us in our troubles, helping us deal with them, helping us discover solutions to them, helping us deal with the new problems inevitably created by those solutions, and so on. Through it all, we discover God's faithful desire to help the downtrodden, the oppressed, the exploited and the forgotten.

We're all like Moses in a lot of ways. We all have choices to make – who we will become, whose side we'll stand on, whether we'll give up after our failures and frustrations, whether we'll have the faith to get up and keep moving forward when we sense God's call. Life may not be easy – but it can certainly be an exciting path to walk, if we go through life with God!

The story of Moses and the escape, or exodus, from Egypt glows at the core of the whole biblical story. It makes one of history's most audacious and unprecedented claims: *God is on the side of slaves, not slave owners*! God doesn't uphold an unjust status quo, but works to undermine it so that a better future can come. That revolutionary message is still unknown or rejected in much of the world today. If you believe it, you will live one way. If you don't, you'll live another way.

Jesus, as one of the descendants of those slaves, was formed in this story of liberation. Every year he gathered around a table to remember these events and to situate his life in the ongoing march from slavery and into freedom. All who ate that Passover meal, as it was called, were demonstrating that they were not part of the slave-owning economy, but were among those seeking freedom from it. They wanted God's judgement to pass over them – which is the source of the meal's name, *Passover* – so they could pass over from slavery to freedom. As part of this community, united in this meal, Jesus learned a profound way of seeing God and others. Where others used their gods to defend an unjust status quo, Jesus believed in the God of justice and liberation. Where others saw a worthless slave, an exploitable asset, a damnable sinner, a disgusting outsider, Jesus saw someone to set free.

The night before his crucifixion, Jesus and his disciples were celebrating the Passover meal. He urged his disciples to keep doing so – not just annually, but frequently, and not just in memory of Moses in ancient Egypt, but also in memory of his own life and message. That's why followers of Jesus continue to gather around a simple meal of bread and wine today. By participating in that meal, we are making the same choice Moses made – and the same choice Jesus made: to join God in the ongoing struggle to be free and to set others free. That's what it means to be alive in God's story of creation and non-violent liberation. It's a road into the wild, a road we make by walking.

Engage

1. What one thought or idea from today's lesson especially intrigued, provoked, disturbed, challenged, encouraged, warmed, warned, helped or surprised you?

2. Share a story about a time you took the side of a vulnerable person, or the time you were the vulnerable person and others took your side . . . or didn't.

3. Name the Hebrew slaves of today's world. Who today is being exploited and crying out for help? Who does back-breaking work for which others reap the rewards? How can we join in solidarity with them, seeking liberation?

4. For children: What's your favourite meal and what do you like most about it? What special meaning does that meal have for you?

5. Activate: This week, seek to have 'Moses eyes' – looking for people who are being oppressed or mistreated. Be open to ways God may call you to intervene.

6. Meditate: Hold this question open before God: 'Loving Creator, help my small heart to join your great heart in having compassion for those most in need.'

CHAPTER 10

Getting Slavery out of the People

Exodus 20:1–21
Matthew 22:34–40
Hebrews 10:1–18

I will put my laws in their hearts, and I will write them on their minds . . .

Most of us spend a lot of our lives trying to get out of something old and confining and into something new and free. That's why we so easily identify with Moses and the freed Hebrew slaves on their journey through the wild wasteland known as the wilderness.

The truth is that we're all on a wilderness journey out of some form of slavery. On a personal level, we know what it is to be enslaved to fear, alcohol, food, rage, worry, lust, shame, inferiority or control. On a social level, in today's version of Pharaoh's economy, millions at the bottom of the pyramid work like slaves from before dawn to after dark and still never get ahead. And even those at the top of the pyramid don't feel free. They wake up each day driven by the need to acquire what others desire, and they fear the lash of their own inner slave-drivers: greed, debt, competition, expectation and a desperate, addictive craving for more, more, more.

From top to bottom, the whole system survives by plundering the planet, purchasing this generation's luxuries at the expense of future generations' necessities. Exiting from today's personal and social slavery won't be easy. It will require something like a wilderness journey into the unknown. We know who we have been: slaves. We know who we're going to be: free men and women, experiencing aliveness as God intended. And right now, we're a little bit of both, in need of the identity transformation that comes as we walk the road to freedom.

So we have much to learn from the stories of Moses and his companions. We too must remember that the road to freedom doesn't follow a straight line from point A to point B. Instead, it zigzags and backtracks through a discomfort zone of lack, delay, distress and strain. In those wild places, character is formed – the personal and social character needed for people to enjoy freedom and aliveness. Like those who have walked before us, we need to know that grumbling and complaining can be more dangerous than poisonous snakes or the hot desert sun. Like them, we must be forewarned about the danger of catastrophising the present and romanticising the past. Like them, we must remember that going forward may be difficult, but going back is disastrous.

As they made a road through the wilderness, Moses and his fellow travellers received a mysterious food that fell from the sky each morning like dew. They called it *manna*, which in Hebrew, somewhat humorously, meant, 'What is this stuff?' Like them, we will receive what we need for each day, too – often in mysterious and sometimes even humorous ways, just enough for today, provided one day at a time. And like them, we will learn that we can't survive on bread alone: we also need moral guidance, spiritual nourishment, manna for the soul.

So along with bread for their bodies, God gave the travellers inner nourishment in the form of ten commands that would become the moral basis for their lives in freedom.

1. Put the God of liberation first, not the gods of slavery.
2. Don't reduce God to the manageable size of an idol – certainly not one made of wood and stone by human hands, and not one made by human minds of rituals and words either, and certainly not one in whose name people are enslaved, dehumanised or killed!
3. Do not use God for your own agendas by throwing around God's holy name. If you make a vow in God's name, keep it!
4. Honour the God of liberation by taking and giving everyone a day off. Don't keep the old 24/7 slave economy going.
5. Turn from self-centredness by honouring your parents. (After all, honour is the basis of freedom.)
6. Don't kill people, and don't do the things that frequently incite violence, including:
7. Don't cheat with others' spouses,
8. Don't steal others' possessions, and
9. Don't lie about others' behaviours or characters.
10. In fact, if you really want to avoid the violence of the old slave economy, deal with its root source – in the drama of desire. Don't let the competitive desire to acquire tempt you off the road of freedom.

Through the ten plagues, we might say, God got the people out of slavery. Through the ten commands, God got the slavery out of the people. God also gave them a set of additional practices – rituals, holidays and so on – to help them develop and deepen the character of free people. One of those practices was setting aside a special holy place. They started with a simple 'tent of meeting' that was replaced by a larger, more elaborate gathering place called the 'tabernacle'. That holy space in the centre of their encampment reminded them that the God of liberation was journeying with them – not only above them, visualised as a cloud of smoke and fire, but among them, walking with them in the desert dust as they made the road to freedom.

In that central holy space the people offered sacrifices. Animal sacrifice had already replaced more primitive and brutal rituals of human sacrifice. But the whole idea of appeasing God through blood-shedding of any kind was gradually being replaced with the idea of communing with God over a meal. So sacrifices were seen increasingly as gifts of food, as if to say, 'God is calling us to gather around the family table.' At certain times of the year, and at special moments when the people realised they had done something horrible, they would come to God's big tent. They would bring the makings of a feast, as if to say, 'God, we're sorry for our wrongs. We want to have our family meal again – reconciling with you and with one another. So here's some food to express our desire to sit down at the table of fellowship. We won't turn back. We'll keeping walking this long road to freedom . . . together.'

Of course, Jesus gathered his companions around a table one night and encouraged them to do the same. We call it a meal of communion. We could also call it a meal of liberation and reconciliation. Around this table, we remember where we've been, where we are, whom we're with and where we're headed, as we make a new road by walking . . . together.

The wilderness journey is always difficult and seems to last for ever. Like children on a car journey, we keep whining, 'Aren't we there yet?' But the truth is, if we arrive before we've learned the lessons of the wilderness, we won't be able to enjoy the freedom that awaits us in the promised land beyond it. There is wisdom we will need there that we can gain only right here. There is strength and skill we will need in the future that we can develop only here and now, on the wilderness road. There is moral muscle we will need then that we can exercise and strengthen only through our struggles on this road, here and now. There is a depth of connection with God that will be there when we need it in the future – if we learn to trust and follow God now, on the long wild road to freedom.

The struggles will make us either bitter or better. The trials will lead to either breakdown or breakthrough. We will often be tempted to return to our old lives, but in that tension between a backward pull and a forward call, we will discover unexplainable sustenance (like manna) and unexpected refreshment (like springs in the desert). Against all odds, walking by faith, we will survive – and more: we will learn what it means to be alive.

There are no shortcuts. The road cannot be made by wishing, by whining or by talking. It can be made only by walking, day after day, step by step, struggle by struggle. It's easier, it turns out, to get people out of slavery than it is to get slavery out of people. So, people, let us walk the road – right through the middle of the desert.

Engage

1. What one thought or idea from today's lesson especially intrigued, provoked, disturbed, challenged, encouraged, warmed, warned, helped or surprised you?

2. Share a story about a significant wilderness experience in your life – either literal or figurative.

3. What do you think it means in today's world to 'get the slavery out of the people'? What kinds of slavery do you think we are still stuck in?

4. For children: What's the longest trip you've ever taken? What was one of the best parts of the trip? What was one of the worst parts?

5. Activate: Each day this week, reread the ten commandments as worded in this chapter. (Maybe send them to yourself and

others via e-mail or social media.) Look for ways this ancient moral code is relevant in today's world – and in your life.

6. Meditate: Relax for a few moments in God's presence in silence. Think of the Sabbath not as being deprived of activity, but as a day of liberation from the 24/7 work-week of a slave. Breathe deep. Let go. Thank God for rest.

CHAPTER 11

From Ugliness, a Beauty Emerges

Deuteronomy 7:1–11
Psalm 137:1–9; 149

By the rivers of Babylon, there we sat down and there we wept . . . For there our captors asked us for songs, and our tormentors asked for mirth . . .

Matthew 15:21–39

We've come a long way in our story already. We've discovered . . .

Creation – God brings into being this beautiful, evolving world of wonders.
Crisis – we step out of the dance and enter into rivalry with God and our fellow creatures, throwing this planet into disarray.
Calling – God calls people to join in a global conspiracy of goodness and blessing, to heal and restore whatever human evil destroys.
Captivity – the people who have joined God's global conspiracy of goodness experience the horrors of slavery, but God eventually leads them by the wilderness road out of captivity towards freedom.

And now we come to a fifth major episode. It's the story of *conquest*, as the Israelites finally reach the land their ancestors had inhabited four centuries earlier. There's just one problem: others have moved into the land and made it their home for many generations. To possess the land, the Israelites will have to displace these current residents through a war of invasion and conquest. Wars like these are the most bloody and difficult of all, but the Israelites trust that their God will give them victory.

This episode in the biblical story, more than any other, forces us to deal with one of life's most problematic questions: the question of violence. By violence, we mean an act that intends to violate the well-being of a person or people. To help some, is God willing to harm others? Is God part of the violence in the world, and is violence part of God?

Or is God the voice calling to us in our violence to move to a new place, to join God beyond violence, in kindness, reconciliation and peace?

Today, as in the ancient world, many people sincerely believe that God loves *us* and wants peace for *us* so much that God has no trouble harming or destroying *them* for our benefit. We find a lot of that kind of thinking in the Bible, giving God credit and praise for *our* victories and *their* defeats. Before we go too far in condemning ancient people for that exclusive way of thinking, we should realise how easy it is for us to do the same – when we create a superior *us* that looks down on *them* for thinking so exclusively!

We should also notice that where we see this kind of thinking embedded in the Bible, we also find important qualifications. For example, God's favour towards *the insiders* is dependent on the insiders living good and humble lives. If the insiders become oppressors, they should not expect God's help. And God gives the freed slaves the right to conquer just enough land for themselves, just one time. They are never given a licence to create an empire, expanding to enslave others as they had previously been enslaved.

Even as they prepare for war, they are told again and again

that after the conquest ends, they must treat 'aliens and strangers' as neighbours, with honour and respect, remembering that they once were 'aliens and strangers' themselves in Egypt. Their ultimate dream is to be farmers, not warriors – so that swords can be beaten into ploughshares and spears into pruning hooks, as soon as possible.

But even with these provisos in mind, we can't ignore the brutality found in many Bible passages. From Deuteronomy 7 to Leviticus 25 to 1 Samuel 15 to Psalms 137 and 149, we hear claims that 'God' or 'the LORD' actively commands or blesses actions that we would call crimes against humanity. Many religious scholars have assumed that because the Bible makes these claims, we must defend them as true and good. That approach, however, is morally unacceptable for growing numbers of us, and fortunately we have another option.

We can acknowledge that in the minds of the originators of these stories, God as they understood God did indeed command these things. We can acknowledge that in their way of thinking, divine involvement in war was to be expected. We can allow that they were telling the truth as they best understood it when they found comfort and reassurance in a vision of a God who would harm or kill *them* to defend, help or avenge *us*. We can try to empathise, remembering that when human beings suffer indignity, injustice, dehumanisation and violence, they naturally pray for revenge and dream of retribution against those who harm them. Without condoning, we can at least understand why they saw God as they did, knowing that if we had walked in their sandals, we would have been no different.

But we don't need to stop there. We can then turn to other voices in the biblical library who, in different circumstances, told competing stories to give a different – and we would say *better* – vision of God.

For example, take the passage in Deuteronomy 7 where God

commands Joshua to slaughter the seven Canaanite nations. They must be shown no mercy. Even their little girls must be seen as a threat. Then we can consider a story from Matthew's Gospel which offers itself as a response to the earlier passage. There we meet a woman who is identified by Matthew as a Canaanite. This identification is significant, since Canaanites no longer existed as an identifiable culture in Jesus' day. Calling this woman a Canaanite would be like calling someone a Viking or Aztec today. She asks for the one thing that had been denied her ancestors: *mercy* . . . mercy for her daughter who is in great need.

Up until this point, Jesus has understood his mission only in relation to his own people. After all, they're pretty lost and they need a lot of help. So he hesitates. How can he extend himself to this Canaanite? But how can he refuse her? In her persistence, he senses genuine faith, and he hears God's call to extend mercy even to her. So he says 'yes' to the mother, and the daughter is healed. From there, Jesus goes to an area to the north-west of the Sea of Galilee. He teaches and heals a large crowd of people there who, like the woman and her daughter, are not members of his own religion and culture. Their non-Jewish identity is clear in their response to Jesus' kindness: 'And they praised the God of Israel.' What was an exception yesterday is now the new rule: *Don't kill the other. Show mercy to them.*

Then Jesus repeats a miracle for these outsiders that he had done previously for his fellow Jews, multiplying loaves and fish so they can eat. In the previous miracle, there were twelve baskets left over, suggesting the twelve tribes of Israel – the descendants, that is, of Jacob and his twelve sons. In this miracle, there are seven baskets left over – suggesting, it seems quite clear, the seven Canaanite nations that Jesus' ancestors had been commanded to destroy.

Matthew's version of this story makes a confession: *Our ancestors, led by Moses and Joshua, believed God sent them into the world in conquest, to show no mercy to their enemies, to defeat and kill them. But now, following Christ, we hear God giving us a higher mission. Now we believe God sends us into the world in compassion, to show mercy, to heal, to feed – to nurture and protect life rather than take it.*

We begin with pre-biblical visions of many warring gods who are all violent and capricious. In much of the Bible, we advance to a vision of a single God who uses violence against *them* in the service of justice for *us*. Eventually, through the biblical library, we find a beautiful new vision of God being revealed. God desires justice for all, not just for *us*. God is leading both *us* and *them* out of injustice and violence into a new way of reconciliation and peace. God loves everyone, everywhere, no exceptions.

Violence, like slavery and racism, was normative in our past and it is still all too common in the present. How will we tell the stories of our past in ways that make our future less violent? We must not defend those stories or give them the final word. Nor can we cover them up, hiding them like a loaded gun in a drawer that can be found and used to harm. Instead, we must expose these violent stories to the light of day. And then we must tell new stories beside them, stories so beautiful and good that they will turn us towards a better vision of kindness, reconciliation and peace for our future and for our children's future.

The stories of Jesus' life and teaching, wisely told, can help us imagine and create a more peaceful future. They help us see the glory of God shining in the face of a kind, forgiving, gentle and non-violent man, and in the smiles and tears, words and deeds of those who radiate his love.

Engage

1. What one thought or idea from today's lesson especially intrigued, provoked, disturbed, challenged, encouraged, warmed, warned, helped or surprised you?

2. Share a story about a film you've seen or a book you've read that upheld violence as the way to prosperity and peace. Can you share an alternative film or story that pointed to a non-violent way to peace?

3. How do you respond to Matthew's story of the Canaanite woman in conversation with the Deuteronomy story of Canaanite slaughter? Can you think of other paired stories like this?

4. For children: Who do you think is stronger – a person who can punch a bad guy and scare him away, or a person who can convince a bad guy to become good?

5. Activate: This week, listen for situations when people use God (or some other 'good reason') to justify violence or unkindness. Try to understand why they would see God and violence this way. Seek to see the world through their eyes and to imagine how hard it would be for them to see God differently.

6. Meditate: Hold in silence the tension between a violent world and a God who calls us to reconciliation, mutual understanding and respect, and peace.

CHAPTER 12

Stories that Shape Us

2 Kings 2:1–15

Psalm 23

Even though I walk through the darkest valley, I fear no evil; for you are with me; your rod and your staff—they comfort me.

Acts 1:1–11

A little girl once asked her mother if the Bible story of Elijah flying to heaven on a chariot of fire was 'real or pretend'. How would you have answered her question?

You might try to explain that sometimes a 'pretend' story can tell more truth and do more good than a 'real' one – as Jesus' parables exemplify so powerfully. You might explain how real stories are often embellished with pretend elements. Or you might respond as that little girl's wise mother did: 'That's a great question! Some stories are real, some are pretend, and some of the very best ones use a mix of both reality and make-believe to tell us something important. What do you think about the Elijah story?' The mother's answer didn't tell the little girl *what* to think. It invited her *to* think – as a bona fide member of the interpretive community.

Whenever we engage with the stories of the Bible, we become members of the interpretive community. And that's a big responsibility, especially when we remember how stories from the Bible have been used to promote both great good and great harm. We might say that good interpretation begins with three elements: science, art and heart. First, we need *critical or scientific research* into history, language, anthropology and sociology to interpret the Bible wisely. Second, since the Bible is a literary and therefore an artistic collection, we need an *artist's eye and ear* to draw meaning wisely from ancient stories. But at every step, we must also be guided by a *humble, teachable heart* that listens for the voice of the Spirit.

In that light, the Elijah story addresses an urgent question: *What happens when a great leader dies?* Typically, a blaze of glory surrounds the hero's departure – symbolised by the fiery chariot and horses in the story. After the leader is gone, the actual life and message of the leader are forgotten, obscured by the blaze of fame and glory. People become fans of the leader's reputation, but not followers of his example. That's why the old mentor Elijah puts his young apprentice Elisha through many trials and warns him about the spectacle surrounding his departure. The fireworks are not the point, Elijah explains; they're a distraction, a temptation to be overcome. If the apprentice resists that distraction and remains resolutely focused on the mentor himself, a double portion of the mentor's spirit will rest on him.

We see something very similar in the story of Jesus' departure. Will his followers look up at the sky and speculate about their departed leader with their heads in the clouds? Will they be fans instead of followers? Or will they get down to work and stay focused on living and sharing Jesus' down-to-Earth way of life, empowered with his Spirit?

Like young Elisha, interpreters today must remember that it's easy to miss the point of ancient stories. Those stories didn't merely aim, like a modern textbook, to pass on factual *information*. They sought people's *formation* by engaging their interpretive *imagination*.

As a first step in wisely interpreting Bible stories with science, art and heart, we need to put each in its intended historical context and get a sense for the big narrative in which each story is nested. Roughly speaking, we can locate the stories of Abraham and Sarah somewhere around 2000–1700 BC. We can place the stories of Moses and the Exodus around 1400 BC. We can locate the conquest of the Canaanites around 1300 BC, after which they formed a loose confederacy under a series of leaders who are somewhat misleadingly called *judges* in the Bible. *Tribal leaders* or even *warlords* might be more accurate names.

Those were violent times, and some of the stories from those times are bone-chilling, especially regarding the appallingly low status of women and the appallingly violent behaviour of men. For example, the book of Judges ends with the account of a brutal gang rape, murder and dismemberment of a young woman, followed by a horrific aftermath of intertribal retaliation and kidnapping of innocent young women. Interestingly, in the very next story in the biblical library, the book of Ruth, we find the polar opposite – the poignant tale of two kind and courageous women, Ruth and Naomi. They forged a resilient life of dignity and beauty in the midst of brutality. Where the men failed, the women prevailed.

Around 1050 BC, pressured by aggressive nations around them and brutality among them, the twelve tribes formed a stronger alliance. They united under a king named Saul. Saul turned out to be a disappointment, but in his shadow a more heroic figure named David appeared. The story of David's gradual rise from shepherd boy to king unfolds in great detail, each episode revealing Saul as less strong and noble and David as more clever and charismatic. When Saul was killed in battle, David established his throne in Jerusalem, inaugurating what is still remembered as Israel's golden age.

David was heroic, but far from perfect, and the Bible doesn't cover up his serious failings – including those of a sexual nature. When David wanted to build a temple to honour God, God said 'no': a place of worship should not be associated with a man of bloodshed. David's son Solomon was not a warrior, so he was allowed to fulfil his father's dream by building a temple. But Solomon used slave labour to build that temple – a tragic irony in light of God's identity as the liberator of slaves.

After Solomon's death, around 930 BC, the kingdom split in two. Ten of the original twelve tribes who lived in the northern region broke away from the two tribes who lived to their south. From that time, the Kingdom of Israel in the north, with its capital in Samaria, was governed by its own line of kings. And the Kingdom of Judah in the south continued under the rule of David's descendants in Jerusalem. Nearly all the kings of both nations were corrupt, ineffective and faithful only to their own agendas of gaining and maintaining power at any cost.

Those darker times made the memory of David's reign seem all the more bright. A dream was born in many hearts: that a descendant of David would one day arise and come to the throne, inaugurating a new kingdom, a new golden age, a new day. The old dream of a promised land now was replaced by a new dream – of a promised *time*, a time when the peace, unity, freedom and prosperity of David's reign would return. This expectation kept hope alive in difficult times, but it also created a sense of pious complacency.

That was what Jesus encountered centuries later. Many were still waiting for a 'son of David', a militant Messiah, to swoop in one day, fix everything and usher in Golden Age 2.0. They expected this warrior king to raise a revolutionary army, overthrow their oppressors and restore civil law and religious order. In anticipation of the warrior king's arrival, some were sharpening daggers and swords. But Jesus was living by a different interpretation of the old stories, so he refused to conform to their expectations. Instead of arming his followers with daggers, swords, spears, chariots and war horses, he armed them with faith, hope, service, forgiveness and love. When he healed people, he didn't tell them, 'I will save you!' or 'My faith will save you!' but 'Your faith has saved you.' Working from a fresh interpretation of the past, he freed them from both passive, pious complacency and desperate, violent action. His fresh interpretation empowered them for something better: faithful, peaceful action.

That's the kind of empowerment we need to face our huge challenges today. How will we deal with political and economic systems that are destroying the planet, privileging the super-elite and churning out weapons of unprecedented destruction at an unprecedented rate? How will we deal with religious systems that often have violent extremists on one wing and complacent hypocrites on the other? How will we grapple with complex forces that break down family and community cohesion and leave vulnerable people at great risk – especially women, and especially the very young and the very old? How will we face our personal demons – of greed, lust, anxiety, depression, anger and addiction – especially when people are spending billions to stimulate those demons so we will buy their products?

These aren't pretend problems. To find real-world solutions, we need to be wise interpreters of our past. Like Elijah's apprentice Elisha, we must stay focused on the substance at the centre, undistracted by all the surrounding fireworks. Because the meaning we shape from the stories we interpret will, in turn, shape us.

Engage

1. What one thought or idea from today's lesson especially intrigued, provoked, disturbed, challenged, encouraged, warmed, warned, helped or surprised you?
2. Share a story about a 'golden age' you learned about in your family, your school or some other group you've been part of.

3. How do you respond to the comparison between the story of Jesus' departure in Acts and the story of Elijah's departure in 2 Kings?

4. For children: Do you have a favourite superhero? Tell us why you like him or her so much.

5. Activate: This week, try to read the gruesome story of the Levite's concubine (Judges 19 – 21) and then the gentle story of Ruth and Naomi (book of Ruth). Do you see similar stories in this week's headlines?

6. Meditate: In silence, hold the phrases 'passive, pious complacency', 'desperate, violent action' and 'faithful, peaceful action' in your mind for a few minutes. Ask God to make you an agent of faithful, peaceful action.

CHAPTER 13

The Great Conversation

Isaiah 1:1 – 2:5

. . . seek justice, rescue the oppressed, defend the orphan, plead for the widow. Come now, let us argue it out.

Romans 15:1–13
Matthew 9:10–17

It was about 800 BC. The Israelites and Judeans had already survived so much. In addition to all the trouble within their respective borders – much of it caused by corrupt leaders – even bigger trouble was brewing outside. The two tiny nations were dwarfed by superpower neighbours, each of which had desires to expand. To the north and east were the Assyrians. To the east were the Babylonians, and to their east, the Persians. To the south were the Egyptians, and to the West, the Mediterranean Sea. How could Israel and Judah, each smaller than present-day Jamaica, Qatar or Connecticut, hope to survive, surrounded in this way?

The northern Kingdom of Israel fell first. In 722 BC, the Assyrians invaded and deported many of the Israelites into Assyria. These displaced Israelites eventually intermarried and lost their distinct identity as children of Abraham. They're remembered today as 'the ten lost tribes of Israel'. The Assyrians quickly repopulated the conquered kingdom with large numbers of their own, who then intermarried with the remaining Israelites. The mixed descendants, later known as Samaritans, would experience a long-standing tension with the 'pure' descendants of Abraham in Judah to the south.

Judah resisted conquest for just over another century, during which Assyrian power declined and Babylonian power increased. Finally, around 587 BC, Judah was conquered by the Babylonians. Jerusalem and its temple were destroyed. The nation's 'brightest and best' were deported as exiles to the Babylonian capital. The peasants were left to till the land and 'share' their harvest with the occupying regime. For about seventy years, this sorry state of affairs continued.

Babylon, meanwhile, was being pressured by their neighbour to the east, the Persians. Soon the Persians conquered the Babylonians. They had a more lenient policy for managing the nations under their power, so in 538 they allowed the exiled Judeans to return and rebuild their capital city. But even with this increased freedom, the people remained under the heel of foreigners. They had survived, but they still felt defeated.

How should they interpret their plight? Some feared that God had failed or abandoned them. Others blamed themselves for displeasing God in some way. Those who felt abandoned by God expressed their devastation in heart-rending poetry. Those who felt they had displeased God tried to identify their offences, assign blame and call for repentance. It was during this devastating period of exile and return that much of the oral tradition known to us as the Old Testament was either written down for the first time, or re-edited and compiled. No wonder, arising in such times of turmoil and tumult, the Bible is such a dynamic collection!

As the people changed and evolved, their understanding of God changed and evolved. For example, when they were nomadic wanderers in the desert, they envisioned God as a pillar of cloud and fire, cooling them by day and warming them by night. When they were involved in conquest, God was the Lord of Hosts, the commander of armies. When they were being pursued by enemies, God was pictured as a hiding place in the rocks. When they became a unified kingdom, God was their ultimate King. When they returned to their land and felt more secure, more gentle images of God took centre stage – God as their Shepherd, for example. When they suffered defeat, they saw God as their avenger. When they suffered injustice, God was the judge who would convict their oppressors and restore justice. When they felt abandoned and alone in a foreign land, they imagined God as a loving mother who could never forget her nursing child.

Not only do we see their understanding of God evolve under evolving circumstances, we also see their understanding of human affairs mature. For example, to immature minds, there are two kinds of leaders: those who have been set in place by God, and those who haven't. The former deserve absolute obedience, since to disobey them would be to disobey God. But in the Bible we see this simplistic thinking challenged. Moses, for example, was a God-anointed leader, and people were indeed urged to obey him and they were punished when they didn't. Yet when Moses made mistakes of his own, he got no special treatment. The same with Saul, and the same even with David.

As their understanding of human affairs matured, their moral reasoning matured as well. In the Garden of Eden story, Adam and Eve wanted to grasp the fruit of knowing good and evil, as if that were a simple thing. But as the biblical story unfolded, first it became clear that the line between good and evil didn't run between groups of *us* and *them*. There were good guys among *them* – including people like Melchizedek, Abimelech, Jethro, Rahab and Ruth. And there were plenty of bad guys among *us* – including most of the kings of Israel and Judah. It became clear that the dividing line doesn't simply run between good and bad individuals, as many people today still believe.

Some of the Bible's best 'good guys' – like David and Solomon – did really bad things. So the Bible presents a morally complex and dynamic world where the best of us can do wrong and the worst of us can do right. The line between good and evil runs – and moves – within each of us.

The Bible often conveys this growing moral wisdom by drawing a third option from two irreconcilable viewpoints on an issue. For example, some biblical voices interpreted the move from an alliance of tribes to a kingdom as a tragic sign that the people had rejected God as their king. Others saw the monarchy as a gift from God, a big improvement over the previous chaos. When both sets of voices are heard, it's clear that each had some of the truth: a strong central government can be both a curse and a blessing, not just one or the other.

Similarly, some biblical voices argued that God required animals to be slaughtered so their blood could be offered as a sacrifice. Without sacrifice, they believed, sins could not be forgiven, so they gave detailed instructions for sacrifice that, they claimed, were dictated by God. Other voices said no, God never really desired bloody sacrifices, but instead wanted another kind of holy gift from humanity: contrite and compassionate hearts, and justice, kindness and humility. When we give both sets of voices a fair hearing, we can agree that sacrifices fulfilled a necessary function for the people at one point in their development, even though ultimately sacrifices weren't an absolute and eternal necessity.

Meanwhile, many voices claimed that Abraham's descendants were God's only chosen and favoured people. Others countered that God created and loves all people and has chosen and guided all nations for various purposes. If we listen to both claims, we can conclude that just as a little girl feels she is uniquely loved by her parents, even as her little brother feels the same way, each nation is intended to feel it is special to God – not to the exclusion of others, but along with others.

From Genesis to Job, the Bible is full of conversations like these – with differing viewpoints making their case, point and counterpoint, statement and counterstatement. Sadly, through-out history people have often quoted one side or the other to prove that their view alone is 'biblical'. That's why it's important for us to remain humble as we read the Bible, not to seek ammu-nition for the side of an argument we already stand on, but to seek the wisdom that comes when we listen humbly to all the different voices arising in the biblical library. Wisdom emerges from the conversation among these voices, voices we could arrange in five broad categories.

First, there are the voices of the *priests* who emphasise keep-ing the law, maintaining order, offering sacrifices and faithfully maintaining traditions and taboos. Then there are the voices of the *prophets*, often in tension with the priests, who emphasise social justice, care for the poor and the condition of the heart. Next are the *poets*, who express the full range of human emotion and opinion – the good, the bad and the ugly. Then come the *sages*, who, in proverb, essay and creative fiction, record their theories, observations, questions and doubts. And linking them together are *storytellers*, each with varying agen-das, who try to tell the stories of the people who look back to Abraham as their father, Moses as their liberator, David as their greatest king and God as their Creator and faithful companion. To be alive is to seek wisdom in this great conver-sation . . . and to keep it going today.

Could it be that we are doing just that, here and now, walking this road in conversation together?

Engage

1. What one thought or idea from today's lesson especially intrigued, provoked, disturbed, challenged, encouraged, warmed, warned, helped or surprised you?

2. Share a story about an argument where both sides were partly right.

3. How do you respond to this vision of the Bible as a library full of difference of opinion, yet carrying on an essential conversation about what it means to be alive? Which set of voices do you identify with most – priests, prophets, poets, sages or storytellers?

4. For children: What's one of your favourite stories – one that you like to hear again and again? What's your favourite thing about that story?

5. Activate: This week, listen for voices who fit in the tradition of the priests, prophets, poets, sages and storytellers in today's culture. See if you perceive points of agreement and disagreement with their counterparts in the biblical library.

6. Meditate: In silence, imagine hearing a vigorous conversation going on. Then let the conversation gradually fade away so that silence envelops you. In that silence, open your heart to God's wisdom.

First Quarter Queries

If possible, compose honest and heartfelt replies to these queries in a journal before gathering with one or two others to share what you have written. When you discuss your replies, you may choose to follow the Five Guidelines for Learning Circles in Appendix II. Or you may invite a trusted mentor to serve as 'catechist' so he or she can listen to and respond to your replies. Make it safe for one another to speak freely, and let your conversation build conviction in each of you as individuals and among you as a community.

1. What does it mean to you to live within the story of creation?
2. What does it mean to you to live within the story of crisis?
3. What does it mean to you to live within the story of calling?
4. What does it mean to you to live in a world of captivity and conquest?

5. What does it mean to you to be a part of the great conversation? What do you learn from the priests, prophets, sages, poets and storytellers?
6. In what ways are you integrating into your daily life your identity in God's unfolding story?
7. What are some significant changes you've experienced from being part of this learning circle?

PART 2

ALIVE IN THE ADVENTURE OF JESUS

In Part 1, we explored what it means to be alive in the story of creation ... a story that includes crisis, calling, captivity, conquest and conversation. Into that conversation comes a man named Jesus, a man whose character, words and example changed history. In Part 2, we will explore what it means to be alive in the adventure of Jesus.

We begin with the story of his birth (during the traditional seasons of Advent and Christmas), and then we follow him through childhood to adulthood, as the light of God shines brightly through him (during the season of Epiphany). Our exploration will lead to this life-changing choice: will we identify ourselves as honest and sincere followers of Jesus today?

You may need to rearrange the order of chapters so that Chapter 17 comes the week before Christmas. Then you can use Chapter 17A on Christmas Eve, and Chapter 18 the Sunday (or whatever day you gather) on or after Christmas. At the end of each of the first five chapters, you'll be invited to light a candle. Whether you do so alone or in a learning circle, use that simple tradition as an invitation to joyful, hopeful, reverent contemplation.

CHAPTER 14

Promised Land, Promised Time

Daniel 7:9–28

Isaiah 40:9–11

He will feed his flock like a shepherd; he will gather the lambs in his arms, and carry them in his bosom, and gently lead the mother sheep.

Luke 1:67–79

To be alive is to desire, to hope and to dream, and the Bible is a book about desires, hopes and dreams. The story begins with God's desire for a good and beautiful world, of which we are a part. Soon, some of us desire the power to kill, enslave or oppress others. Enslaved and oppressed people hope for liberation. Wilderness wanderers desire a promised land where they can settle. Settled people dream of a promised time when they won't be torn apart by internal factions, ruled by corrupt elites or dominated by stronger nations nearby.

Desires, hopes and dreams inspire action, and that's what makes them so different from a wish. Wishing is a substitute for action. Wishing creates a kind of passive optimism that can paralyse people in a happy fog of complacency: 'Everything will turn out fine. Why work, struggle, sacrifice or plan?' Guess what happens to people who never work, struggle, sacrifice or plan? Things don't normally turn out the way they wish!

In contrast, our desires, hopes and dreams for the future guide us in how to act now. If a girl hopes to be a doctor one day, she'll study hard and prepare for medical school. If a boy dreams of being a marine biologist one day, he'll spend time around the sea and learn to snorkel and scuba-dive. Their hope for the future guides them in how to act now. They align their lives by their hope, and in that way their lives are shaped by hope. Without action, they would be wishing, not hoping.

Prophets in the Bible have a fascinating role as custodians of the best hopes, desires and dreams of their society. They challenge people to act in ways consistent with those hopes, desires and dreams. And when they see people behaving in harmful ways, they warn them by picturing the future to which that harmful behaviour will lead.

One of the most important prophetic compositions was the book of Isaiah. Most scholars today agree that at least three people contributed to the book over a long period of time, but their combined work has traditionally been attributed to one author. The first thirty-nine chapters of Isaiah were situated in the southern Kingdom of Judah, just before the northern Kingdom of Israel was invaded and colonised by the Assyrians. The prophet saw deep spiritual corruption and complacency among his people and warned them that this kind of behaviour would lead to decline and defeat.

That defeat came in 587 BC at the hand of the Babylonians. After the invasion, many survivors were taken as exiles to Babylon. Chapters 40 – 55, often called 'Second Isaiah', addressed those Judean exiles, inspiring hope that they would one day return to their homeland and rebuild it. That soon happened, beginning in 538 BC under the leadership of Ezra and Nehemiah. That era of rebuilding was the setting for 'Third Isaiah', chapters 56 – 66.

For readers in later generations, ingredients from these three different settings blend into one rich recipe for hope, full of imagery that still energises our imagination today.

> They shall beat their swords into ploughshares,
> and their spears into pruning-hooks;
> nation shall not lift up sword against nation,
> neither shall they learn war any more. (2:4)
> A shoot shall come out from the stock of [David's father] Jesse,
> and a branch shall grow out of his roots.
> The Spirit of the LORD shall rest on him . . .
> The wolf shall live with the lamb,
> the leopard shall lie down with the kid,
> the calf and the lion and the fatling together,
> and a little child shall lead them . . .
> They will not hurt or destroy
> on all my holy mountain;
> for the earth will be full of the knowledge of the LORD
> as the waters cover the sea. (11:1–2, 6, 9)
> Here is my servant, whom I uphold,
> my chosen, in whom my soul delights;
> I have put my spirit upon him;
> he will bring forth justice to the nations.
> He will not cry or lift up his voice,
> or make it heard in the street;
> a bruised reed he will not break,
> and a dimly burning wick he will not quench;
> he will faithfully bring forth justice. (42:1–3)

Isaiah's descriptions of that better day were so inspiring that Jesus and his early followers quoted Isaiah more than any other writer. But many other prophets added their own colours to this beautiful vision of hope. In Ezekiel's vision, people's hearts of stone will be replaced with hearts of flesh. For Malachi, the hearts of parents would turn to their children, and children to their parents. Joel describes the Spirit of God being poured out on all humanity – young and old, men and women, Jew and Gentile. Amos paints the vivid scene of justice rolling down like a river, filling all the lowest places. And Daniel envisioned the world's beast-like empires of violence being overcome by a simple unarmed human being, a new generation of humanity.

In the centuries between the time of the prophets and the birth of Jesus, these prophetic dreams never completely died. But they were never completely fulfilled either. Yes, conditions for the Jews improved under the Persians, but things still weren't as good as the prophets promised. Next the Greek and Seleucid empires took control of the region, and for a time the Jews threw off their oppressors. But their independence was brief, and the full dream of the prophets remained unfulfilled. Next the Romans seized power, subjugating and humiliating the Jews and testing their hope as never before. Yet their dream lived on. It remained alive in people like Elizabeth and Zechariah, Mary and Joseph, and Anna and Simeon, and even among humble shepherds who lived at the margins of society.

To be alive in the adventure of Jesus is to have a desire, a dream, a hope for the future. It is to translate that hope for the future into action in the present and to keep acting in light of it, no matter the disappointments, no matter the setbacks and delays. So let us begin this Advent season by lighting a candle for the prophets who proclaimed their hopes, desires and dreams. Let us keep their flame glowing strong in our hearts, even now.

Engage

1. What one thought or idea from today's lesson especially intrigued, provoked, disturbed, challenged, encouraged, warmed, warned, helped or surprised you?
2. Share a story about a time when you kept hope or lost hope.

3. How do you respond to the imagery of Isaiah, and how would you translate some of that imagery from the ancient Middle East into imagery from today's world?

4. For children: What do you hope to be or do when you grow up?

5. Activate: This week, look for discouragement or cynicism in your own thinking. Challenge yourself to become cynical about your cynicism, and challenge yourself towards prophetic hope.

6. Meditate: Light a candle and choose one image from the prophets mentioned in this chapter. Simply hold that image in your heart, in God's presence. Let it inspire a simple prayer that you may wish to speak aloud.

CHAPTER 15

Women on the Edge

Luke 1:5–55

He has brought down the powerful from their thrones, and lifted up the lowly; he has filled the hungry with good things, and sent the rich away empty.

Isaiah 7:14; 9:2–7
Romans 12:1–2

Imagine a woman in the ancient world who all her life longed to have children. She married young, maybe around the age of fifteen. At sixteen, still no pregnancy. At twenty, still no pregnancy. At twenty-five, imagine how she prayed. By thirty, imagine her anxiety as her prayers were mixed with tears of shame and disappointment – for herself, for her husband. At forty, imagine hope slipping away as she wondered if it even made sense to pray any more. Imagine her sense of loss and regret at fifty. Why pray now?

Of course, this was the story of Abraham's wife, Sarah, back in the book of Genesis. That ancient story was echoed in the Gospel of Luke. Luke tells us of a woman named Elizabeth who was married to a priest named Zechariah. They prayed for a child, but none came, year after year. One day as Zechariah was doing his priestly duties, he had a vision of an angelic messenger from God. Zechariah's prayers for a son would be answered, the messenger said. When Elizabeth gave birth, they should name their child John. Zechariah found this impossible to believe. 'I'm an old man,' he said, 'and Elizabeth is past her prime as well!' The messenger told him that because of his scepticism, he would not be able to speak until the promised baby was born.

In a way, the stories of Sarah and Elizabeth are a picture of the experience of the Jewish people. The prophets had inspired them to dream of a better day. Their prophecies echoed the first promise to Abraham: that everyone everywhere would be blessed through Abraham's descendants. But those promises and prophecies had been delayed and frustrated and delayed again, until it seemed ridiculous to keep the dream alive.

All of us experience this sense of frustration, disappointment, impatience and despair at times. We all feel that we have the capacity to give birth to something beautiful and good and needed and wonderful in the world. But our potential goes unfulfilled, or our promising hopes miscarry. So we live on one side and then on the other of the border of despair.

And then the impossible happens.

Elizabeth had a young relative named Mary. Mary was engaged but not yet married. Significantly, she was a descendant of King David, whose memory inspired the hope of a David-like king who would bring the better days long hoped for among her people. When Elizabeth was about six months pregnant, an angelic messenger – the same one who appeared to Zechariah, it turns out – now appeared to Mary. 'Greetings, favoured one!' he said. 'The Lord is with you!' Mary felt, as any of us would, amazed and confused by this greeting.

The messenger said, 'Don't be afraid, Mary. You will conceive and bear a son . . .' And the messenger's words echoed the promises of the prophets from centuries past – promises of a leader who would bring the people into the promised time. Mary asked, 'How can this be, since I am a virgin?' The angel replied that the

Holy Spirit would come upon her, so the child would be conceived by the power of God. And he added that Elizabeth, her old and barren relative, was also pregnant. 'Nothing will be impossible with God,' he said.

Many of us today will suspect that Luke made up this story about Mary to echo Isaiah's prophecy about a son being born to a virgin, just as he invented the story of Elizabeth conceiving in old age to echo the story of Sarah. It's tempting to quickly assign both stories to the category of primitive, pre-scientific legend and be done with them. After all, both stories are, to scientific minds, simply impossible.

But what if that's the point? What if their purpose is to challenge us to blur the line between what we think is possible and what we think is impossible? Could we ever come to a time when swords would be beaten into ploughshares? When the predatory people in power – the lions – would lie down in peace with the vulnerable and the poor – the lambs? When God's justice would flow like a river – to the lowest and most 'God-forsaken' places on Earth? When the broken-hearted would be comforted and the poor would receive good news? If you think, *Never – it's impossible*, then maybe you need to think again. Maybe it's not too late for something beautiful to be born. Maybe it's not too soon, either. Maybe the present moment is pregnant with possibilities we can't see or even imagine.

In this light, the *actual* point of these pregnancy stories – however we interpret their *factual* status – is a challenge to us all: to dare to hope, like Elizabeth and Mary, that the seemingly impossible is possible. They challenge us to align our lives around the 'impossible possibilities' hidden in this present, pregnant moment.

The image of a virgin birth has other meanings as well. The leaders of ancient empires typically presented themselves as divine-human hybrids with superpowers. Pharaohs and Caesars were 'sons of gods'. In them, the violent power of the gods was fused with the violent power of humans to create superhuman superviolence – which allowed them to create superpower nations. But here is God gently inviting – not coercing – a young woman to produce a child who will be known not for his violence but for his kindness. This is a different kind of leader entirely – one who doesn't rule with the masculine power of swords and spears, but with a mother's sense of justice and compassion.

In Luke's telling of the birth of Jesus, God aligns with the creative feminine power of womanhood rather than the violent masculine power of statehood. The doctrine of the virgin birth, it turns out, isn't about bypassing sex but about subverting violence. The violent power of top-down patriarchy is subverted not by counterviolence but by the creative power of pregnancy. It is through what proud men have considered 'the weaker sex' that God's true power enters and changes the world. That, it turns out, is exactly what Mary understood the messenger to be saying:

> God has looked with favour on the lowliness of his servant . . . scattered the proud . . . brought down the powerful . . . lifted up the lowly . . . filled the hungry with good things, and sent the rich away empty. (Luke 1:48, 51, 52, 53)

So Mary presents herself to the Holy Spirit to receive and co-operate with God's creative power. She surrenders and receives, she nurtures and gives her all . . . because she dares to believe the impossible is possible. Her son Jesus will consistently model her self-surrender and receptivity to God, and he will consistently prefer the insightful kindness of motherhood to the violent blindness of statehood.

That's what it means to be alive in the adventure of Jesus. We present ourselves to God – our bodies, our stories, our futures, our possibilities, even our limitations. 'Here I am,' we say with Mary, 'the Lord's servant. Let it be with me according to your will.'

So in this Advent season – this season of awaiting and pondering the coming of God in Christ – let us light a candle for Mary. And let us, in our own hearts, dare to believe the impossible by surrendering ourselves to God, courageously co-operating with God's creative, pregnant power – in us, for us and through us. If we do, then we, like Mary, will become pregnant with holy aliveness.

Engage

1. What one thought or idea from today's lesson especially intrigued, provoked, disturbed, challenged, encouraged, warmed, warned, helped or surprised you?

2. Share a story about a woman in your life who had a powerful influence.

3. How do you respond to these reflections on the meaning of the virgin birth?

4. For children: Tell us about a time you were surprised in a good and happy way.

5. Activate: Start each day this week putting Mary's prayer of commitment and surrender, 'Let it be to me according to your will', into your own words. Let this be a week of presenting your life to God so that 'holy aliveness' grows in you.

6. Meditate: After lighting a candle, hold the words 'Here I am, the Lord's servant' in your heart for a few minutes in silence. Try to return to those words many times in the week ahead.

CHAPTER 16

Keep Herod in Christmas

Jeremiah 32:31–35
Micah 5:2–5a
Matthew 1:18 – 2:15

. . . the child conceived in her is from the Holy Spirit. She will bear a son, and you are to name him Jesus, for he will save his people from their sins.'

Right in the middle of Matthew's version of the Christmas story comes a shock. It is disturbing, terrifying and horrific. And it is essential to understanding the adventure and mission of Jesus.

King Herod, or Herod the Great, ruled over Judea in the years leading up to Jesus' birth. Although he rebuilt the temple in Jerusalem – a sign of his Jewish identity – he was a puppet king who also depended on the Roman Empire for his status. He was, like many biblical characters – and like many of us, too – a man with an identity crisis. Cruel and ruthless, he used slave labour for his huge building projects. He had a reputation for assassinating anyone he considered a threat – including his wife and two of his own sons. Late in his reign, he began hearing rumours . . . rumours that the long-awaited liberator prophesied by Isaiah and others had been born. While a pious man might have greeted this news with hope and joy, Herod only saw it as a threat – a threat to political stability and to his own status as king.

In recent years, there had been a lot of resistance, unrest and revolt in Jerusalem, so Rome wasn't in a tolerant frame of mind. Any talk of rebellion, Herod knew, would bring crushing retaliation against the city. So Herod enquired of the religious scholars to find out if the holy texts gave any indication of where this long-anticipated child would be born. Their answer came from the book of Micah: Bethlehem.

Herod did what any desperate, ruthless dictator would do. First, he tried to enlist some foreign mystics, known to us as 'the wise men from the East'. He wanted them to be his spies to help him discover the child's identity and whereabouts so he could have the child killed. But the wise men were warned of his deceit in a dream and so avoided becoming his unwitting accomplices. Realising that his 'Plan A' had failed, Herod launched 'Plan B'. He sent his henchmen to find and kill any young boy living in the area of Bethlehem. But the particular boy he sought had already been removed from Bethlehem and taken elsewhere.

The result? A slaughter of innocent children in Bethlehem. As is the case with many biblical stories, some scholars doubt this mass slaughter occurred, since none is recorded in other histories of the time. Others argue that Bethlehem was a small town, so the total number of casualties may have been twenty or thirty. Dictators certainly have their ways of keeping atrocities secret – just as they have their ways of making their exploits known. Whatever the infant death count in Bethlehem, we know Herod killed some of his own children when they became a threat to his agenda. So even if the story has been fictionalised to some degree, there is a deeper truth that has much to say to us today.

In his slaughter of innocent children, King Herod has now emulated the horrible behaviour of Pharaoh centuries before, in the days of Moses. A descendant of the slaves has behaved like the ancient slave-master. The story of Herod tells us once again that the world can't be simply divided between the good guys

– *us* – and the bad guys – *them* – because like Herod, members of *us* will behave no differently from *them*, given the power and provocation. So all people face the same profound questions: *How will we manage power? How will we deal with violence?*

Herod – and Pharaoh before him – model one way: violence is simply one tool, used in varying degrees, to gain or maintain power.

The baby whom Herod seeks to kill will model another way. His tool will be service, not violence. And his goal will not be gaining and maintaining power, but using his power to heal and empower others. He will reveal a vision of God that is reflected more in the vulnerability of children than in the violence of men, more in the caring of mothers than in the cruelty of kings.

All this can sound quite abstract and theoretical unless we go one step deeper. The next war – whoever wages it – will most likely resemble every war in the past. It will be planned by powerful older men in their comfortable offices, and it will be fought on the ground by people the age of their children and grandchildren. Most of the casualties will probably be between eighteen and twenty-two years old – in some places, much younger. So the old, sad music of the ancient story of Herod and the slaughter of the children will be replayed again. And again, the tears of mothers will fall.

The sacrifice of children for the well-being and security of adults has a long history among human beings. For example, in the ancient Middle East there was a religion dedicated to an idol named Molech. Faithful adherents would sacrifice infants to Molech every year, a horrible display of twisted religiosity to appease their god's wrath and earn his favour. In contrast, beginning with the story of Abraham and Isaac, we gradually discover that the true God doesn't require appeasement at all. In fact, God exemplifies true, loving, mature parenthood . . . self-giving for the sake of one's children, not sacrificing children for one's own selfish interests.

This is why it matters so much for us to grapple with what we believe about God. Does God promote or demand violence? Does God favour the sacrifice of children for the well-being of adults? Is God best reflected in the image of powerful old men who send the young and vulnerable to die on their behalf? Or is God best seen in the image of a helpless baby, identifying with the victims, sharing their vulnerability, full of fragile but limitless promise?

We do not live in an ideal world. To be alive in the adventure of Jesus is to face at every turn the destructive reality of violence. To be alive in the adventure of Jesus is to side with vulnerable children in defiance of the adults who see them as expendable. To walk the road with Jesus is to withhold consent and co-operation from the powerful, and to invest it instead with the vulnerable. It is to refuse to bow to all the Herods and all their ruthless regimes – and to reserve our loyalty for a better King and a better Kingdom.

Jesus has truly come, but each year during the Advent season we acknowledge that the dream for which he gave his all has not yet fully come true. As long as elites plot violence, as long as children pay the price and as long as mothers weep, we cannot be satisfied.

So let us light a candle for the children who suffer in our world because of greedy, power-hungry and insecure elites. And let us light a candle for grieving mothers who weep for lost sons and daughters, throughout history and today. And let us light a candle for all people everywhere to hear their weeping. In this Advent season, we dare to believe that God feels their pain and comes near to bring comfort. If we believe that is true, then of course we must join God and come near, too. That is why we must keep Herod and the ugliness of his mass murder in the beautiful Christmas story.

Engage

1. What one thought or idea from today's lesson especially intrigued, provoked, disturbed, challenged, encouraged, warmed, warned, helped or surprised you?

2. Share a story about a time when you were a child and an adult other than a parent showed you great respect or kindness.

3. How do you respond to Matthew's decision to include this story that none of the other Gospels recount?

4. For children: If you could ask grown-ups to do one thing to help children, what would it be?

5. Activate: This week, try to look at personal and political situations from the vantage point of how they will affect children and their mothers.

6. Meditate: Light a candle, and hold in your mind both the image of Herod, ruthless and power-hungry, and the image of Jesus, a vulnerable baby. Observe what happens in your heart and express a prayer in response.

CHAPTER 17

Surprising People

Psalm 34:1–18

The Lord is near to the broken-hearted, and saves the crushed in spirit.

Matthew 1:1–17
Luke 2:8–20

And Abraham was the father of Isaac, and Isaac the father of Jacob, and Jacob . . . To modern readers, the ancestor lists that are so common in the Bible seem pretty tedious and pointless. But to ancient people, they were full of meaning. They were shorthand ways of showing connections, helping people remember how they were related, and reminding them of the story that they found themselves in.

Both Matthew's and Luke's Gospels give us ancestor lists for Jesus. Although they are very different lists, both agree on two essential points. First, Jesus was a descendant of Sarah and Abraham. That reminded people of God's original promise to Abraham and Sarah – that through their lineage, all nations of the world would be blessed. Second, Jesus was a descendant of King David. That brought to mind all the nostalgia for the golden age of David's reign, together with all the hope from the prophets about a promised time under the benevolent reign of a descendant of David.

Apart from these similarities, the two lists offer distinct treasures. Luke's Gospel starts with the present and goes back, all the way to Abraham, and then all the way to Adam, the original human in the Genesis story: 'son of Enoch, son of Jared, son of Mahalaleel, son of Cainan, son of Enos, son of Seth, son of Adam, son of God.' The use of that phrase 'son of God' is fascinating. It suggests a primary meaning of the term: to be *the son of* is to 'find your origin in'. It also suggests that Jesus, as the son of Adam, is in some way a new beginning for the human race – a new genesis, we might say. Just as Adam bore the image of God as the original human, Jesus will now reflect the image of God. We might say he is Adam 2.0.

That understanding is reinforced by what comes immediately before Luke's ancestor list. A voice comes from heaven and says, 'You are my Son, the Beloved; with you I am well pleased.' Just as *Son of David* prepares us to expect Jesus to model leadership, and just as *Son of Abraham* prepares us to expect Jesus to model blessing and promise for all, *Son of God* sets us up to expect Jesus to model true humanity as Adam did.

Matthew's version, which starts in the distant past and moves to the present, holds lots of treasures, too. Most surprising is his inclusion of five women. In the ancient world, people were unaware of the existence of the human egg and assumed that a man provided the only seed of a new life. So ancestor lists naturally focused on men. It's surprising enough for Matthew to include women at all, but the women he selects are quite astonishing.

First, there is Tamar. She had once posed as a prostitute in a web of sexual and family intrigue. Then there is Rahab – a Gentile of Jericho who was actually a prostitute. Then there is Ruth, another Gentile who entered into a sexual liaison with a wealthy Jew named Boaz. Then there is Bathsheba who was married to a foreigner – Uriah the Hittite – and with whom King

David committed adultery. Finally there is Mary, who claims to be pregnant without the help of Joseph. These are not the kind of women whose names were typically included in ancestor lists of the past!

But that, of course, must be Matthew's point. Jesus isn't entering into a pristine story of ideal people. He is part of the story of Gentiles as well as Jews, broken and messy families as well as noble ones, normal people as well as kings and priests and heroes. We might say that Jesus isn't entering humanity from the top with a kind of trickle-down grace, but rather from the bottom, with grace that rises from the grass roots up.

That theme is beautifully embodied in the unsung heroes of Luke's Christmas story: shepherds. They're the ones who, along with Joseph and Mary, have a front-row seat to welcome the 'good news of great joy for all the people'. They're the down-to-Earth people who hear the celestial announcement from angelic messengers.

Shepherds were marginal people in society – a lot like Tamar, Rahab, Ruth, Bathsheba and Mary. They weren't normal 'family men' because they lived outdoors most of the time, guarding sheep from wolves and thieves, and guiding sheep to suitable pasture. A younger son, for whom there was no hope of inheriting the family farm, might become a shepherd, as would a man who for some reason was not suitable for marriage. It was among poor men like these that Jesus' birth was first celebrated.

The poor, of course, have a special place in the Bible. The priests and prophets of Israel agreed that God had a special concern for the poor. God commanded all right-living people to be generous to them. Provision was made for the landless to be able to glean from the fields of the prosperous. According to Proverbs, those who exploited the poor – or simply didn't care about them – would not prosper, and those who were good to the poor would be blessed.

The poor were especially central to the life and ministry of Jesus. Jesus understood himself to be empowered by the Spirit to bring good news to the poor. In Jesus' parables, God cared for the poor and confronted the rich who showed the poor no compassion. Jesus taught rich people to give generously to the poor, and even though others considered the poor to be cursed, Jesus pronounced the poor and those who are in solidarity with them to be blessed. When Jesus said, 'The poor you will always have with you,' he was echoing Deuteronomy 15:4 (NLT), which says, 'There should be no poor among you,' for there is actually enough in God's world for everyone.

Although much has changed from Jesus' day to ours, this has not: a small percentage of the world's population lives in luxury, and the majority live in poverty. For example, about half the people in today's world struggle to survive on less than $2.50 (£1.50) per day. Those who subsist on $1.25 (75p) per day make up over a billion of the world's 7 billion people. About half of the people in sub-Saharan Africa and over 35 per cent of people in South-east Asia fit in this category. They are today's shepherds, working the rice fields, streaming into slums, sleeping on pavements, struggling to survive.

So let us light a candle for surprising people like the women of the ancestor lists and the shepherds of the ancient world, and for their counterparts today – all who are marginalised, dispossessed, vulnerable, hungry for good nutrition, thirsty for drinkable water, desperate to know they are not forgotten. Let us join them in their vigil of hope – waiting for good news of great joy for all people, all people, all people. Amen.

Engage

1. What one thought or idea from today's lesson especially intrigued, provoked, disturbed, challenged, encouraged, warmed, warned, helped or surprised you?

2. Share a story about a shady or colourful character from your family history.

3. How do you respond to this approach to the meaning of 'son of God'?

4. For children: Imagine you are a shepherd in the time of Jesus. What do you think your life would be like?

5. Activate: This week, look for surprising people to whom you can show uncommon respect and unexpected kindness.

6. Meditate: After lighting a candle, hold the words 'good news of great joy for all people' in your heart in God's presence for a few moments of silence. Break the silence with a short prayer.

CHAPTER 17A

The Light Has Come (Christmas Eve)

Isaiah 60:1–3
John 1:1–5, 9–10; 3:19–21; 8:12; 9:5; 12:35–36, 46

The true light, which enlightens everyone, was coming into the world.

Do you remember how the whole biblical story begins? 'In the . . .' And do you remember the first creation that is spoken into being? 'Let there be . . .'

On Christmas Eve, we celebrate a new *beginning*. We welcome the dawning of a new *light*.

A new day begins with sunrise. A new year begins with lengthening days. A new life begins with infant eyes taking in their first view of a world bathed in light. And a new era in human history began when God's light came shining into our world through Jesus.

The Fourth Gospel tells us that what came into being through Jesus was not merely a new religion, a new theology or a new set of principles or teachings – although all these things did indeed happen. The real point of it all, according to John, was *life*, vitality, *aliveness* – and now that Jesus has come, that radiant aliveness is here to enlighten all people everywhere.

Some people don't see it yet. Some don't want to see it. They've got some shady plans that they want to preserve undercover, in darkness. From pickpockets to corrupt politicians, from human traffickers to exploitative business sharks, from terrorists plotting in hidden cells to racists spreading messages of hate, they don't welcome the light, because transparency exposes their plans and deeds for what they are: evil. So they prefer darkness.

But others welcome the light. They receive it as a gift, and in that receiving they let God's holy, radiant aliveness stream into their lives. They become portals of light in our world and they start living as members of God's family – which means they're related to all of God's creation. That relatedness is the essence of enlightenment.

What do we mean when we say Jesus is the light? Just as a glow on the eastern horizon tells us that a long night is almost over, Jesus' birth signals the beginning of the end for the dark night of fear, hostility, violence and greed that has descended on our world. Jesus' birth signals the start of a new day, a new way, a new understanding of what it means to be alive.

Aliveness, he will teach, is a gift available to all by God's grace. It flows not from taking but from giving, not from fear but from faith, not from conflict but from reconciliation, not from domination but from service. It isn't found in the outward trappings of religion – rules and rituals, controversies and scruples, temples and traditions. No, it springs up from our innermost being like a fountain of living water. It intoxicates us like the best wine ever and so turns life from a disappointment into a banquet. This new light of aliveness and love opens us up to rethink everything – to go back and become like little children again. Then we can rediscover the world with a fresh, child-like wonder – seeing the world in a new light, the light of Christ.

On Christmas Eve, then, we remember a silent, holy night long ago when Luke tells us of a young and very pregnant woman and a weary man walking beside her. They had travelled over eighty miles, a journey of several days, from Nazareth in the province of Galilee to Bethlehem in the province of Judea. Mary went into labour, and because nobody could provide them with a normal bed in a normal house, she had to give birth in a stable. We can imagine oxen and donkeys and cattle filling the air with their sounds and scent as Mary wrapped the baby in rags and laid him in a manger, a food trough for farm animals. On that dark night, in such a humble place, enfleshed in a tiny, vulnerable, homeless, helpless baby . . . God's light began to glow.

Politicians compete for the highest offices. Business tycoons scramble for a bigger and bigger piece of the pie. Armies march and scientists study and philosophers philosophise and preachers preach and labourers sweat. But in that silent baby, lying in that humble manger, there pulses more potential power and wisdom and grace and aliveness than all the rest of us can imagine.

To be alive in the adventure of Jesus is to kneel at the manger and gaze upon that little baby who is radiant with so much promise for our world today.

So let us light a candle for the Christ child, for the infant Jesus, the Word made flesh. Let our hearts glow with that light that was in him, so that we become candles through which his light shines still. For Christmas is a process as well as an event. Your heart and mine can become the little town, the stable, the manger . . . even now. Let a new day, a new creation, a new you, a new me, begin. Let there be light.

Engage

The gathering can be concluded with a candle-lighting ceremony. If an Advent wreath is being used, the central Christ candle is lit at the beginning of the gathering, and at the end the light is passed from candle to candle, person to person – in silence, or while singing an appropriate carol.

You may wish to walk together to a public place with your candles lit, in silence or while singing carols, as a visible witness to the light that has come into the world. You could also hold some small signs, lettered with simple words of peace from the Christmas story. You could even bring gifts of sweets or fruit to give to people who pass by, along with a sincere 'Merry Christmas'.

CHAPTER 18

Sharing Gifts (Sunday on or after Christmas Day)

Psalm 117
Matthew 2:1–12

Then, opening their treasure-chests, they offered him gifts of gold, frankincense, and myrrh.

Luke 2:25–32

They were called Magi . . . we know them as wise men. They were astrologers, holy men of a foreign religion. They had observed a strange celestial phenomenon, which they interpreted to mean that a new king had been born in Judea. According to Matthew's Gospel, they travelled to honour him, bringing valuable treasures of gold, frankincense and myrrh – precious gifts indeed.

In their giving of gifts they were wiser than they realised. Gift-giving, it turns out, was at the heart of all Jesus would say and do. God is like a parent, Jesus would teach, who loves to shower their sons and daughters with good gifts. The kingdom or commonwealth of God that Jesus constantly proclaimed was characterised by an abundant, gracious, extravagant economy of grace, of generosity, of gift-giving. 'It is better to give than to receive,' Jesus taught, and his followers came to understand Jesus himself as a gift expressing God's love to the whole world.

So, in memory of the wise men's gift-giving to Jesus, in honour of Jesus' teaching and example of giving, and as an echo of God's self-giving in Jesus, we joyfully give one another gifts when we celebrate the birth of Jesus.

Not everyone felt generosity in response to this new baby. King Herod was furious about anyone who might unsettle the status quo. When he deployed troops to the Bethlehem region with orders to kill all infant boys, Joseph was warned in a dream to escape. So the family fled south to Egypt, where Jesus spent part of his childhood as a refugee.

How meaningful it is that members of other religions – the Magi from the east and the Egyptians to the south – help save Jesus' life. Could their role in the Christmas story be a gift to us today? Could they be telling us that God has a better way for religions to relate to one another?

Through the centuries, religions have repeatedly divided people. Religions – including the Christian religion – have too often spread fear, prejudice, hate and violence in our world. But in the Magi's offering of gifts to honour the infant Jesus, and in the Egyptians' protective hospitality for Jesus and his refugee family, we can see a better way, a way Jesus himself embodied and taught as a man. They remind us that members of Earth's religions don't need to see their counterparts as competitors or enemies. Instead, we can approach one another with the spirit of gift-giving and honour, as exemplified by the Magi. We can be there to welcome and protect one another, as exemplified by the Egyptians.

Instead of looking for faults and errors by which other religions can be discredited, insulted and excluded, we can ask other questions: *What good can be discovered in this religion? Let us honour it. What treasures have they been given to share with us? Let us warmly welcome them. What dangers do they face? Let us protect them. What gifts do we have to share with them? Let us generously offer them.*

According to Matthew, when King Herod died, Joseph had another dream telling him it was safe to return to his homeland. But Herod's son still ruled Judea, the region around Bethlehem, so the family went further north to another region, Galilee. They resettled in Nazareth, Galilee – which would be Jesus' address throughout the rest of his childhood and young adulthood.

So, having been protected by the Magi and the Egyptians, Jesus grew up as a Galilean Jew. The Jews were the descendants of the Judeans who had survived the Babylonian invasion over five centuries earlier. They had not lost their identity while living under exile in Babylon. Nor had they lost that identity over the following centuries, when they survived occupation and oppression by the Persians, Greeks and Romans. Because the Jews had so courageously survived oppression and mistreatment by others, and because they believed God had given them special blessings to enjoy and share with everyone, no wonder Jewish identity was highly cherished. No wonder it was repeatedly affirmed and celebrated through holidays like Passover and rites of passage like circumcision.

Luke's Gospel doesn't tell us about the Magi or the Egyptians. For Luke, the next big event after Jesus' birth came eight days later, when Jesus' parents took him to the temple in Jerusalem to be circumcised, a primary sign of Jewish identity for every newborn son. You can imagine his parents' surprise when an old man, a perfect stranger named Simeon, came up to them in the temple and took Jesus from their arms and began praising God. 'This child will be a light for revelation to the Gentiles, and a glory to God's people, Israel,' Simeon said. He was seeing in Jesus a gift for *us* and for *them* both, not one against the other or one without the other.

Old Simeon the Jew in Luke's Gospel and the non-Jewish Magi from the east in Matthew's Gospel agree: this child is special. He is worthy of honour. He has gifts that will bring blessing to his own people, and to all people everywhere.

To be alive in the adventure of Jesus is to know ourselves as part of a tradition and, through that tradition, to have a history and an identity to enjoy, preserve and share. And to be alive in the adventure of Jesus is to see others as part of their unique traditions too, with their own history, identity and gifts. Like the Magi, like the Egyptians, like old Simeon . . . we don't have to see people of other religions in terms of us versus them. We can see people of other religions as beloved neighbours, us with them, them with us, with gifts to share.

May we who follow Jesus discover the gifts of our tradition and share them generously, and may we joyfully receive the gifts that others bring as well. For every good gift and every perfect gift comes from God.

Engage

1. What one thought or idea from today's lesson especially intrigued, provoked, disturbed, challenged, encouraged, warmed, warned, helped or surprised you?

2. Share a story of a meaningful encounter you've had with a member of another religion. Who might be today's Magi – people from other religions (or no religion) who honour Jesus without wanting to leave the religion into which they were born?

3. How do you respond to the idea that members of different religions can see one another as neighbours with whom to exchange gifts rather than as enemies or competitors?

4. For children: What was one of your favourite Christmas presents that you received or that you gave? Why was it your favourite?

5. Activate: This week, look for someone of another faith to spend some time with. Get to know them. Learn about their

tradition. Ask them what they value in their heritage and answer any questions they ask about yours. Perhaps tell them the story of the Magi.

6. Meditate: In silence, think of the different religions in today's world. Hold in your heart the idea that each has gifts to give and each can receive gifts, too. Conclude your meditation with a prayer.

CHAPTER 19

Jesus Coming of Age

1 Kings 3
Luke 2:39 – 3:14; 3:21–22

And Jesus increased in wisdom and in years, and in divine and human favour.

1 Timothy 4:6–16

What were you like when you were twelve? In what ways are you the same today? How have you changed?

We have only this one glimpse into Jesus' childhood. Jesus was twelve, when boys came of age in ancient Jewish culture. He joined his family on their annual pilgrimage south to Jerusalem for the Passover holiday. This was a journey of over sixty miles – not a short trip on foot, maybe taking four or five days each way. This year, as at each Passover holiday, the Jewish people would celebrate the story of God liberating their ancestors from slavery in Egypt. Because the Romans now ruled over them, making them feel like slaves again, the holiday kept alive the hopes that a new Moses might arise among them and lead them to expel the Romans. Like every good holiday, then, this Passover was to be about both the past and the present.

People travelled to and from the Passover festival in large groups, so Mary and Joseph assumed that Jesus was among their fellow travellers when they began the long trek home. When Jesus couldn't be found, they rushed back to Jerusalem, where they looked for him for three long days. Finally they came to the temple, and there Jesus sat, a twelve-year-old boy among the religious scholars and teachers. He was asking questions of them and answering questions they posed in return. Everyone was amazed at this young spiritual prodigy. He was like a modern-day Solomon, King David's son who was famous for his wisdom.

His mother pulled him aside and gave him exactly the lecture you would expect. 'Child!' she began, as if to remind this young adolescent that he wasn't grown up yet. 'Why have you treated us like this? Listen! Your father and I have been worried sick. We've been looking everywhere for you!' Jesus replied, 'Didn't you know that it was necessary for me to be in my Father's house?'

The reply tells us a lot about Jesus. By the age of twelve, he saw God in tender, fatherly terms. He saw himself as God's child. He was already deeply curious – demonstrated by his questions to the religious scholars. And he was deeply thoughtful – demonstrated by his wise answers to their questions. Like most parents of teenagers, of course, Mary and Joseph were completely baffled by his behaviour and his explanation of it. He went back to Nazareth with them, and the next eighteen years were summarised by Luke in these fourteen words: 'Jesus matured in wisdom and years, and in favour with God and with people' (CEB).

As Jesus was maturing in Nazareth, his relative John, son of Elizabeth and Zechariah, was coming of age back in Jerusalem. As the son of a priest, he would have lived the comfortable, privileged life of the upper classes. We would expect him to follow in his father's footsteps at the temple in Jerusalem, offering sacrifices, officiating at festivals and performing ritual cleansings called baptisms.

Baptisms were essential, because pilgrims who came from distant lands to the temple were understood to be 'unclean' as a result of their contact with people of other religions and cultures. Several special baths had been constructed around the temple so that worshippers could ceremonially wash off that contamination and present themselves to God as 'clean people' again. It was another way to preserve religious identity during a time of occupation and domination by 'unclean foreigners'.

Can you imagine how shocking it is for Zechariah's son to burst onto the scene, preaching and performing baptisms – not in Jerusalem, but over eighty miles to the north and east? Can you imagine the disruption of him performing ritual cleansing – not in the private, holy baths near the temple, but in public, out in the countryside, along the banks of the River Jordan? Can you imagine the gossip about his choice to trade the luxurious robes of the priesthood for the rough garments of a beggar, and the high-class menu of Jerusalem for the subsistence fare of the wilderness? What would such actions mean?

John's departure from both family and temple suggested that John was protesting against the religious establishment his father faithfully served. Jerusalem's temple was not all it was held up to be, he would have been saying. A new kind of baptism – with a radical new meaning – was needed. Travelling to a special city and an opulent building could not make people clean and holy. What they needed most was not a change in location, but a change in orientation, a change in heart. People needed a different kind of cleanness – one that couldn't come through a conventional ceremonial bath in a holy temple.

According to John, the identity that mattered most wasn't one you could inherit through tribe, nationality or religion – as descendants of Abraham, for example. The identity that mattered most was one you created through your actions . . . by sharing your wealth, possessions and food with those in need, by refusing to participate in the corruption so common in government and business, by treating others fairly and respectfully, and by not being driven by greed. One word summarised John's message: *repent*, which meant 'rethink everything', or 'question your assumptions', or 'have a deep turnaround in your thinking and values'. His baptism of repentance symbolised being immersed in a flowing river of love, in solidarity not just with the clean, privileged, superior *us* – but with everyone, everywhere.

Like prophets of old, John issued a powerful warning: God would soon intervene to confront wrong and set things right, and the status quo would soon come to an end. Crowds started streaming out to the countryside to be baptised by John. His protest movement grew, and with it expectation and hope. Maybe John would be the long-awaited liberator, the people whispered – like Moses and Joshua, leading people to freedom; like David, instituting a new reign and a new golden age. John quickly squashed those expectations. 'I'm not the one you're waiting for,' he said. 'I'm preparing the way for someone who is coming after me. He will really clean things up. He will bring the change we need.'

John kept thundering out his message of warning and hope, week after week, month after month. He dared to confront the powerful and name their hypocrisy. (Herod Antipas, the son of the Herod who tried to kill Jesus, couldn't withstand the agitation of John's protest movement, so he ultimately would have John arrested and, eventually, beheaded.)

Among the crowds coming to be baptised one day was a young man of about John's age. By receiving John's baptism, this young man identified himself with this growing protest movement in the Galilean countryside. As he came out of the water, people heard a sound, as if the sky was cracking open with a rumble of thunder. They saw something descending from the sky . . . it looked like a dove landing on his head. Some claimed to hear the voice of God saying, 'You are my Son, whom I dearly love. In you I find pleasure' (Mark 1:11, author's paraphrase).

What Jesus had said about God at the age of twelve in the temple, God now echoed about Jesus at the age of thirty at the riverside: they shared a special parent-child relationship, a deep connection of love and joy. And in that relationship there was an invitation for us all, because Jesus taught that all of us could enter into that warm and secure parent-child relationship with God.

That dove is full of meaning as well. Jesus came, not under the sign of the lion or tiger, not under the sign of the bull or bear, not under the sign of the hawk or eagle or viper . . . but under the sign of the dove – a sign of peace and non-violence. Similarly, when John first saw Jesus, he didn't say, 'Behold the Lion of God, come to avenge our enemies,' but rather, 'Behold the Lamb of God, who takes away the sin of the world.' To remove sin rather than get revenge for it – that was an agenda of peace indeed.

So now, Jesus had come of age and stepped onto the stage: a man with a dove-like spirit, a man with the gentleness of a lamb, a man of peace whose identity was rooted in this profound reality: *God's beloved child.*

When we awaken within that deep relationship of mutual love and pleasure, we are ready to join in God's peace movement today – an adventure of protest, hope and creative, non-violent, world-transforming change.

Engage

1. What one thought or idea from today's lesson especially intrigued, provoked, disturbed, challenged, encouraged, warmed, warned, helped or surprised you?

2. Share the story of your baptism or some other initiation experience you've had.

3. How do you respond to this explanation of John the Baptist and baptism? In breaking with tradition, what kind of challenges do you think he encountered?

4. For children: When you think of a dove and a lamb, what do you think of?

5. Activate: This week, look for every chance to 'grow in wisdom' by listening, learning and asking questions.

6. Meditate: Imagine God asking you, 'What one thing would you like me to do for you?' As Solomon asked for wisdom, hold one request up to God in silence. Then receive God's message to Jesus as a message to you by saying these words, silently or aloud, one time or several times: '[Your name], you are my child, whom I dearly love. In you I find pleasure.' Finally, make these words your own: 'I am [my name], your child, whom you dearly love. In me you find pleasure.'

CHAPTER 20

Join the Adventure!

Isaiah 61:1–4
Luke 4:1–30; 5:1–11

The Spirit of the Lord is upon me, because he has anointed me to bring good news to the poor.

2 Timothy 2:1–9

Never to be given a chance to succeed – that's a tragedy. But in some ways it's even worse to have your chance and not be ready for it. That's why in almost every story of a great hero, there is an ordeal or a test that must be passed before the hero's adventure can begin.

That was the case with Jesus. Before he could begin his public adventure, Jesus felt the Holy Spirit leading him away from the crowds, away from the cities and away from the fertile Jordan Valley, out into the solitude of the harsh, dry, barren Judean desert.

By saying Jesus fasted in the desert for forty days, Luke's Gospel is inviting us to remember Moses who, before becoming the liberator of the Hebrew slaves, spent forty years in the wilderness, where he eventually encountered God in the burning bush. Luke's Gospel is also inviting us to remember the story of the newly liberated Hebrew slaves who, after leaving Egypt, were tested for forty years in the wilderness before they were prepared to enter the promised land. Once again the Gospel writers present Jesus as mirroring the experience of his ancestral people.

Luke describes Jesus' testing in the vivid language of an encounter with the devil. Some take this language literally. Others see the devil as a literary figure who developed over time among ancient storytellers to personify all that is dark, evil and violent in human nature and human culture.

'Turn these stones into bread,' the devil says in his first temptation. In other words, *Who needs the character formation and self-control that come from spiritual disciplines like fasting? That's a long, hard process. You can have it all, right now – public influence and private self-indulgence – if you just use your miraculous powers to acquire whatever you desire!* In the second temptation, Jesus is offered the chance to get on the fast track to power by acknowledging that self-seeking power, not self-giving love, reigns supreme: 'You can rule over all the kingdoms of the world – if you'll simply worship me!' In the third temptation, the devil tells him, 'Prove yourself as God's beloved child by throwing yourself off the temple!' This seemingly suicidal move, with angelic intervention at the last moment before impact, would provide just the kind of public-relations spectacle that showmen love. But Jesus is not a showman, and he isn't interested in shortcuts. Besides, he doesn't need to prove he is God's beloved child. He knows that already.

So he will not use his power for personal comfort and pleasure. He will refuse unscrupulous means to achieve just and peaceful ends. He will not reach for spectacle over substance. And so Jesus sets the course for the great work before him – not driven by a human lust for pleasure, power or prestige, but empowered by the Spirit. And of course, if we want to join Jesus in his great work, we must face our own inner demons and discover the same Spirit-empowerment.

He soon comes to his home town, Nazareth. Like any good Jewish man, he goes to the synagogue on the Sabbath day. There is a time in the synagogue gathering where men can read a passage of Scripture and offer comment upon it. So on this day, Jesus stands and asks for the scroll of the prophet Isaiah. He unrolls the scroll until he comes to the passage that speaks of the Spirit anointing someone to bring good news to the poor, release to the captives, healing to the blind, freedom to the oppressed.

By quoting these words, Jesus stirs the hopes of his people – hopes for the time Isaiah and other prophets had urged the people to wait for, pray for and prepare for. Then he sits – a teacher's customary posture in those days. He offers this amazing commentary – notable for its brevity and even more for its astonishing claim: 'Today this Scripture has been fulfilled in your hearing.'

If he had said, 'One day this Scripture will be fulfilled,' everyone would have felt it was a good, comforting sermon. If he had said, 'This Scripture is already fulfilled in some ways, not yet in others,' that would also have been interesting and acceptable. But either commentary would postpone until the future any need for real change in his hearers' lives. For Jesus to say the promised time was here already, fulfilled, today . . . that was astonishing. That required deep rethinking and radical adjustment.

The same is true for us today.

Imagine if a prophet arose today in Panama, Sierra Leone or Sri Lanka. In an interview on the BBC or Al Jazeera he says, 'Now is the time! It's time to dismantle the military-industrial complex and reconcile with enemies! It's time for CEOs to slash their mammoth salaries and give generous pay rises to all their lowest-paid employees! It's time for criminals, militias, weapons factories and armies to turn in their bullets and guns so they can be melted down and recast as trumpets, swings and garden tools. It's time to stop plundering the Earth for quick corporate profit and to start healing the Earth for long-term universal benefit.

Don't say "one day" or "tomorrow". The time is today!'[16] Imagine how the talking heads would spin!

The Nazareth crowd is impressed that their home-town boy is so articulate and intelligent and bold. But Jesus won't let them simply be impressed or appreciative for long. He quickly reminds them of two stories from the Scriptures, one involving a Sidonian widow in the time of Elijah and one involving a Syrian general in the time of Elisha. God bypassed many needy people of our religion and nation, Jesus says, to help those foreigners, those Gentiles, those outsiders. You can almost hear the snap as people are jolted by this unexpected turn.

Clearly, the good news proclaimed by the home-town prophet is for *them* as well as *us*, for all humankind and not just for *our kind*. Somehow, that seems disloyal to the Nazarenes. That seems like a betrayal of their unique and hard-won identity. In just a few minutes, the crowd quickly flips from proud to concerned to disturbed to furious. They are transformed by their fury from a congregation into a lynch mob, and they push Jesus out of the door and over to the edge of a cliff. They're ready to execute this heretical traitor.

Again, imagine if a pope, a patriarch or a famous TV preacher today were to declare that God is just as devoted to Muslims, Hindus and atheists as to Christians. They might not be thrown off a cliff, but one can easily imagine tense brows and grave voices advocating for them to be thrown out of office or taken off the air!

No wonder Jesus needed that time of preparation in the wilderness. He needed to get his mission clear in his own heart so that he wouldn't be captivated by the expectations of adoring fans or intimidated by the threats of furious critics. If we dare to

---

16 This section is adapted from my book *The Secret Message of Jesus* (Nashville: W Publishing/Thomas Nelson, 2006), pp. 24–25.

follow Jesus and proclaim the radical dimensions of God's good news as he did, we will face the same twin dangers of domestication and intimidation.

Jesus managed to avoid execution that day. But he knew it wouldn't be his last brush with hostile opposition. Soon he began inviting select individuals to become his followers. As with aspiring musicians who are invited to become the students of a master-musician, this was a momentous decision for them. To become disciples of a rabbi meant entering a rigorous programme of transformation, learning a new way of life, a new set of values, a new set of skills. It meant leaving behind the comforts of home and facing a new set of dangers on the road. Once they were thoroughly apprenticed as disciples, they would then be sent out as apostles to spread the rabbi's controversial and challenging message everywhere. One did not say 'yes' to discipleship lightly.

The word *Christian* is more familiar to us today than the word *disciple*. These days, *Christian* often seems to apply more to the kinds of people who would push Jesus off a cliff than it does to his true followers. Perhaps the time has come to rediscover the power and challenge of that earlier, more primary word *disciple*. The word *disciple* occurs over 250 times in the New Testament, in contrast to the word *Christian*, which occurs only three times. Maybe those statistics are trying to tell us something.

To be alive in the adventure of Jesus is to hear that challenging good news of *today*, and to receive that thrilling invitation to follow him . . . and to take the first intrepid step on the road as a *disciple*.

Engage

1. What one thought or idea from today's lesson especially intrigued, provoked, disturbed, challenged, encouraged, warmed, warned, helped or surprised you?

2. Share a story about a time when you went through some hardship or temptation that prepared you for a later opportunity, or a time when you missed an opportunity because you were unprepared.

3. How do you respond to the idea that you can be captivated by the expectations of your loyal fans and intimidated by the threats of your hostile critics? Which is a greater danger for you?

4. For children: What's something you can't do right now that you hope you will be able to do one day? What will you have to learn in order to do that thing?

5. Activate: This week, write the word *disciple* in prominent places to remind yourself of Jesus' invitation to you.

6. Meditate: In silence, imagine Jesus calling your name and saying two words: *Follow me.* Allow that invitation to stir a response in you at the deepest part of your being.

CHAPTER 21

Significant and Wonderful

2 Samuel 11:26 – 12:15
John 2:1–12
Mark 1:21–28

They were all amazed, and they kept on asking one another,
'What is this? A new teaching—with authority!

You can't go many pages in the Gospels without encountering a
miracle. Some of us find it easy and exciting to believe in miracles. Others of us find them highly problematic.

If you find it easy to believe in miracles, the Gospels are a treasure of inspiration. But you still have to deal with one big problem:
the miracles in the Gospels easily stir hopes that are almost always
dashed in people's lives today. For example, in Matthew 9 you read
about a little girl being raised from the dead, but since that time
millions of faithful, praying parents have grieved lost children
without a miraculous happy ending. Why not? In Matthew 14,
you read about fish and bread being multiplied to feed the hungry,
but since that day, how many millions of faithful, praying people
have slowly starved, and no miracle came? Doesn't the possibility
of miracles only make our suffering worse when God could grant
them but doesn't? It's all so much worse if accusatory people then
blame the victim for not having enough faith.

If you are sceptical about miracles, you avoid these problems. But you have another problem, no less significant: if you're not careful, you can be left with a reduced world, a disenchanted, mechanistic world where the impossible is always and forever impossible. You may judge the miracle stories in the Gospels as silly legends, childish make-believe, false advertising or deceitful propaganda. But in banishing what you regard as superstition, you may also banish meaning and hope. If you lock out miracles, you can easily lock yourself in – into a closed mechanistic system, a small box where God's existence doesn't seem to make much difference.

There is a third alternative, a response to the question of miracles that is open to both sceptics and believers in miracles alike. Instead of 'Yes, miracles actually happened', or 'No, they didn't really happen', we could ask another question: *What happens to us when we imagine miracles happening?* In other words, perhaps the story of a miracle is intended to do more than inform us about an event that supposedly happened in the past, an event that if you were to believe it, might prove something else.

Perhaps a miracle story is meant to shake up our normal assumptions, inspire our imagination about the present and the future, and make it possible for us to see something we couldn't see before. Perhaps the miracle that really counts isn't one that happened to *them* back then, but one that could happen in *us* right now as we reflect upon the story.

Perhaps, by challenging us to consider impossible possibilities, these stories can stretch our imagination, and in so doing can empower us to play a catalytic role in co-creating new possibilities for the world of tomorrow. Doesn't that sound rather . . . miraculous?

Consider Jesus' first miracle in the Fourth Gospel. The story begins, 'On the third day there was a wedding in Cana of Galilee.' Jesus' mother notices that the wedding host has run out of wine and she nudges Jesus to do something about it. Jesus resists, but Mary doubts his resistance. She tells the servants to get ready to do whatever Jesus instructs.

Jesus points them to some nearby stone containers – six of them, used to hold water for ceremonial cleansing. These cleansings express the intention to live as 'clean people', in contrast to 'unclean people'. The containers are huge – potentially holding twenty or thirty gallons each. But they are empty. 'Fill them with water,' Jesus says. So the servants get to work drawing 120–180 gallons of water and filling the huge containers. Jesus instructs them to draw out a sample to give to the banquet master. He takes a taste. He's amazed! 'You've saved the best wine until last!' he says.

John says this was the first of the signs by which Jesus revealed his glory. That word *signs* is important. Signs point. They signify. They mean something. Often the word *signs* is linked with *wonders* – which make you wonder and astonish you with awe. So having warmed up our imagination by picturing a story about a far-away place in a long-ago time, let's now apply our inspired imagination to our lives, our world, here and now. Let's consider the significance of the sign. Let's do some wondering.

In what ways are our lives – and our religions and our cultures – like a wedding banquet that is running out of wine? What are we running out of? What are the stone containers in our day – huge but empty vessels used for religious purposes? What would it mean for those empty containers to be filled – with wine? And why so much wine? Can you imagine what 180 gallons of wine would mean in a small Galilean village? What might that supera-bundance signify? What might it mean for Jesus to re-purpose containers used to separate the clean from the unclean? And what might it mean for God to save the best for last?

Questions like these show us a way of engaging with the mira-cle stories as signs and wonders, without reducing them to the level of 'mere facts' on the one hand or 'mere superstition' on the other. They stir us to imagine new ways of seeing, leading to new ways of acting, leading to new ways of being alive.

In Mark's Gospel, the first miracle is very different. It happens in Capernaum, Jesus' home base, in the synagogue on the Sabbath day. The people have gathered and Jesus is teaching with his trademark authority. Suddenly, a man 'with an unclean spirit' screams: 'What do you want with us, Jesus of Nazareth? Have you come to destroy us? I know who you are – the Holy One of God!' Jesus tells the spirit to be quiet and leave the man, and the spirit shakes the man violently and leaves.

Today we would probably diagnose the man as being mentally or emotionally unwell, anxiety-ridden, maybe even paranoid. Instead of being possessed by a demon, we would understand him to be possessed by a chemical imbalance, a psychiatric disorder, a neurological malady or a powerful delirium. But even with our difference in diagnosing and understanding human behaviour, we can imagine how we would respond to seeing Jesus return this man to mental well-being with one impromptu therapy session lasting less than ten seconds!

Again, the story stimulates us to ask questions about our own lives, our own times. What unhealthy, polluting spirits are troubling us as individuals and as a people? What fears, false beliefs and emotional imbalances reside within us and distort our behaviour? What unclean or unhealthy thought patterns, value systems and ideologies inhabit, oppress and possess us as a community or culture? What in us feels threatened and intimidated by the presence of a supremely 'clean' or 'holy' spirit or presence, like the one in Jesus? In what way might this individual symbolise our whole society? In what ways might our society lose its health, its balance, its sanity, its 'clean spirit', to something unclean or unhealthy?

And what would it mean for faith in the power of God to liberate us from these unhealthy, imbalanced, self-destructive disorders? Dare we believe that we could be set free? Dare we trust that we could be restored to health? Dare we have faith that such a miracle could happen to us – today?

There is a time and place for arguments about whether this or that miracle story literally happened. But in this literary approach, we turn from arguments about history to conversations about meaning. We accept that miracle stories intentionally stand on the line between believable and dismissible. In so doing, they throw us off balance so that we see, think, imagine and feel in a new way.

After people met Jesus, they started telling wild, inspiring stories like these . . . stories full of gritty detail, profound meaning and audacious hope. They felt their emptiness being filled to overflowing. They watched as their lifelong obsession with *clean* and *unclean* was replaced with a superabundant, supercelebrative joy. They felt their anxiety and paranoia fade, and in their place faith and courage grew. They experienced their blindness ending, and they began to see everything in a new light. That was why these stories had to be told. And that's why they have to be told today. You may or may not believe in literal miracles, but faith still works wonders.

Engage

1. What one thought or idea from today's lesson especially intrigued, provoked, disturbed, challenged, encouraged, warmed, warned, helped or surprised you?
2. Share a story about a time when you felt you experienced a miracle, or when you prayed for a miracle that never came.
3. How do you respond to the literary approach that looks for meaning in miracle stories? Can you apply it to some other miracle stories?
4. For children: If you could have a magical power, what would it be, and why?

5. Activate: Keep these two miracle stories in mind throughout this week, and see if they bring new insights to situations you face.

6. Meditate: Hold in silence the image of an empty ceremonial stone container being filled with water that is transformed to wine. Hear the sound of water filling to the brim. See the water change in colour, and taste the change in flavour as it becomes wine. Hear the sound of people celebrating in the background. Sit with the words *empty*, *full* and *transformed*. See what prayer takes shape in your heart.

CHAPTER 22

Jesus the Teacher

Proverbs 3:1–26
Jeremiah 31:31–34
Mark 4:1–34

When he was alone, those who were around him along with the twelve asked him about the parables.

Who was Jesus? People in his day would have given many answers – a healer, a troublemaker, a liberator, a threat to law and order, a heretic, a prophet, a community organiser. His friends and foes would have agreed on this: he was a powerful teacher. When we scan the pages of the Gospels, we find Jesus teaching in many different ways.

First, he instructed through signs and wonders. By healing blindness, for example, Jesus dramatised God's desire to heal our distorted vision of life. By healing paralysis, he showed how God's reign empowers people who are weak or trapped. By calming a storm, he displayed God's desire to bring peace. And by casting out unclean spirits, he conveyed God's commitment to liberate people from occupying and oppressive forces – whether those forces were military, political, economic, social or personal.

Second, he gave what we might call public lectures. Crowds would gather for a mass teach-in on a hillside near the Sea of

Galilee. Whole neighbourhoods might jam into a single house, and then spread around the open doors and windows, eager to catch even a few words. People came to hear him at weekly synagogue gatherings. Or they might catch word that he was down at the beach, sitting in a boat, his voice rising above the sounds of lapping waves and calling gulls to engage the minds and hearts of thousands standing on the sand.

Third, he taught at surprising, unplanned, impromptu moments – in transit from here to there, at a well along a road, at a dinner party when an uninvited guest showed up, in some public place when a group of his critics tried to ambush him with a 'gotcha' question. You always needed to pay attention, because with Jesus any moment could become a teaching moment.

Fourth, he saved much of his most important teaching for private retreats and field trips with his disciples. He worked hard to break away from the crowds so he could mentor those who would carry on his work. Certain places seemed the ideal setting for certain lessons.

Fifth, Jesus taught through what we might call public demonstrations. For example, he once led a protest march into Jerusalem, performing a kind of guerrilla-theatre dramatisation of a royal entry, while denouncing with tears the city's ignorance of what makes for peace. Once he staged an act of civil disobedience in the temple, stopping business as usual and dramatically delivering some important words of instruction and warning. Once he demonstrated an alternative economy based on generosity rather than greed, inspired by a small boy's fish-sandwich donation.

Sixth, Jesus loved to teach through finely crafted works of short fiction called parables. He often introduced these parables with these words: 'Whoever has ears to hear, let him hear.' He knew that most adults quickly sort messages into either/or categories – agree/disagree, like/dislike, familiar/strange. In so doing, they react and argue without actually hearing and thinking about what is being said. His parables drew his hearers into deeper thought by engaging their imagination and by inviting interpretation instead of reaction and argument. In this way, parables put people in the position of children who are more attracted to stories than to arguments. Faced with a parable, listeners were invited to give matters a second thought. They could then ask questions, stay curious and seek something deeper than agreement or disagreement – namely, *meaning*.

In all these overlapping ways, Jesus truly was a master-rabbi, capable of transforming people's lives with a message of unfathomed depth and unexpected imagination. But what was the substance of his message? What was his point? Sooner or later, anyone who came to listen to Jesus would hear one phrase repeated again and again: *the kingdom of God*, or *the kingdom of heaven*. Sadly, people today hear these words and frequently have no idea what they originally meant. Or even worse, they misunderstand the phrase with complete and unquestioning certainty.

For example, many think *kingdom of God* or *kingdom of heaven* means 'where righteous people go when they die', or 'the perfect new world God will create after destroying this hopeless mess'. But for Jesus, the kingdom of heaven wasn't a place we *go up to one day*; it was a reality we pray to *come down here now*. It wasn't a distant future reality. It was *at hand*, or within reach, today. To better understand this pregnant term, we have to realise that kingdoms were the dominant social, political and economic reality of Jesus' day. Contemporary concepts like nation, state, government, society, economic system, culture, superpower, empire and civilisation all resonate in that one word: *kingdom*.

The kingdom, or empire, of Rome in which Jesus lived and died was a top-down power structure in which the few on top maintained order and control over the many at the bottom. They did so with a mix of rewards and punishments. The punishments included imprisonment, banishment, torture and execution. And the ultimate form of torture and execution, reserved for rebels who dared to challenge the authority of the regime, was crucifixion. It was through his crucifixion at the hands of the Roman Empire that Jesus did his most radical teaching of all.

Yes, he taught great truths through signs and wonders, public lectures, impromptu teachings, special retreats and field trips, public demonstrations and parables. But when he mounted Rome's most powerful weapon, he taught his most powerful lesson.

By being crucified, Jesus exposed the heartless violence and illegitimacy of the whole top-down, fear-based dictatorship that nearly everyone assumed was humanity's best or only option. He demonstrated the revolutionary truth that God's kingdom wins not through shedding the blood of its enemies, but through gracious self-giving on behalf of its enemies. He taught that God's kingdom grows through apparent weakness rather than conquest. It expands through reconciliation rather than humiliation and intimidation. It triumphs through a willingness to suffer rather than a readiness to inflict suffering. In short, on the cross Jesus demonstrated God's non-violent non-compliance with the world's brutal powers-that-be. He showed God to be a different kind of king, and God's kingdom to be a different kind of kingdom.

How would we translate Jesus' radical and dynamic understanding of *the kingdom of God* into our context today?

Perhaps a term like *global commonwealth of God* comes close – not a world divided up and ruled by nations, corporations and privileged individuals, but a world with enough abundance for everyone to share. Maybe *God's regenerative economy* would work – challenging our economies based on competition, greed and extraction. Maybe *God's beloved community* or *God's holy ecosystem* could help – suggesting a reverent connectedness in dynamic and creative harmony. Or perhaps *God's sustainable society* or *God's movement for mutual liberation* could communicate the dynamism of this radical new vision of life, freedom and community.

Today, as in Jesus' day, not everybody seems interested in the good news that Jesus taught. Some are more interested in revenge or isolation or gaining a competitive advantage over others. Some are obsessed with sex or a drug or another addiction. Many are desperate for fame or wealth. Still others can think of nothing more than relief from the pain that plagues them at the moment. But underneath even the ugliest of these desires, we can often discern a spark of something pure, something good, something holy – a primal desire for *aliveness*, which may well be a portal into the *kingdom of God*.

Interestingly, when the Gospel of John was written some years after its three counterparts, the term *kingdom of God* was usually translated into other terms: *life, life of the ages, life to the full* – which is clearly resonant with this word *aliveness*. However we name it – kingdom of God, life to the full, global commonwealth of God, God's sustainable society, or holy aliveness – it is the one thing most worth seeking in life, because in seeking it we will find everything else worth having.

To be alive in the adventure of Jesus is to seek first the kingdom and justice of God . . . to become a student of the one great subject Jesus came to teach in many creative ways.

Engage

1. What one thought or idea from today's lesson especially intrigued, provoked, disturbed, challenged, encouraged, warmed, warned, helped or surprised you?
2. Share a story about one of the most important teachers in your life and what made him or her so significant.

3. How do you respond to the explanation of the term *king-dom of God*? How would you translate it into words or images that make sense today?

4. For children: What makes a good teacher so good? Who is one of your favourite teachers so far?

5. Activate: This week, notice where you seek and find aliveness. Relate that thirst for aliveness to the kingdom of God.

6. Meditate: Choose one of the synonyms for *kingdom of God* from this chapter and simply hold it in silence for a few moments. Conclude the silence with these words: 'Let it come.'

CHAPTER 23

Jesus and the Multitudes

Ezekiel 34
Luke 5:17–32; 18:15 – 19:9

Jesus answered, 'Those who are well have no need of a physician, but those who are sick; I have come to call not the righteous but sinners to repentance.'

Most human societies are divided between the elites and the masses. The elites are the 1 or 3 or 5 per cent at the top that have and hoard the most money, weapons, power, influence and opportunities. They make the rules and usually rig the game to protect their interests. They forge alliances across sectors – in government, business, religion, media, the arts, sciences and the military. As a result, they have loyal allies across all sectors of a society and they reward those allies to keep them loyal.

Down at the bottom, we find the masses – commonly called 'the multitude' in the Gospels. They provide cheap labour in the system run by the elites. They work with little pay, little security, little prestige and little notice. They live in geographically distant regions or in socially distant slums. So to the elites, the multitudes can remain surprisingly invisible and insignificant most of the time.

In the middle, between the elites and the multitudes, we find those loyal allies who function as mediators between the few above them and the many below them. As such, they make a little more money than the masses, and they live in hope that they or their children can climb up the pyramid, closer to the elites. But those above them generally don't want too much competition from below, so they make sure the pyramid isn't too easy to climb.

These dynamics were at work in Jesus' day, and he was well aware of them. In his parables he constantly made heroes of people from the multitudes: day labourers, small farmers, women working in the home, slaves and children. He captured the dilemma of what we would call middle management – the stewards, tax collectors and their associates who extracted income from the poor and powerless below them for the sake of the rich and powerful above them. And he exposed the duplicity and greed of those at the top – especially the religious leaders who enjoyed a cozy, lucrative alliance with the rich elites.

In addressing the social realities of his day, Jesus constantly turned the normal dominance pyramid on its head, confusing even his disciples.

Take, for example, the time a group of parents brought their little children to Jesus to be blessed (Mark 10:13–16). Their great teacher had important places to go and important people to see, so the disciples tried to send them away. But Jesus rebuked them. 'Let those little children come to me,' he said. 'For of such is God's kingdom.'

Or take the time Jesus and his disciples were passing through Samaria, a region that 'proper folks' hated to pass through because its inhabitants were considered religiously and culturally 'unclean' (John 4:4–42). Jesus decided to wait outside the city while his companions went into town to buy lunch. When they returned, Jesus was sitting by a well, deep in a spiritual and theological conversation with a Samaritan woman . . . and one with a sketchy reputation at that. The sight of Jesus and this woman talking respectfully was a triple shock to the disciples: men didn't normally speak with women as peers, Jews didn't normally associate with Samaritans, and 'clean' people didn't normally interact with those they considered morally stained.

Or take the time Jesus and his disciples, accompanied by a large crowd, passed a blind man along the road (Mark 10:46–52). The man seemed marginal and insignificant, just another beggar, and the people around told him to quiet down when he started crying out for mercy. But to Jesus, he mattered. The same thing happened when Jesus was on his way to heal the daughter of a synagogue official named Jairus (Mark 5:21–43). Along the way, Jesus was touched by a woman with an embarrassing 'female problem' that rendered her 'unclean'. She didn't even think she was important enough to ask for Jesus' help. Jesus healed her, publicly affirmed her value, and then he healed the official's little girl. Little children, a Samaritan, a man who might today be classified as 'disabled' and 'unemployed', a frightened and 'unclean' woman, a little girl . . . they all mattered to Jesus.

It wasn't just weak or vulnerable people whom Jesus considered important. Even more scandalous, he saw value in those considered by everyone to be notorious and sinful. Once, for example, Jesus and his companions were invited to a formal banquet (Luke 7:36–50). Imagine their shock when a woman known to be a prostitute sneaked into the gathering uninvited. Imagine their disgust when she came and honoured Jesus by washing his feet with her tears and drying them with her hair. When the host indulged in predictably judgemental thinking about both the woman and Jesus, Jesus turned the tables and held her up as an example for all at the banquet to follow.

That host was a member of the Pharisees, a religious reform movement in Jesus' day. The Pharisees were pious, fastidious and religiously knowledgeable. They maintained a close association with 'the scribes', or religious scholars. Today some might call them 'hyper-orthodox' or 'fundamentalist'. But back then most would have considered them pure and faithful people, the moral backbone of society.

From the start, the Pharisees seemed strangely fascinated with Jesus. When Jesus once claimed his disciples needed a moral rightness that surpassed their own, they must have been unsettled. How could anyone possibly be more upright than they? He further troubled them by his refusal to follow their practice of monitoring every action of every person as clean or unclean, biblical or unbiblical, legal or illegal. To make matters worse, he not only associated with 'unclean' people – he seemed to enjoy their company! The Pharisees just didn't know what to do with a man like this. So they kept throwing questions at him, hoping to trap him in some misstatement.

Once they criticised Jesus for healing someone on the Sabbath, their name for the seventh day of the week when no work was supposed to be done (Luke 14:1–6). Jesus asked them a question: If your son – or even your ox – falls into a hole on the Sabbath, will you wait until the next day to rescue him/it? By appealing to their basic humanity – kindness to their own children, if not their own beasts of burden – he implied that God must possess at least that level of 'humanity'. In so doing, Jesus proposed that basic human kindness and compassion are more absolute than religious rules and laws. 'The Sabbath was made for human beings,' Jesus said in another debate with the Pharisees (Mark 2:27). 'Human beings weren't made for the Sabbath.'

Jesus often turned the condemning language of the Pharisees back on them (Matthew 23). 'You travel over land and sea to make a single convert,' he said, 'and convert him into twice the son of hell he was before you converted him! You wash the outside of the cup but leave the inside filthy and putrid. You are like those who make beautiful tombs . . . slapping lots of white paint on the outside, only to hide rot and death inside!'

The contrast between Jesus and the Pharisees was nowhere clearer than in their attitude towards the multitudes. The

Pharisees once looked at the multitudes and said, 'This crowd doesn't know the Scriptures – damn them all' (John 7:49). But when Jesus looked at the multitudes, 'he had compassion for them, because they were harassed and helpless, like sheep without a shepherd' (Matthew 9:36).

There are always multitudes at the bottom being marginalised, scapegoated, shunned, ignored and forgotten by elites at the top. And there are always those in the middle torn between the two. To be alive in the adventure of Jesus is to stand with the multitudes, even if doing so means being marginalised, criticised and misunderstood right along with them.

Engage

1. What one thought or idea from today's lesson especially intrigued, provoked, disturbed, challenged, encouraged, warmed, warned, helped or surprised you?

2. Share a story about a time when you felt like one of the multitude, or when you behaved like one of the Pharisees.

3. How do you respond to the stories of Jesus engaging with 'the multitudes' and the Pharisees in this chapter?

4. For children: Think of one of the children in your class who is the least popular or who seems to have the fewest friends. What do you think that child wishes other children would do for him or her?

5. Activate: Make an opportunity this week to spend time with some member of 'the multitude'.

6. Meditate: Think of some group of people you normally turn away from. Imagine them, in silence, and repeat these words: 'They are harassed and helpless, like sheep without a shepherd.' Notice what happens to your heart as you do so.

CHAPTER 24

Jesus and Hell

Jonah 4
Luke 16:19–31
Matthew 25:31–40

Truly I tell you, just as you did it to one of the least of these who are members of my family, you did it to me.

Jesus was boring, if you go by the tame and uninteresting caricature many of us were given. He was a quiet, gentle, excessively nice, somewhat fragile man on whose lap children liked to sit. He walked around in flowing robes in pastel colours, never dirty, always freshly washed and pressed. He liked to hold a small sheep in one arm and raise the other as if hailing a taxi. Or he was like an x or n – an abstract part of a mathematical equation, not important primarily because of what he said or how he lived, but only because he filled a role in the cosmic calculus of damnation and forgiveness.

The real Jesus was far more complex and interesting than any of these caricatures. And nowhere was he more defiant, subversive, courageous and creative than when he took the language of fire and brimstone from his greatest critics and used it for a very different purpose.

The idea of hell entered Jewish thought rather late. In Jesus' day, as in our own, more traditional Jews – especially those of a political and religious group known as the Sadducees – had little to say about the afterlife and about miracles, angels and the like. Their focus was on this life and on how to be good and faithful human beings within it. Other Jews – especially the Pharisees, the Sadducees' great rivals – had welcomed ideas on the afterlife from neighbouring cultures and religions.

To the north and east in Mesopotamia, people believed that the souls of the dead migrated to an underworld whose geography resembled an ancient walled city. Good and evil, high-born and lowly, all descended to this shadowy, scary, dark, inescapable realm. For the Egyptians to the south, the newly departed faced a ritual trial of judgement. Bad people who failed the test were then devoured by a crocodile-headed deity, and good people who passed the test settled in the land beyond the sunset.

To the west, the Greeks had a more elaborate schema. Although there were many permutations, in general souls were sorted into four groups at death: the holy and heroic, the indeterminate, the curably evil and the incurably evil. The incurably evil went to Tartarus where they would experience eternal conscious torment. The holy and heroic were admitted to the Elysian Fields, a place of joy and peace. Those in between might be sent back to Earth for multiple reincarnations until they could be properly sorted for shipment to Tartarus or the Elysian Fields.

Then there were the Persian Zoroastrians to the east. In Zoroastrianism, recently departed souls would be judged by two angels, Rashnu and Mithra. The worthy would be welcomed into the Zoroastrian version of heaven. The unworthy would be banished to the realm of the satanic figure Ahriman – their version of hell.

A large number of Jews had been exiles in the Persian Empire in the sixth century BC, and the Persians ruled over the Jews for about 150 years after they returned to rebuild Jerusalem. After that, the Greeks ruled and tried to impose their culture and religion. So it's not surprising that many Jews adopted a mix of Persian and Greek ideas of the afterlife. In fact, the Pharisees may have picked up their name from the old word for Persian – *Parsi* or *Farsi*. For Jews who integrated Greek, Persian and other ideas into their vision of the afterlife, the heaven-bound could be easily identified. They were like the Pharisees – religiously knowledgeable and observant, socially respected, economically prosperous and healthy in body. The hell-bound were just as easily identified: the opposite of the Pharisees – uninformed about religious lore, careless about religious rules, socially suspect, economically poor and physically sick or disabled.

Jesus clearly agreed with the Pharisees that there was an afterlife. Death was not the end for Jesus. But one of the most striking facets of his life and ministry was the way he took the Pharisees' understanding of the afterlife and turned it on its head.

Who was going to hell? Rich and successful people who lived in fancy houses and stepped over their destitute neighbours who slept in the gutters outside their gates! Proud people who judged, insulted, excluded, avoided and accused others! Hypocrites who 'strained out gnats and swallowed camels'! In other words, who was going to hell? People just like the Pharisees! The judgement they so freely pronounced on others, Jesus turned back on them.

And who, according to Jesus, was going to heaven? The very people whom the religious elite despised, deprived, avoided, excluded and condemned. Heaven's gates opened wide for the poor and destitute who shared in few of life's blessings; the sinners, the sick and the homeless who felt superior to nobody and who therefore appreciated God's grace and forgiveness all the more; even the prostitutes and tax collectors. Imagine how this overturning of the conventional understanding of hell must have shocked everyone – multitudes and Pharisees alike.

Again and again, Jesus took conventional language and

imagery for hell and reversed it. We might say he wasn't so much teaching about hell as he was *un-teaching* about hell. In so doing, he wasn't simply arguing for a different understanding of the afterlife. He was doing something far more important and radical: proclaiming a transformative vision of God. God is not the one who condemns the poor and weak, nor is God the one who favours the rich and righteous. God is the one who loves everyone, including the people the rest of us think don't count. Those fire-and-brimstone passages that countless preachers have used to scare people about hell, it turns out, weren't intended to teach us about hell: Jesus used the language of hell to teach us a radical new vision of God!

Jesus used fire-and-brimstone language in another way as well. He used it to warn his countrymen about the catastrophe of following their current road – a wide and smooth highway leading to another violent uprising against the Romans. Violence won't produce peace, he warned; it will produce only more violence. If his countrymen persisted in their current path, Jesus warned, the Romans would get revenge on them by taking their greatest pride – the temple – and reducing it to ashes and rubble. The Babylonians had done it once, and the Romans could do it again. That was why he advocated a different path – a 'rough and narrow path' of non-violent social change instead of the familiar broad highway of hate and violence.

For a time, the Pharisees rejected both Jesus' alternative portrayal of God and his warnings about a violent uprising. In fact, the Pharisees joined with the Zealots and became leaders in a rebellion against the Roman Empire in AD 67. Their grand scheme succeeded for a time, but three years later the Romans marched in and crushed the rebellion. Jerusalem was devastated and the temple was destroyed. The nation was even worse off after its revolution than before.

And that was when the Pharisees changed. In many ways,

after their failed revolution, they followed a path more like the one Jesus had taught. They showed that it wasn't too late to change, even for the Pharisees.

In that outcome, we see the real purpose of Jesus' fire-and-brimstone language. Its purpose was not to predict the destruction of the universe or to make absolute for all eternity the insider-outsider categories of *us* and *them*. Its purpose was to wake up complacent people, to warn them of the danger of their current path, and to challenge them to change – using the strongest language and imagery available. As in the ancient story of Jonah, God's intent was not to destroy but to save. Neither a great big fish nor a great big fire gets the last word, but rather God's great big love and grace.

Sadly, many religious people still use the imagery of hell more in the conventional way Jesus sought to reverse. Like Jonah, they seem disappointed that God's grace might get the final word. If more of us would re-examine this fascinating dimension of Jesus' teaching and come to a deeper understanding of it, we would see what a courageous, subversive and fascinating leader he was, pointing us to a radically different way of seeing God, life and being alive.

Engage

1. What one thought or idea from today's lesson especially intrigued, provoked, disturbed, challenged, encouraged, warmed, warned, helped or surprised you?
2. Share a story about a time someone confronted you with a mistake or fault and you didn't respond well.
3. How do you respond to the parable of the rich man and Lazarus?
4. For children: What are some of the ways that grown-ups try to keep children from doing harmful or dangerous things? What ways do you think work the best?

5. Activate: This week, look for people like Lazarus in the parable and refuse to imitate the rich man in your response to them.

6. Meditate: Imagine the rich man walking by Lazarus in the gutter. In silence, ask God if you are stepping over anyone in your life.

CHAPTER 25

Jesus, Violence and Power

Isaiah 42:1–9; 53

. . . a bruised reed he will not break, and a dimly burning wick he will not quench; he will faithfully bring forth justice.

Matthew 16:13 – 17:9

Once Jesus took his disciples on a field trip.[17] There was something he wanted them to learn, and there was a perfect place for them to learn it. So he led them on a twenty-five-mile trek north from their base in Galilee to a city called Caesarea Philippi, a regional centre of the Roman Empire.

The city was built beside a dramatic escarpment or cliff face. A famous spring emerged from the base of the cliff. Before Roman occupation, the spring had been known as Panias, because it was a centre for worship of the Canaanite god Baal, and later for the Greek god Pan. Worshippers carved elaborate niches, still visible today, into the cliff face. There they placed statues of Pan and other Greek deities. Panias also had a reputation as the site of a devastating military defeat. At Panias,

---

17 This chapter is adapted from my book *Everything Must Change* (Nashville: Thomas Nelson, 2007).

invading armies affiliated with Alexander the Great took the whole region for the Greek Empire.

Eventually the Romans replaced the Greeks, and when their regional ruler Herod the Great died, his son Herod Philip was given control of the region around Panias. He changed the name to Caesarea Philippi. By the first name he honoured Caesar Augustus, the Roman Emperor. By the second name, he honoured himself and distinguished the city from another city named Caesarea Maritima – on the coast. The city was, in effect, Philip's Caesar-ville.

Imagine what it would be like to enter Caesar-ville with Jesus and his team. Today we might imagine a Jewish leader bringing his followers to Auschwitz, a Japanese leader to Hiroshima, a Native American leader to Wounded Knee, or a Palestinian leader to the wall of separation. There, in the shadow of the cliff face with its idols set into their finely carved niches, in the presence of all these terrible associations, Jesus asks his disciples a carefully crafted question: 'Who do people say the Son of Man is?'

We can imagine that an awkward silence might follow this rather strange and self-conscious question. But soon the answers flow. 'Some people say you're John the Baptist raised from the dead; others say Elijah; and still others, Jeremiah or one of the prophets.'

Jesus sharpens the question: 'What about you? Who do you say I am?' Another silence, and then Peter, a leader among them, speaks: 'You are the Christ, the Son of the living God.'

It may sound like Peter is making a theological claim with these words. But in this setting, they're as much a political statement as a theological one. *Christ* is the Greek translation for the Hebrew term *Messiah*, which means 'the one anointed as liberating king'. To say 'liberating king' anywhere in the Roman Empire is dangerous, even more so in a city bearing

Caesar's name. By evoking the term *Christ*, Peter is saying, 'You are the liberator promised by God long ago, the one for whom we have long waited. You are King Jesus, who will liberate us from King Caesar.'

Similarly, *Son of the living God* takes on an incandescent glow in this setting. Caesars called themselves 'sons of the gods', but Peter's confession asserts that their false, idolatrous claim is now trumped by Jesus' true identity as one with authority from the true and living God. The Greek and Roman gods in their little niches in the cliff face may be called on to support the dominating rule of the Caesars. But the true and living God stands behind the liberating authority of Jesus.

Jesus says that God has blessed Peter with this revelation. He speaks in dazzling terms of Peter's foundational role in Jesus' mission. 'The gates of hell' will not prevail against their joint project, Jesus says, using a phrase that could aptly be paraphrased 'the authority structures and control centres of evil'. Again, imagine the impact of those words in this politically charged setting.

Surely this Caesar-ville field trip has raised the disciples' hopes and expectations about Jesus to sky-high levels. But Jesus quickly brings them back down to Earth. Soon, he says, he will travel south to Jerusalem. There he will be captured, imprisoned, tortured and killed by the religious and political establishment of their nation, after which he will be raised. Peter appears not to hear the happy ending, only the horrible middle. So he responds just as we would have, with shock and denial: 'Never, Lord! This shall never happen to you!' (Matt. 16:22, NIV).

Do you feel Peter's confusion? Jesus just said that Peter 'gets it' – that Jesus is indeed the liberating king, the revolutionary leader anointed and authorised by the living God to set oppressed people free. If that's true, then the one thing Jesus can*not* do is be defeated. He must conquer and capture, not *be* conquered and captured. He must torture and kill his enemies, not *be* tortured and killed by them. So Peter corrects Jesus: 'Stop talking this nonsense! This could never happen!'

At that moment, Jesus turns to Peter in one of the most dramatic cases of conceptual whiplash ever recorded in literature anywhere. 'Get behind me, Satan!' Jesus says. It's a stunning reversal. Jesus has just identified Peter as the blessed recipient of divine revelation. Now he identifies Peter as a mouthpiece of the dark side. Jesus has just named Peter as a foundational leader in a movement that will defeat the gates of hell. Now he claims Peter is working on the side of hell. Do you feel the agony of this moment?

Like most of his countrymen, Peter knows with unquestioned certainty that God will send a Messiah to lead an armed uprising to defeat and expel the occupying Roman regime and all who collaborate with it. But no, Jesus says. That way of thinking is human, satanic, the opposite of God's plan. Since the beginning, Jesus has taught that the non-violent will inherit the Earth. Violence cannot defeat violence. Hate cannot defeat hate. Fear cannot defeat fear. Domination cannot defeat domination. God's way is different. God must achieve victory through defeat, glory through shame, strength through weakness, leadership through servanthood, and life through death. The finely constructed mental architecture in which Peter has lived his whole adult life is threatened by this paradoxical message. It's not the kind of change of perspective that happens quickly or easily.

But isn't that why a master-teacher takes students on a field trip? By removing students from familiar surroundings, the teacher can dislodge them from conventional thinking. By taking them to a new place, the teacher can help them see from a new vantage point, a new perspective.

It was less than a week later that Jesus took three of his disciples on another field trip, this time to the top of a mountain. There they had a vision of Jesus, shining in glory, conversing with two of the greatest leaders in Jewish history. Again, Peter was bold to speak up, offering to make three shrines to the three great men, elevating Jesus to the same elite level as the great liberator Moses and the great prophet Elijah. This time, God's own voice rebuked Peter, as if to say, 'Moses and Elijah were fine for their time, but my beloved Son Jesus is on another level entirely, revealing my true heart in a unique and unprecedented way. Listen to him!'

Moses the law-giver and Elijah the prophet, great as they were, differed from Jesus in one important way: they had both engaged in violence in God's name. But in God's name Jesus will undergo violence, and in so doing he will overcome it. And that was why, as they came down the mountain, Jesus once again spoke of suffering, death and resurrection – a different kind of strategy for a different kind of victory.

In many ways, we're all like Peter. We speak with great insight one minute and we make complete fools of ourselves the next. We're clueless about how many of our pious and popular assumptions are actually illusions. We don't know how little we know, and we have no idea how many of our ideas are wrong. Like Peter, we may use the right words to describe Jesus – *Christ, Son of the living God.* But we still don't understand his heart, his wisdom, his way. But that's OK. Peter was still learning, and so are we. After all, life with Jesus is one big field trip that we're taking together. So let's keep walking.

Engage

1. What one thought or idea from today's lesson especially intrigued, provoked, disturbed, challenged, encouraged, warmed, warned, helped or surprised you?

2. Share a story about a time when you were completely certain about something, and then you realised you were completely (or at least partly) wrong.

3. How do you respond to this interpretation of the Caesar-ville field trip?

4. For children: What's one of the nicest compliments you have ever received? Why did that mean a lot to you?

5. Activate: Look for situations this week when your initial reaction should be questioned, especially in relation to power dynamics.

6. Meditate: Imagine you are Peter after he hears the words, 'Get behind me, Satan!' In silence, listen for ways your thinking is out of sync with God's ways. Imagine what you would want to say to Jesus in reply.

CHAPTER 26

Making It Real

Mark 2:1–19

[Jesus] said to him, 'Follow me.' And he got up and followed him.

Hebrews 11:1–8
1 John 1:1 – 2:6

Let's imagine ourselves visitors in a small village in Galilee, just at the time Jesus was passing through.[18] A crowd has completely filled a house. An even bigger crowd surrounds the house, with people crammed around every open window and door. We approach but can only hear a word or two. We ask a woman on the edge of the crowd about what's going on inside. She whispers that inside the house is a rabbi everyone wants to hear. We ask her who he is. She motions for us to follow her and whispers, 'I am Mary. I come from Magdala, a town not far from here. I don't want to disturb those who are trying to listen. I will be glad to tell you what I know.'

When we get a stone's throw from the crowd, Mary explains that the rabbi inside is the son of a tradesman from Nazareth.

---

18 This chapter is adapted from my book *The Secret Message of Jesus* (Nashville: Thomas Nelson, 2006).

He has no credentials or status, no army or weapons, no nobility or wealth. He travels from village to village with a dozen of his friends plus a substantial number of supportive women, teaching deep truths to the peasants of Galilee.

'Look around at us,' she says. 'We are poor. Many of us are unemployed, and some are homeless. See how many of us are disabled, and how many are, like me, women. Few of us can afford an education. But to be uneducated is not the same as being stupid. Stupid people cannot survive in times like these. So we are hungry to learn. And wherever this rabbi goes, it is like a free school for everyone – even women like me. Do you see why we love him?'

We ask, 'Do you think he is starting a new religion?'

She thinks for a moment and whispers, 'I think Rabbi Jesus is doing something far more dangerous than starting a new religion. He says he is announcing a new kingdom.'

We continue, 'So he is a rebel?'

'His kingdom is not like the regimes of this world that take up daggers, swords and spears,' Mary says. 'He heals the sick, teaches the unschooled and inspires the downtrodden with hope. So no, I would not say that he is a rebel. Nor would I say that this is a revolution. I would call it an uprising, an uprising of learning and hope.'

We look curious, so she continues: 'According to Rabbi Jesus, you cannot point to this land or that region and say, "The kingdom of God is located here," because it exists in us, among us. It does not come crashing in like an army, he says. It grows slowly, quietly, under the surface, like the roots of a tree, like yeast in dough, like seeds in soil. Our faith waters the seed and makes it grow. Do you see this? When people trust it is true, they act upon it and it becomes true. Our faith unlocks its potential. Our faith makes it real. You can see why this message is unlike anything people around here have ever heard.' Mary looks concerned. She asks, 'And where are you from? You aren't spies from Jerusalem, are you, looking for a reason to arrest the rabbi?'

'No, we are travellers,' we reply, 'passing through.' We quickly turn the subject back to her: 'You are one of his disciples?'

She looks down for a moment and replies, 'Not yet. But I am considering it.'

We wait for her to continue: 'Most of my friends in Magdala are just trying to survive. Some of them are indeed dreaming about a holy war against Rome and their puppets in Jerusalem. Even little boys are sharpening their knives and talking of war. But I think that is foolish. My father was killed in the rebellion in Sepphoris, so I know. There must be another way. Another kind of uprising. An uprising of peace. If Rabbi Jesus can lead that kind of uprising, I will join it gladly.'

'You seem to have a lot of faith,' we observe. 'Do you ever have doubts?'

She laughs. 'Sometimes I think his message is the crazy dream of poets and artists, the fantasy of children at play, or old men who drink too much. But then I ask, what other message could possibly change the world? Perhaps what is truly crazy is what we are doing instead – thinking that a little more hate can conquer hate, a little more war can cure war, a little more pride can overcome pride, a little more revenge can end revenge, a little more gold can cure greed, or a little more division can create cohesion.'

Mary is silent for a moment, lost in her thoughts. She turns again to us. 'What about you? Are you beginning to believe in him? Do you trust him?'

That question has a peculiar power, doesn't it? 'Do you trust him?' is not the same as 'Do you believe he existed?' or 'Do you believe certain doctrines about him?' It's a question about commitment, about confidence. For Jesus, the call to trust him was closely linked to the call to follow him. If we truly trust him, we will follow him on the road, imitate him, learn from his example, live by his way. Because his message was and is so radical on so many levels, believing and following can't be treated lightly. They are costly. They require us to rethink everything. They change the course of our lives.

This time, we have been lost in our own thoughts, so Mary asks again: 'Maybe you believe he is misguided and only misleads others? That is what the religious scholars from Jerusalem think.'

'We're like you,' we respond. 'We want to learn more. We feel our hearts being drawn towards him. Maybe we are beginning to trust him.'

'So we must go back and listen,' she says. We return with our new companion to the edge of the crowd. While we were away, it appears there has been some kind of commotion on the roof of the house. The crowd is buzzing about a paralysed man being healed.

Mary leans towards us and whispers: 'Often when he heals someone, he says, "Your faith has healed you." So there it is again. With him, faith is where it all begins. When you believe, you make it real.'

'You change this' – she points to her head – 'and this' – she points to her heart – 'and you change all this.' She gestures to indicate the whole world.

We hear in her words a summons, a challenge, a life-changing invitation. Do we dare to step out and follow Jesus, to make the road by walking, to risk everything on an uprising of peace, an uprising of generosity, an uprising of forgiveness, an uprising of love? If we believe, we will make it real.

Engage

1. What one thought or idea from today's lesson especially intrigued, provoked, disturbed, challenged, encouraged, warmed, warned, helped or surprised you?
2. Share a story about one of your biggest decisions – how you reached it, how it felt before and after making the choice.

3. How do you respond to the idea that *faith makes it real*?

4. For children: Who is someone you want to be like when you grow up?

5. Activate: This week, consider beginning each day with the words 'I believe'. If you would like, add the words 'Help my unbelief'. Echo them throughout the day when they arise in your heart.

6. Meditate: Sit in silence with Jesus' words: 'Your faith has made you well.' What in you feels like it is being made well? End the silence with a simple prayer.

Second Quarter Queries

If possible, compose prayerful, honest and heartfelt replies to these queries in private, and then gather to share what you have written. The Five Guidelines for Learning Circles in Appendix II may be helpful to guide your sharing. You may also find it helpful to invite a trusted spiritual leader to serve as 'catechist' and ask him or her for additional guidance, feedback and instruction. Make it safe for one another to speak freely, and let your conversation build conviction in each of you as individuals and among you as a community.

1. Here is the meaning I find in the stories of John the Baptist, the virgin birth, Herod's slaughter of innocent children, the ancestor lists, the coming of the Magi, and Jesus in the temple at the age of twelve . . .
2. Here is why Jesus' parables, miracles and teaching about hell are important to me . . .

3. Here is how I respond to Jesus' care for the multitudes and Jesus' attitudes towards Caesar . . .

4. Here is my understanding of 'the kingdom of God' . . .

5. I believe in Jesus. I have confidence in Jesus. Here is what that means to me . . .

6. If you have been baptised, what does that baptism mean to you? If you have not been baptised, what would it mean for you to choose to be baptised now?

7. What do you appreciate most about this learning circle?

ALIVE IN A GLOBAL UPRISING

Joining the adventure of Jesus is a starting line, not a finish line. It leads us into a lifetime of learning and action. It challenges us to stand up against the way things have been and the way things are, to help create new possibilities for the way things can and should be. It enlists us as contemplative activists in an ongoing uprising of peace, freedom, justice and compassion. In Part 3 we focus on what it means for us to join in his adventure.

The first five chapters have been written for use in the traditional season of Lent. They are dedicated to Jesus' most concentrated teaching in the Sermon on the Mount (Matthew 5 – 7). Rather than having multiple Scripture readings during this season, we will read one passage multiple times to encourage deeper reflection.

Then, for Passion Week, we will imagine ourselves in and around Jerusalem. Beginning with Easter, we'll travel with the growing company of disciples as their uprising spreads across the Mediterranean world.

Because the date of Easter changes from year to year, learning circle organisers may need to adjust the order of chapters so that chapters 32 and 33 are read on Palm Sunday and Easter Sunday respectively. Note also that Passion Week includes lessons for special gatherings on Thursday, Friday and Saturday (chapters 32A, 32B and 32C).

CHAPTER 27

A New Identity

Matthew 5:1–16 (Read this passage reflectively two or three times.)

Let your light shine before others, so that they may see your good works and give glory to your Father in heaven.

Imagine yourself in Galilee, on a windswept hillside near a little fishing town called Capernaum. Flocks of birds circle and land. Wildflowers bloom among the grasses between rock outcrops. The Sea of Galilee glistens blue below us, reflecting the clear midday sky above.

A small group of disciples circles a young man who appears to be about thirty. He is sitting, as rabbis in this time and culture normally do. Huge crowds extend beyond the inner circle of disciples, in a sense eavesdropping on what he is teaching them. This is the day they've been waiting for. This is the day Jesus is going to pass on to them the heart of his message.

Jesus begins in a fascinating way. He uses the term *blessed* to address the question of identity, the question of who we want to be. In Jesus' day, to say 'Blessed are these people' is to say 'Pay attention: these are the people you should aspire to be like. This is the group you want to belong to.' It's the opposite of saying 'Woe to those people' or 'Cursed are those people', which means 'Take note: you definitely don't want to be like those people or counted among their number.'

His words no doubt surprise everyone, because we normally play by these rules of the game: Do everything you can to be rich and powerful. Toughen up and harden yourself against all feelings of loss. Measure your success by how much of the time you are thinking only of yourself and your own happiness. Be independent and aggressive, hungry and thirsty for higher status in the social pecking order. Strike back quickly when others strike you, and guard your image so you'll always be popular.

But Jesus defines success and well-being in a profoundly different way. Who are blessed? What kinds of people should we seek to be identified with?

The poor and those in solidarity with them.

Those who mourn, who feel grief and loss.

The non-violent and gentle.

Those who hunger and thirst for the common good and aren't satisfied with the status quo.

The merciful and compassionate.

Those characterised by openness, sincerity and unadulterated motives.

Those who work for peace and reconciliation.

Those who keep seeking justice even when they're misunderstood and misjudged.

Those who stand for justice as the prophets did, who refuse to back down or quieten down when they are slandered, mocked, misrepresented, threatened and harmed.

Jesus has been speaking for only a matter of seconds, and he has already turned our normal status ladders and social pyramids upside down. He advocates an identity characterised by solidarity, sensitivity and non-violence. He celebrates those who long for justice, embody compassion and manifest integrity and non-duplicity. He creates a new kind of hero: not warriors, corporate executives or politicians, but brave and determined activists for pre-emptive peace, willing to suffer with him in the prophetic tradition of justice.

Our choice is clear from the start. If we want to be his disciples, we won't be able to simply coast along and conform to the norms of our society. We must choose a different definition of well-being, a different model of success, a new identity with a new set of values.

Jesus promises we will pay a price for making that choice. But he also promises we will discover many priceless rewards. If we seek the kind of unconventional blessedness he proposes, we will experience the true aliveness of God's kingdom, the warmth of God's comfort, the enjoyment of the gift of this Earth, the satisfaction of seeing God's restorative justice come more fully, the joy of receiving mercy, the direct experience of God's presence, the honour of association with God and of being in league with the prophets of old. That is the identity he invites us to seek.

That identity will give us a very important role in the world. As creative non-conformists, we will be difference makers, aliveness activists, catalysts for change. Like salt that brings out the best flavours in food, we will bring out the best in our community and society. Also like salt, we will have a preservative function – opposing corruption and decay. Like light that penetrates and eradicates darkness, we will radiate health, goodness and well-being to warm and enlighten those around us. Simply by being who we are – living boldly and freely in this new identity as salt and light – we will make a difference, as long as we don't lose our 'saltiness' or try to hide our light.

We'll be tempted, no doubt, to let ourselves be tamed, toned down, shut up and glossed over. But Jesus means us to stand *apart* from the status quo, to stand *up* for what matters, and to stand *out* as part of the solution rather than part of the problem. He means our lives to overcome the blandness and darkness of evil with the salt and light of good works. Instead of drawing attention to ourselves, those good works will point towards God. 'Wow!' people will say. 'When I see the goodness and kindness of your lives, I can believe there's a good and kind God out there too.'

The way Jesus phrases these memorable lines tells us something important about him. Like all great leaders, he isn't preoccupied with himself. He puts others – *us* – in the spotlight when he says, '*You* are the salt of the Earth. *You* are the light of the world.' Yes, there's a place and time for him to declare who *he* is, but he begins by declaring who *we* are.

It's hot in the Galilean sunshine. Still, the crowds are hanging on Jesus' every word. They can tell something profound and life-changing is happening within them and among them. Jesus is not simply trying to restore their religion to some ideal state in the past. Nor is he agitating unrest to start a new religion to compete with the old one. No, it's abundantly clear that he's here to start something bigger, deeper and more subversive: a global uprising that can spread to and through every religion and culture. This uprising begins not with a new strategy but with a new identity. So he spurs his hearers into reflection about who they are, who they want to be, what kind of people they will become, what they want to make of their lives.

As we consider Jesus' message today, we join those people on that hillside, grappling with the question of who we are now and who we want to become in the future. Some of us are young, with our whole lives ahead of us. Some of us are further along, with a lot of hopes left and not a lot of time to fulfil them. As we listen to Jesus, each of us knows, deep inside: *If I accept this new identity, everything will change for me. Everything will change.*

Engage

1. What one thought or idea from today's lesson especially intrigued, provoked, disturbed, challenged, encouraged, warmed, warned, helped or surprised you?

2. Share a story about someone who has impressed you as being the kind of salt and light Jesus spoke of.

3. How do you respond to the reversal of status ladders and social pyramids described in this chapter?

4. For children: Lots of people ask children what they want to be when they grow up. But what kind of child do you want to be right now?

5. Activate: This week, look for ways to be a non-conformist – resisting the pressures of your environment and conforming your life to the alternative values of the beatitudes.

6. Meditate: In silence, imagine darkness, and into that darkness, imagine light coming from a candle, a sunrise, a fire or a torch. Hold these questions open before God: Which is more fragile and which is more powerful, light or darkness? How can my life become like light?

CHAPTER 28

A New Path to Aliveness

Matthew 5:17–48 (Read this passage reflectively two or three times.)

Do not think that I have come to abolish the law or the prophets;
I have come not to abolish but to fulfill.

Anyone present that day would have felt some tension in the air. Many in the crowd stuck to the familiar road of tradition, playing by the rules, leading conservative, conventional and respectable lives. They were worried that Jesus was too . . . different, too non-compliant. Others ran on a very different road. Unfettered by tradition, they gladly bent any rule that got in their way. They were worried that Jesus wasn't different and defiant enough.

According to Jesus, neither group was on the road to true aliveness.

When Jesus said, 'Do not think that I have come to abolish the law or the prophets,' you can imagine the traditionalists in the crowd felt relieved, because that was just what they feared he was about to do. When he added, 'I have come not to abolish but to fulfil,' they must have tensed up again, wondering what he could possibly mean by 'fulfil'. Then, when he said, 'Unless your righteousness *exceeds* that of the scribes and Pharisees, you will never enter the kingdom of heaven,' the non-traditionalists would have looked dismayed. How could anyone be more righteous than that fastidious crowd?

As Jesus continued, it became clear he was proposing a third way that neither the compliant nor the non-compliant had ever considered before. Aliveness won't come through unthinking conformity to tradition, he tells them. And it won't come from defying tradition either. It will come only if we discern and fulfil the highest intent of tradition – even if doing so means breaking with the details of tradition in the process.

If tradition could be compared to a road that began in the distant past and continues to the present, Jesus dares to propose that the road isn't finished yet. To extend the road of tradition into the future – to fulfil its potential – we must first look back to discern its general direction. Then, informed by the past, we must look forward and dare to step beyond where the road currently ends, venturing off the map, so to speak, into new territory. To stop where the road of tradition currently ends, Jesus realises, would actually end the adventure and bring the tradition to a standstill. So faithfulness doesn't simply *allow* us to extend the tradition and seek to fulfil its unexplored potential; it *requires* us to do so.

But what does it mean to fulfil the tradition? Jesus answers that question with a series of examples. Each example begins, 'You have heard that it was said . . .' which introduces what the tradition has taught. Then Jesus dares to say, 'But I say . . .' This is not, as his critics will claim, an act of abolishment or destruction. His 'but I say' will creatively fulfil the intent of the tradition.

The tradition said, 'Don't murder.' That was a good start. However, the tradition didn't want us to stop merely at the point of avoiding murder. So as a first step beyond what the tradition required, Jesus calls us to root out the anger that precedes the physical violence that leads to murder. As a second step, he calls us to deal with the verbal violence of name-calling that precedes the physical violence that leads to murder. As a third step, he urges us to engage in pre-emptive reconciliation. In other words, whenever we detect a breach in a relationship, we don't need to determine who is at fault. The intent of tradition isn't merely to be 'in the right'; the goal is to be in a right relationship. So we are to deal with the breach quickly and proactively, seeking true reconciliation. Being in a right relationship – not merely avoiding murder – was the intent of the tradition all along.

That kind of pre-emptive reconciliation, Jesus teaches, will help us avoid the chain reactions of offence, revenge and counter-offence that lead to murder, and that keep our court systems busy and our prison systems full.

After extending the road in the area of violence, Jesus moves to four more issues, each deeply important both to individuals and societies – sexuality, marriage, oaths and revenge. In each case, conventional religious morality – which Jesus calls the righteousness of the scribes and Pharisees – focuses on *not doing external wrong*: not murdering, not committing adultery, not committing illegal divorce, not breaking sacred oaths, not getting revenge. For Jesus, true aliveness focuses on *transforming our deeper desires*.

So, regarding sexuality, the tradition requires you to avoid adultery. But Jesus says to extend the road, to go further and deeper by learning to manage your internal lustful desires. Regarding divorce, you can try to 'make it legal' in the eyes of society as the tradition requires. But Jesus challenges you to go further and deeper by desiring true fidelity in your heart. Regarding oaths, you can play a lot of silly verbal games to shade the truth. Or you can go further and deeper, desiring simple, true speech, saying what you mean and meaning what you say. And regarding retaliation against injustice, you can react in ways that play right into unjust systems. Or you can go further and deeper, transcending those systems entirely.

Here Jesus gets very practical. As people living under Roman occupation, his hearers were used to getting shoved around. It was not uncommon for a Roman soldier to give one of them a backhand slap – the insulting whack of a superior to an inferior. When this happened, some would skulk away in humiliation or beg the bully not to hit them again. But that rewarded the oppressor's violence, and it made them complicit in their own diminishment.

That was why others dreamed of retaliation, of pulling out a dagger and slitting the throat of the oppressor. But that would reduce them to the same violent level as their oppressors. So Jesus offered them a creative alternative: *stand tall and courageously turn the other cheek*, he said. In so doing, they would choose non-violence, strength, courage and dignity . . . and they would model a better way of life for their oppressors, rather than mirroring the violent example they were setting.

Another problem they frequently faced was that rich landowners would often take tenant farmers to court. If they hadn't paid their rent or tribute, the landowners would start suing them for their personal belongings. So, Jesus said, if someone takes you to court and they sue for your outer garment, go ahead and strip down naked and give them your underwear as well. Yes, your 'generosity' leaves you exposed – but your nakedness also exposes the naked greed of your oppressor.

Often, a Roman soldier would order a civilian of an occupied nation to carry his pack for a mile. If the civilian refused to do so, he would show courage and self-respect, but he would probably end up dead or in jail. Most would comply, but once again, doing so would reinforce the oppressor's sense of superiority and their own sense of humiliation. Jesus tells his disciples to surprise their oppressors by volunteering to take the pack a second mile. The first mile may be forced upon them, but the second mile they'll walk free. The first mile they are oppressed, but the second mile they transcend their oppression and treat their oppressor as a human being, demonstrating the very human kindness that he fails to practise.

Neither the compliant nor the defiant typically imagine such creative responses. Jesus is helping their moral and social imagination come alive.

Jesus employs his 'you have heard it said . . . but I say . . .' pattern once more, perhaps the most radical example of all. Tradition always requires love and responsibility towards friends and neighbours, people we like, people like us, people 'of our kind'. That is a big step beyond utter selfishness and narcissism. But Jesus says that the road of tradition was never meant to end there. Love should now be extended further than before, to outsiders as well as insiders, to *them* as well as *us*, even to our enemies. We may not have walked the road that far yet, but that is God's intent for us.

Again, using example after example, Jesus directs his disciples beyond what the tradition requires to what the Creator desires. 'Be perfect, therefore, as your heavenly Father is perfect,' he says. Some people might assume that by 'be perfect' he means 'achieve external technical perfection', which is what the scribes and Pharisees aim for. But Jesus means something far deeper and wiser. He tells them that God doesn't let rain and sunshine fall only on good people's lands, leaving bad people to starve. No, God is good to all, no exceptions. God's perfection is a compassionate and gracious perfection. It goes far beyond the traditional requirements of the scribes and Pharisees.

For us today, as for the disciples on that Galilean hillside, this is our better option – better than mere technical compliance to tradition, better than defiance of tradition. This is our third way. God is out ahead of us, calling us forward – not to stay where tradition has brought us so far, and not to defy tradition

166

reactively, but to fulfil the highest and best intent of tradition, to make the road by walking forward together.

Engage

1. What one thought or idea from today's lesson especially intrigued, provoked, disturbed, challenged, encouraged, warmed, warned, helped or surprised you?

2. Share a story about a time when someone knew you had done wrong but loved you anyway.

3. How do you respond to the comparison between a tradition and a road? Where do you think you are being called to move beyond where you are right now?

4. For children: Are there times when you want to do better than 'good enough'? What makes you want to do your very best?

5. Activate: This week, look for opportunities to practise Jesus' teaching in regard to violence, lust, marriage, oaths and revenge.

6. Meditate: In silence, ponder God's perfection as a compassionate perfection. Let a prayer of praise arise from your heart to break the silence.

CHAPTER 29

Your Secret Life

Matthew 6:1–18 (Read this passage reflectively two or three times.)

Your kingdom come. Your will be done, on earth as it is in heaven.

All of us agree: the world isn't what it should be. We all wish the world would change. But how? How can we change the world, when we can hardly change ourselves? The forces of conformity and peer pressure are so strong. We set out to change the world, and time and time again the reverse happens. Or we resist the status quo with such fury that we become bitter, cynical, angry – hardly models of a better world. That's why we aren't surprised when Jesus turns to the dynamics of change in our personal lives. He shows us how to *be* the change we want to *see* in the world.

The key concept, according to Jesus, is the opposite of what we might expect. If you want to see change in the outside world, the first step is to withdraw into your inner world. Connect with God in secret, and the results will occur 'openly'.

Jesus offers three specific examples of how this withdrawal process works: giving in secret, praying in secret and fasting in secret. Giving, praying and fasting are often called spiritual disciplines or practices: actions within our power by which we become capable of things currently beyond our power.

For example, can you run twenty miles? If you haven't trained, no matter how well intentioned you are, you will be reduced to a quivering mass of cramps and exhaustion before you reach the finish line. But, as thousands of people have learned, you can start training. You can start running shorter distances in private, and gradually increase them. A few months from now you could cross the finish line in full public view!

If through physical practice a lazy slug can end up a lean and energetic runner, then through spiritual practice an impatient and self-obsessed egotist can become a gentle, generous and mature human being. But Jesus makes clear that not just any practices will do: we need the right practices, employed with the right motives. 'Practice makes perfect', it turns out, isn't quite accurate. It's truer to say practice makes *habit*. That's why Jesus emphasises the importance of practising prayer, fasting and generosity in secret. If we don't withdraw from public view, we'll habitually turn our spiritual practices into a show for others, which will sabotage their power to bring deep change in us. So, instead of seeking to appear more holy or spiritual in public than we are in private, Jesus urges us to become more holy or spiritual in private than we appear to be in public.

When it comes to *giving to the poor*, Jesus says, don't publicise your generosity like the hypocrites do. Don't let your left hand know how generous your right hand is. By giving in secret, you'll experience the true reward of giving. A lot of us have found that a good way to make secret giving habitual is to give on a regular basis, as a percentage of our income. As our income increases over time, we can increase our standard of giving and not just our standard of living. It's kind of ironic: a lot of people do ugly things in secret – they steal, lie, cheat and so on. Jesus reverses things, urging us to plot goodness in secret, to do good and beautiful things without getting caught.

It's the same when it comes to *prayer*, Jesus says. Prayer can either strengthen your soul in private or raise your profile in public, but not both. So don't parrot the empty phrases of those who pray as if they were being paid by the word. A few simple words, uttered in secret, make much more sense . . . especially since God knows what you need before you even ask. Jesus offers a model for the kind of simple, concise, private prayer that he recommends. His model prayer consists of four simple but profound moves.

First, we orient ourselves to God. We acknowledge God as the loving parent whose infinite embrace puts us in a family relationship with all people, and with all creation. And we acknowledge God as the glorious holy mystery whom we can name but who can never be contained by our words or concepts.

Second, we align our greatest desire with God's greatest desire. We want the world to be the kind of place where God's dreams come true, where God's justice and compassion reign.

Third, we bring to God our needs and concerns – our physical needs for things like food and shelter, and our social and spiritual needs for things like forgiveness for our wrongs and reconciliation with those who have wronged us.

Finally, we prepare ourselves for the public world which we will soon re-enter. We ask to be guided away from the trials and temptations that could ruin us, and we ask to be liberated from evil.

Immediately after the model prayer, Jesus adds a reminder that God isn't interested in creating a forgiveness market where people come and acquire cheap forgiveness for themselves. God is interested in creating a whole forgiveness economy – where forgiveness is freely received and freely given, unleashing waves of reconciliation in our world that is so ravaged by waves of resentment and revenge.

Jesus takes us through the same pattern with the spiritual practice of *fasting*: 'Whenever you . . . do not . . . but do . . .' he says. Whenever you fast, don't try to look all sad and dishevelled like those who make spirituality a performance. Instead, keep your hunger a secret. Let every minute when your stomach is growling be a moment where you affirm to God, 'More than my body desires food, I desire you, Lord! More than my stomach craves fullness, I crave to be full of you! More than my tongue desires sweetness or salt, my soul desires your goodness!'

So, Jesus teaches, if we make our lives a show staged for others to avoid their criticism or gain their praise, we won't experience the reward of true aliveness. It's only in secret, in the presence of God alone, that we begin the journey to aliveness.

Jesus now turns to the subject of wealth. Just as we can practise giving, prayer and fasting for social enhancement or spiritual benefit, we can build our lives around public, external, financial wealth or a higher kind of 'secret' wealth. Jesus calls this higher wealth 'treasure in heaven'. Not only is this hidden wealth more secure, it also re-centres our lives in God's presence, and that brings a shift to our whole value system so that we see everything differently. When we see and measure everything in life in terms of money, all of life falls into a kind of dismal shadow. When we seek to be rich in generosity and kindness instead, life is full of light.

Some people shame the poor, as if the only reason poor people are poor is that they're lazy or stupid. Some shame the rich, as if the only reason they're rich is that they're selfish and greedy. Jesus doesn't shame anyone, but calls everyone to a higher kind of wealth and a deeper kind of ambition. And that ambition begins not with how we want to appear in public, but with who we want to be in secret.

The world won't change unless we change, and we won't change unless we pull away from the world's games and pressures. In secrecy, in solitude, in God's presence, a new aliveness can, like a seed, begin to take root. And if that life takes root in us, we can be sure it will bear fruit through us . . . fruit that can change the world.

Engage

1. What one thought or idea from today's lesson especially intrigued, provoked, disturbed, challenged, encouraged, warmed, warned, helped or surprised you?

2. Share a story about a time when you did something good – but for a less-than-ideal motive.

3. How do you respond to the four-part summary of Jesus' model prayer?

4. For children: Why do you think grown-ups think about money so much? What do you think about money? Do you get an allowance? Is that important to you? Why?

5. Activate: This week, decide whether you'd like to experiment with giving to the poor, fasting or praying in secret. But don't tell anyone!

6. Meditate: Hold the phrase 'treasure in heaven' in silence in God's presence, and notice how your heart responds.

CHAPTER 30

Why We Worry, Why We Judge

Matthew 6:19 – 7:12 (Read this passage reflectively two or three times.)

But strive first for the kingdom of God and his righteousness, and all these things will be given to you as well.

Wise parents soon learn what makes their children cranky: not getting enough sleep, too much sugar, being hungry, not getting time alone, too much time alone, lack of stimulation, too much stimulation. Have you ever wondered what makes grown-ups cranky?

In the next section of Jesus' core teaching, he strips away layer after layer until he exposes three core problems that turn us into dismal grouches and keep us from enjoying life to the full.

Our first core problem is anxiety. Driven by anxiety, we act out scripts of destruction and cruelty rather than life and creativity. We worry about things beyond our control – and in so doing we often miss things within our control. For example, you may fear losing someone you love. As a result, driven by your anxiety, you grasp, cling and smother, and in that way you drive away the person you love. Do you catch the irony? If you're anxious about your life, you won't enjoy or experience your life – you'll only experience your anxiety! So to be alive is to be on guard against anxiety.

Jesus names some of the things we tend to be anxious about. First, we obsess about our bodies. Are we too fat or thin, too tall or short, or too young or old, and how is our hair? Then we obsess about our food, our drink and our clothing. Are we eating at the best restaurants, drinking the finest wines, wearing the most enviable styles? Our anxieties show us how little we trust God: *God must be either so incompetent or uncaring that we might end up miserable or starving or naked or dead!* So we worry and worry, as if anxiety will somehow make us taller, thinner, better looking, better dressed or more healthy!

Not only are our anxieties ridiculous and counterproductive, Jesus explains, they're also unnecessary. He points to the flowers that surround his hearers on the hillside. See how beautiful they are? Then he gestures to the flock of birds flying across the sky above them. See how alive and free they are? God knows what they need, Jesus says. God cares for them. God sustains them through the natural order of things. And God does the same for us, but we are too anxious to appreciate it.

Anxiety doesn't stop its dirty work at the individual level. It makes whole communities tense and toxic. Anxiety-driven systems produce a pecking order as anxious people compete and use each other in their pursuit of more stuff to stave off their anxiety. Soon, participants in such a system feel they can't trust anybody, because everyone's out for himself or herself, driven by fear. Eventually, anxiety-driven people find a vulnerable person or group to vent their anxiety upon. The result? Bullying, scapegoating, oppression, injustice. And still they will be anxious. Before long, they'll be making threats and launching wars so they can project their internal anxiety on an external enemy. No doubt many of Jesus' original hearers would have thought, *He's describing the Romans!* But to some degree, the diagnosis applies to us all.

Jesus advocates the opposite of an anxiety-driven system. He describes a faith-sustained system that he calls *God's kingdom and justice*. He makes this staggering promise: if we seek God's kingdom and justice first, everything that we truly need – financially, physically or socially – will be given to us. His promise makes sense. When we each focus anxiously on our own individual well-being without concern for our neighbour, we enter into rivalry and everyone is worse off. But when we learn from the songbirds and wildflowers to live by faith in God's abundance, we collaborate and share. We watch out for each other rather than compete with each other. We bless each other rather than oppress each other. We desire what God's desires – for all to be safe, for all to be truly alive – so we work for the common good. When that happens, it's easy to see how everyone will be better off. Contagious aliveness will spread across the land!

After anxiety, Jesus moves to a second core problem we all face. Anxious people are *judgemental* people. Worried that someone is judging them, they constantly judge others, which, of course, intensifies the environment of judgement for everyone. Just as anxiety quickly becomes contagious and creates an anxiety-driven system, judgement easily creates accusatory systems in which no one can rest, no one can be himself or herself, no one can feel free.

We can't help but remember the story from Genesis – the choice between two trees, the tree of life that nourishes us to see the goodness in everything, and the tree whose fruit we grasp to know and judge everything and everyone around us as good or evil. When we see in these dualistic terms, we constantly judge *us* as good and condemn *them* as evil. In response, others do the same to us. In the shade of that tempting tree, soon nobody is safe. Nobody is free. Nobody is truly and fully alive.

So Jesus calls us back to the tree of life where we stop creating a *them* to condemn as evil people and an *us* to privilege as good people. If Jesus' antidote to anxiety is to seek God's kingdom and justice first, his antidote to judging is self-examination. Instead of trying to take splinters out of other people's eyes – that is, focus on their faults – we should first deal with the planks in our own eyes. When we have experienced how difficult and delicate it is to deal with our own problems, we will be much more sensitive in helping others deal with theirs.

It's interesting that Jesus refers again to eyes: so much about being truly alive is about seeing in a new way.

To refrain from judging does not mean we stop discerning, as Jesus' tough words about not throwing pearls before swine make clear. Put simply, if we want to experience non-judgemental aliveness, then in everything – with no exceptions – we will do unto all others – with no exceptions – as we would have them do to us. In these words, Jesus brings us back to the central realisation that we are all connected, all children in the same family, all loved by the same Parent, all precious and beloved. In this way, Jesus leads us out of an anxiety-driven and judgement-driven system, and into a faith-sustained, grace-based system that yields aliveness.

Beneath our anxiety and judging lies an even deeper problem, according to Jesus. We do not realise how deeply we are *loved*. He invites us to imagine a child asking his mum or dad for some bread or fish. No parent would give their hungry child a stone or snake, right? If human parents, with all their faults, know how to give good gifts to their children, can't we trust the living God to be generous and compassionate to all who call out for help?

So next time you're grouchy, angry, anxious and uptight, here is some wisdom to help you come back from being 'out of your mind' to being 'in your right mind' again. Try telling yourself: *My own anxiety is more dangerous to me than whatever I am anxious about. My own habit of condemning is more dangerous to me than what I condemn in others. My misery is unnecessary because I am truly, truly, truly loved.* From that wisdom, unworried, unhurried, unpressured aliveness will flow again.

Engage

1. What one thought or idea from today's lesson especially intrigued, provoked, disturbed, challenged, encouraged, warmed, warned, helped or surprised you?

2. Share a story about a time when you felt anxious, judgemental, or both.

3. How do you respond to the idea that our deepest problem is that we don't know we are loved? In what ways does it help you to think of God's love as fatherly, and in what ways does it help to think of God's love as motherly? Are there ways that imagining God as a loving friend helps you in ways that parental images for God don't?

4. For children: Why do you think little children are often afraid to be left with a babysitter? What is so special about having your parents around?

5. Activate: This week, monitor yourself for anxiety and judgement. Whenever you see them arising in you, bring to mind Jesus' teaching in this lesson.

6. Meditate: In silence, ponder how the love of good parents frees their children from anxiety and the need to judge one another. Savour that feeling of being safe and secure in God's love.

CHAPTER 31

The Choice Is Yours

Matthew 7:13–29 (Read this passage reflectively two or three times.)

. . . the gate is narrow and the road is hard that leads to life, and there are few who find it.

Imagine that hillside in Galilee. Jesus is seated, surrounded by his disciples, a huge crowd circled around them. Perhaps it's the rhythm and tone of his voice. Maybe it's the pace of his words. Somehow they know he is building towards a climax, a moment of decision. He presents a series of vivid images, all in pairs.

First, there are two gates, opening to two roads. We can't travel both. One, he says, is broad and smooth like a Roman highway. It leads to destruction. One is narrow and rocky like a mountain path. It leads to life. 'Go along with the crowd,' Jesus implies, 'and you'll end up in disaster. But dare to be different, dare to follow a new and different path, and you'll learn what it means to be alive.'

Next, there are two vines or two trees producing two different kinds of fruit, each representing aliveness. One approach to life produces thorns, briars and thistles; another approach produces luscious fruits. Get your inner identity straight, he tells them, and your life will be fruitful.

Next there are two groups of people, one entering Jesus' presence, the other going away. One group may boast of all its religious credentials, but Jesus isn't impressed by talk. He's looking for people he *knows*, people he recognises – people, we might say, who 'get' him and understand what he's about. We can identify them because they translate their understanding into action.

Finally there are two builders building two houses, one on sand, one on rock. They both represent people who hear Jesus' message. They both experience falling rain, rising floodwaters and buffeting winds. The big difference? The person who builds on the solid foundation, whose structure withstands the storm, doesn't just *hear* Jesus' message; he translates it into *action*.

Each pair of images challenges us to move beyond mere interest and agreement to commitment and action. And what is the desired action? To take everything Jesus has taught us – all we have considered as we have listened to him here on this hillside – and translate it into our way of living, our way of being alive.

It makes sense, then, to go back and review the substance of Jesus' teaching:

Be among the lowly in spirit, remain sensitive to pain and loss, live in the power of gentleness, hunger and thirst for true righteousness, show mercy to everyone rather than harshness, don't hide hypocrisy or duplicity in your heart, work for peace, be willing to joyfully suffer persecution and insult for doing what is right.

Dare to be a non-conformist by being boldly different, like salt and light in the world. Demonstrate your differentness through works of generosity and beauty.

Reject both mindless conformity to tradition and rebellious rejection of it. Instead, discern the true intent of tradition and pursue that intent into new territory.

Never hate, hold grudges or indulge in anger, but instead, aim to be the first to reach out a hand in reconciliation.

Do not nurture secret fantasies to be sexually unfaithful to your spouse. Ensure fidelity by monitoring your desires – the way you see (symbolised by the eye) and grasp (symbolised by the hand) for pleasure. And do not settle for maintaining the appearance of legality and propriety; aspire to true fidelity in your heart.

Avoid 'word inflation' when making vows. Instead, practise clear, straight speech, so simple words like 'yes' and 'no' retain their full value.

Reject revenge. Instead, pursue creative and non-violent ways to overcome wrongs done to you.

Love your enemies as well as your friends, and so imitate God's big, generous heart for all creatures.

Cultivate a hidden life of goodness by giving to the poor, praying and fasting secretly.

Pray in secret through four movements of your heart. First, orient yourself towards a caring yet mysterious God. Second, align your desires with God's great desire for a just and compassionate world. Third, bring to God your needs and concerns – both physical and spiritual. Finally, prepare to re-enter the public world of temptation and oppression, trusting God to guide you and strengthen you.

Remember that God isn't setting up a forgiveness market but is building a whole forgiveness economy.

Don't let greed cloud your outlook on life, but store up true wealth by investing in a growing portfolio of generosity and kindness.

Be especially vigilant about money becoming your slave-master.

Don't let anxiety run and ruin your life, but instead trust yourself to God's gracious and parental care, and seek first and foremost to build the just and generous society that would fulfil God's best dreams for humanity.

Don't develop a sharp eye for the faults and failures of others, but instead first work on your own blindness to your own faults and failures.

Don't push on people treasures they are not yet ready for or can't yet appreciate the value of.

Go to God with all your needs, and don't be discouraged if you face long delays. Remember that God loves you as a faithful, caring parent and will come through in due time.

Do to others as you would have them do to you.

Realise that aliveness includes tough choices, and that thriving includes suffering.

Don't be misled by religious talk; what counts is actually living by Jesus' teaching.

Some may claim that God is angry and needs to be appeased through sacrifice. Some may claim that God is harsh and demanding, requiring humans to earn God's favour through scrupulous religious rule keeping. Some may claim that God scrutinises our brains and speech for perfect doctrinal correctness. But Jesus, like the prophets before him, proclaims a different vision of God. Based on what Jesus has told us today, God is gracious and compassionate and does not need to be appeased through sacrifice. God's love is freely given and does not have to be earned. What God desires most is that we seek God's commonwealth of justice, live with generosity and kindness, and walk humbly – and secretly – with God.

If you were there that day on the Galilean hillside, what would your decision have been? No doubt you would have been impressed, but would you have said 'yes'?

Engage

1. What one thought or idea from today's lesson especially intrigued, provoked, disturbed, challenged, encouraged, warmed, warned, helped or surprised you?

2. Share a story about a fork in the road that you faced, where you made a life-changing choice.
3. How do you respond to the summary of Jesus' sermon?
4. For children: What do you think of this as a basic rule for life: 'Treat other people the way you wish they would treat you'?
5. Activate: Choose one of the summary statements of Jesus' teaching that you think you most need to focus on. Write it down, or e-mail it to yourself, or put it on your calendar, or in some other way make sure you will be reminded of it several times each day this week.
6. Meditate: After a few moments of holding the image of a house standing strong in a storm, ask God to help you develop this kind of strength as a disciple of Jesus.

CHAPTER 32

Peace March (Palm Sunday)

Zechariah 9:9–10

He will cut off the chariot . . . the warhorse . . . and the battle-bow . . . and he shall command peace to the nations.

Psalm 122
Luke 19:29–46

Let's imagine ourselves just outside Jerusalem. We are with Jesus and his band of disciples early on a Sunday morning. Jesus has walked many a mile since he taught us that day on the hillside in Galilee. He has told many a parable, answered many a question and asked even more. Earlier this morning, he did something really strange.

He sent two of our number into a town on the Mount of Olives, which overlooks Jerusalem from the east. He said they would find a donkey's colt tied to a tree. The two disciples should untie it and bring it to him, and if anyone asked about it, they should simply say, 'The master needs it.' That was exactly what happened, and they brought Jesus the colt. The colt, of course, didn't have a saddle, so we took some of our coats and put them on the donkey. Then we lifted Jesus up onto it. We started down the road that led to Jerusalem.

So now we walk with him. At first it's quiet, with only the

sound of the donkey's hooves clomping on the road. The wind blows through the olive trees. We don't have any idea what he has planned.

Then we hear something up ahead. What is it? A crowd is gathering. Children are shouting. Palm branches are waving. People are taking their coats and spreading them on the dusty road to make a lavish, multicolour carpet, as if Jesus were a king being welcomed to the capital. More and more people join our parade as we descend the hill. Eventually, we feel our confusion giving way to excitement. We shout and dance and praise God together as we descend the road that leads to Jerusalem. Our voices echo across the valley: 'Blessings on the king who comes in the name of the Lord!' we shout. 'Peace in heaven and glory in the highest heavens!'

Some Pharisees who have been part of the crowd are getting uncomfortable. They rush up to Jesus and sternly warn him that this is dangerous. He should order us all to be quiet. They're worried that proclaiming Jesus as king will be seen as a revolutionary act, the kind that might bring the Roman soldiers riding in on their horses, swords and spears in hand, to slaughter us all in the name of law and order. But Jesus refuses to silence us. 'If they are silent, the rocks will start shouting!' he says.

So our parade continues. We shout louder than ever. After our long journey over these last three years, it feels that things are finally reaching their climax. We round a bend, and there is Jerusalem spread before us in all her beauty, the temple glistening in the sun. A reverent silence descends upon our parade. It's a sight that has choked up many a pilgrim.

But Jesus doesn't just get choked up. He begins to weep. The crowd clusters around him, and he begins to speak to Jerusalem. 'If only you knew on this day of all days the things that lead to peace,' he says through his tears. 'But you can't see. A time will come when your enemies will surround you, and you will be crushed and this whole city levelled . . . all because you didn't recognise the meaning of this moment of God's visitation.'

What a shock! From a shouting, celebrating crowd to the sound of Jesus weeping! From the feeling that we were finally about to win to a prediction of massive military defeat! From joyful laughter to tears!

As we continue descending the road towards Jerusalem, we also descend into the quiet of our own thoughts. We begin whispering among ourselves about what's happening. Someone reminds us of the words from the prophet Zechariah (CEB): 'Rejoice greatly, Daughter Zion! Sing aloud, Daughter Jerusalem! Look, your king will come to you. He is righteous and victorious. He is humble and riding on an ass, on a colt, the offspring of a donkey.' A shiver of recognition runs through us.

'What comes next?' one of us asks. 'What did the prophet Zechariah say after that?' Someone else has the passage memorised: 'He will cut off the chariot from Ephraim and the warhorse from Jerusalem. The bow used in battle will be cut off; he will speak peace to the nations. His rule will stretch from sea to sea, and from the river to the ends of the earth.'

Suddenly we feel the full drama of this moment. We recall another parade that frequently occurs on the other side of Jerusalem, whenever Herod rides into the city in full procession from his headquarters in Caesarea Philippi. He enters, not on a young donkey, but on a mighty warhorse. He comes in the name of Caesar, not in the name of the Lord. He isn't surrounded by a ragtag crowd holding palm branches and waving their coats. He's surrounded by chariots, accompanied by uniformed soldiers with their swords and spears and bows held high. His military procession is a show of force intended to inspire fear and compliance, not hope and joy.

And so the meaning of this day begins to become clear to us. Caesar's kingdom, the empire of Rome, rules by fear with threats of violence, demanding submission. God's kingdom, the kingdom of heaven, rules by faith with a promise of peace, inspiring joy. Jesus' tears are telling us something: he knows that our leaders aren't going to listen to him. They're going to respond to Caesar's violence with violence of their own, and that's why Jesus just made that dire prediction.

Our minds are reeling with these realisations as Jesus leads our little parade into Jerusalem and straight to the temple. There he causes a big scene. He drives out the merchants who sell animals for sacrifice. He drives out those who exchange foreign currency for the temple currency. Again, we know there is great meaning in his actions. He is again challenging assumptions about the necessity of sacrifice and about the need for opulent temples and all they represent. This time he links together quotes from two of our greatest prophets, Isaiah and Jeremiah. My house will be a house of prayer for all peoples, Isaiah said. But you have turned it into a hideout for crooks, Jeremiah said.

It has been quite a day, a Sunday we'll never forget, the beginning of a week we'll never forget. What a wild mix of emotions! What a collection of dramatic moments! As we fall asleep, we ponder this: to be alive is to learn what makes for peace. It's not more weapons, more threats, more fear. It's more faith, more freedom, more hope, more love, more joy. Blessed is the one who comes in the name of the Lord!

Engage

1. What one thought or idea from today's lesson especially intrigued, provoked, disturbed, challenged, encouraged, warmed, warned, helped or surprised you?

2. Share a story about a time when you were part of a public parade or demonstration.

3. How do you respond to the idea that on Palm Sunday Jesus was intentionally echoing Zechariah's prophecy?

4. For children: What do you like about parades?

5. Activate: This week, look for moments when you, like Jesus, can see with grief that people are choosing a way of conflict or violence instead of peace. Allow yourself to feel the sadness without vilifying anyone.

6. Meditate: Hold the phrase 'a house of prayer for all people' together with the phrase 'my Father's house'. See what thoughts and emotions arise within you, and express them in prayer.

A Table. A Basin. Some Food. Some Friends. (Holy Thursday)

Selections from John 13 – 17 will be read to conclude this chapter

I have given you an example.

Let's imagine ourselves near Jerusalem. It's Thursday night, and we are walking the road with Jesus' disciples on Thursday of this climactic week. What a week it has been! It all started last Sunday as Jesus led us in that unforgettable parade into Jerusalem. And then there was that scene at the temple. That certainly stirred things up! Every night we have slept outside the city and returned the next morning for more drama. One day there were confrontations with the religious scholars and Pharisees; the next day, more controversy with the Sadducees. Jesus has issued lots of dire warnings about the fate of the temple, which upsets many people because it's the centre of their whole world. And earlier today, just as Jesus sent two of us to find that donkey for our parade last Sunday, he sent Peter and John to find a man carrying a water jar so they could prepare the Passover meal at his guest room tonight.

Every Passover all Jews remember the night before our ancestors were liberated from slavery in Egypt. We celebrate a night of great anticipation. We associate each element of the meal – bitter herbs, unleavened bread, a lamb, fruit and more – with different meanings from the liberation story. In that meal, we feast on meaning. But tonight, at this special Passover, the focus isn't on the distant past. It's on the present and what will soon happen. Jesus draws our attention not to the lamb, but to a simple loaf of bread and a cup of wine. Near the end of the meal, Jesus lifts the bread and gives thanks for it. He says, 'This is my body, given for you. Do this in remembrance of me.' Then he lifts a cup of wine and says, 'This cup is the new covenant by my blood, which is poured out for you for the forgiveness of sins.' He adds, 'Whenever you take this bread and drink from this cup, do so in memory of me.'

Our first reaction is shock. To ask us to remember him suggests he will soon die. We know he has mentioned this several times, but now it hits us: he really means it, and it's coming soon. Our second reaction? To speak of his body and blood this way sounds repulsive – like cannibalism! Why would we want to eat human flesh or drink human blood? That's unkosher in our religion, and downright uncivilised! What could Jesus possibly mean by these strange words?

But before we can ponder the meaning of Jesus' strange words any more, he adds to our shock by speaking about one of us being his betrayer. That quickly gets us arguing about which one of us would do such a terrible thing. Soon, we've moved on from arguing about which of us is the worst disciple to arguing about which of us is the greatest. It's pretty pathetic, when you think about it. It says a lot about us disciples, and a lot about human nature too. Jesus is trying to tell us he's about to suffer and die, and all we can do is think about ourselves, our egos, our status in the pecking order!

Even this becomes a teaching opportunity for Jesus. Gentiles, meaning the Romans who occupy our land and seek to dominate us in every way, play these kinds of status games, he says. They cover up their status games with all kinds of language games.

'That's not the way it will be with you,' Jesus says. 'Instead, the greatest among you must become like a person of lower status and the leader like a servant.'

Years from now, when the Fourth Gospel will tell the story, it will make this theme of service the focal point of this whole evening. It won't even include the bread and the wine and Jesus' solemn words about them. It will put centre stage the dramatic moment when Jesus strips off his normal clothing and puts a towel around his waist. He pours water in a basin, stoops as a servant would, and washes the dust from our feet, one by one. When he finishes, he explains that he has set an example – of humble service, not domination – and he means us to imitate his example. Later, after the meal, he will expand 'Serve one another as I have served you' to 'Love one another as I have loved you'.

Both ways of telling the story of this night lead us to the same meaning. The original Passover recalled one kind of liberation – liberation from slavery in Egypt. This meal suggests another kind of liberation – liberation from playing the shame games of rivalry, pecking order, domination and competition to reach the top of the pyramid of pride. If the first Passover gets people out from under the heel of the slave-master, this holy meal leads people out from the desire to be slave-masters in the first place. This meal celebrates a new model of aliveness – a model of service, of self-giving, of being blessed, broken and given for the well-being of others.

It's pretty predictable, I guess: to see how we disciples completely miss the point and turn that holy supper into an argument, a contest for who will be the greatest, who will have the most status at the table, who will be excluded. But in spite of our anxiety and rivalry . . .

Jesus, the patient teacher . . .

Jesus, the humble leader . . .

Jesus, the king of self-giving sets an example of service. And in that context, he asks us to remember him – not primarily for his great miracles, not primarily for his brilliant teaching, but primarily, essentially, for this: that he gives himself like food for us, and for the whole world.

Some people say that later on that unforgettable night, after the holy supper, after Jesus went to a garden to pray, after his disciples fell asleep, after Judas came to betray Jesus with a kiss, after Peter pulled out his sword and Jesus told him to put it away, after Jesus was taken into custody, after his disciples ran away, Jesus was whipped. They say he received thirty-nine lashes, one fewer than the forty lashes that constituted a death sentence. So let us conclude our time together by observing silence, extinguishing the lights, and pausing to remember thirty-nine of Jesus' sayings from this holy, horrifying night.

1. If I, your Lord and teacher, have washed your feet, you too must wash each other's feet.
2. I give you a new commandment. Love each other. Just as I have loved you, so you also must love each other.
3. This is how everyone will know you are my disciples, when you love each other.
4. Don't be troubled. Trust in God. Trust also in me.
5. I am the way, and the truth, and the life.
6. Whoever has seen me has seen the Father.
7. I assure you that whoever believes in me will do the works that I do. They will do even greater works than these, because I am going to the Father.
8. If you love me, you will keep my commandments.
9. I won't leave you as orphans. I will come to you.
10. Whoever has my commandments and keeps them loves me. Whoever loves me will be loved by my Father, and I will love them and reveal myself to them.
11. Whoever loves me will keep my word. My Father will love them, and we will come to them and make our home with them.

12. The Companion, or the Holy Spirit, whom the Father will send in my name, will teach you everything and will remind you of everything I told you.

13. Peace I leave with you. My peace I give you.

14. I am the true vine, and my Father is the vineyard keeper.

15. Remain in me, and I will remain in you.

16. A branch can't produce fruit by itself, but must remain in the vine.

17. I am the vine; you are the branches. If you remain in me and I in you, you will produce much fruit.

18. If you remain in me and my words remain in you, ask for whatever you want and it will be done for you.

19. As the Father has loved me, I too have loved you. Remain in my love.

20. This is my commandment: love each other just as I have loved you.

21. There is no greater love than to give up one's life for one's friends. You are my friends if you do what I command you.

22. I don't call you servants any longer, because servants don't know what their master is doing. Instead, I call you friends, because everything I heard from my Father I have made known to you.

23. I assure you that it is better for you that I go away. If I don't go away, the Companion won't come to you. But if I go, I will send him to you.

24. I have much more to say to you, but you can't handle it now. However, when the Spirit of Truth comes, he will guide you in all truth.

25. Soon you won't be able to see me; soon after that, you will see me.

26. Ask and you will receive, so that your joy will be complete.

27. I left the Father and came into the world. I tell you again: I am leaving the world and returning to the Father.

28. I have said these things to you so that you will have peace in me. In the world you have distress. But be encouraged! I have conquered the world.

29. This is eternal life: to know you, the only true God, and Jesus Christ whom you sent.

30. Holy Father, watch over them in your name, the name you gave me, that they will be one just as we are one.

31. Make them holy in the truth. Your word is truth.

32. As you sent me into the world, so I have sent them into the world.

33. I pray they will be one, Father, just as you are in me and I am in you. I pray that they also will be in us, so that the world will believe that you sent me.

34. I am in them and you are in me so that they will be made perfectly one. Then the world will know that you sent me and that you have loved them just as you loved me.

35. I have made your name known to them and will continue to make it known so that your love for me will be in them, and I myself will be in them.

36. Put your sword away!

37. My kingdom doesn't originate from this world.

38. I was born and came into the world for this reason: to testify to the truth.

39. Whoever accepts the truth listens to my voice.

Amen.

Note: A hammer or wineglass may be struck, or another kind of loud noise may be used, to punctuate the thirty-nine statements as they are read slowly and reflectively. Or in a more quiet setting, a pebble may be dropped into a pool of water, or a chord strummed on a guitar, or a brief musical interlude played. And the room may be set up with forty candles lit around the room. As each statement is read, one candle can be extinguished, leaving the room in darkness save for one remaining candle.

Everything Must Change (Good Friday)

Psalm 22

Luke 22:39 – 23:56

Then Jesus, crying with a loud voice, said, 'Father, into your hands I commend my spirit.' Having said this, he breathed his last.

Let's imagine ourselves with the disciples just before three o'clock on this Friday afternoon. A few of us have come together to talk about what has happened over the last twenty-four hours.

───────────

It all started falling apart late last night when Judas, accompanied by a band of soldiers, came for Jesus. All we could think about was saving ourselves. Only Peter and John had the courage to stay with Jesus for a while. But by the time dawn came, Peter was having an emotional breakdown and John had run away too. The next thing we knew, about nine this morning, Jesus was carrying his cross through the streets of Jerusalem. It was obvious he had been beaten, scourged mercilessly, mocked and tortured. He was hardly recognisable.

By noon, he was hanging on the cross.

During the last three hours, some of us have gathered at a

distance to watch. We've been silent, lost in our own thoughts, but no doubt all our thoughts have been running the same circuit through the same shared memories.

We've been remembering last night in the garden, before Judas showed up. We kept falling asleep as Jesus prayed: 'My Father, if it is possible, take this cup of suffering away from me. However, not what I want but what you want.' With tears and in great distress, he prayed a second and third time. But the thrust of his prayer shifted from what might be possible to what might *not* be possible: 'My Father, if it is not possible that this cup be taken away unless I drink it, then let it be what you want.' In the second and third prayers, he was clearly preparing to die.

But why? Why was there no other way? Why did this good man – the best we have ever known, the best we have ever imagined – have to face torture and execution as if he were some evil monster?

As the hours drag on from noon to nearly three o'clock, we imagine many reasons. Some are political. The Pharisees were right to be concerned last Sunday when Jesus came marching into the capital. First our little parade – the Romans would have called it a rebellious mob – proclaimed Jesus as king. From there, he marched into the temple and called it a hideout for crooks, turning over the tables and upsetting the religious economy. Only a fool would do things like these without expecting conse-quences. Jesus was no fool.

We think about more spiritual reasons for this to happen. Jesus has told us again and again that God is different from our assumptions. We've assumed that God was righteous and pure in a way that makes God hate the unrighteous and impure. But Jesus has told us that God is pure love, so overflowing in good-ness that God pours out compassion on the pure and impure alike. He has not only told us of God's unbounded compassion – he has embodied it every day as we have walked this road with him. In the way he has sat at table with everyone, in the way he has never been afraid to be called a 'friend of sinners', in the way he has touched untouchables and refused to condemn even the most notorious of sinners, he has embodied for us a very different vision of what God is like.

At dinner last night, when he knelt down and washed our feet, and later when he called us his friends, what was that supposed to mean? Was he trying to show us that God isn't a dictator high in the sky eager for us to cower in fear at his feet? Was he inviting us to think of God as the one who is down here with us, who stoops low and touches our feet – as a servant would? Was he telling us that God would rather cleanse us than condemn us? If that was the case last night, what could this horrible day be trying to show us? Could there be any meaning in this catastrophe playing out before us now?

And then we think: if Jesus is showing us something so radical about God, what is he telling us about ourselves – about human beings and our social and religious institutions? What does it mean when our political leaders and our religious leaders come together to mock and torture and kill God's messenger, God's beloved child, God's best and brightest? How misguided can our nation be? Is this the only way religions and governments maintain order – by threatening us with pain, shame and death if we don't comply? And is this how they unify us – by turning us into a mob that comes together in its shared hatred of the latest failure, loser, rebel, criminal, outcast . . . or prophet? The Romans boast of their peace, and our priests boast of their holiness and justice, but today it all looks like a sham, a fraud, a con game. What kind of world have we made? What kind of people have we become?

One minute the crowds were flocking to Jesus hoping for free bread and healing. The next minute they were shouting, 'Crucify him!' And we, his so-called disciples, we are no better. One minute we were eating a meal with him and he was calling us his friends. Now here we stand at a distance, unwilling to identify ourselves with him and so risk what he is going through.

It has grown strangely dark now, in the middle of the afternoon, and in the darkness, even from this distance, we can hear Jesus. 'Father, forgive them,' he shouts. 'For they don't know what they are doing.'

Forgive them? Forgive us?

Our thoughts bring us again to the garden last night, when Jesus asked if there could be any other way. And now it seems clear. There could be no other way to show us what God is truly like. God is not revealed in killing and conquest . . . in violence and hate. God is revealed in this crucified man – giving of himself to the very last breath, giving and forgiving.

And there could be no other way to show us what we are truly like. We do not know what we are doing, indeed.

If God is like this, and if we are like this . . . everything must change. Everything must change.

Engage

1. What one thought or idea from today's lesson especially intrigued, provoked, disturbed, challenged, encouraged, warmed, warned, helped or surprised you?

2. Share what the crucifixion of Jesus says and means to you today.

3. How do you respond to the idea that 'there couldn't be any other way'?

4. For children: If a friend asked you, 'Why did Jesus die?' what would you say?

5. Activate: Today, try to create or attend a 'stations of the cross' service or visit a 'stations of the cross' installation. Let the horror of the crucifixion story inform you about what God is like and what we are like.

6. Meditate: In silence, let scenes from the crucifixion story play in your imagination. Imagine seeing the story unfold from the vantage point of various characters in the story – Jesus' frightened disciples, the religious leaders, the Roman soldiers, the crowds and Jesus himself. Finally, hold over all these scenes Jesus' words: 'Father, forgive them, for they don't know what they're doing.'

Doubt. Darkness. Despair.
(Holy Saturday)

Psalm 77

I cry aloud to God, . . . my soul refuses to be comforted.

Psalm 88
Ecclesiastes 1:1–11
Job 10

Let us imagine ourselves with the disciples on that Saturday after the crucifixion. We are hiding together in a home, engaged in sober, sombre conversation.

———————

Perhaps our descendants, the disciples of the future, will call this a day of waiting. But we are not waiting. For us, there is nothing to wait for. All we know is what was lost yesterday as Jesus died on the cross. For us, it's all over. This is a day of doubt, despair, disillusionment, devastation.

Certain details of the killing yesterday are hard to shake. Jesus, carrying his cross on the road to Golgotha, surrounded by women who were weeping for him. Jesus telling them, 'Don't weep for me. Weep for yourselves and your children.' What did he mean? Was he telling them that the violence spilling out on him was only a trickle of the reservoir that waited behind the scenes to flood the whole region?

Then there was Peter ... so full of bluster at dinner on Thursday, such a coward later that night, and invisible all of yesterday. And Judas – to think we trusted him as our treasurer! At least the women stayed true ... the women, and John, who was entrusted with Mary's care as her surrogate son. None of us can imagine what yesterday must have been like for Mary. She has carried so much in her heart for so long, and now this.

Then there was that strange darkness, as if the whole world were being uncreated, and there was that strange rumour about the veil in the temple being torn from top to bottom. Was that an image for God in agony, like a man tearing his clothes in fury over the injustice that was happening? Or was it a rejection of the priesthood for their complicity in the crime – a way of saying that God was done with the priests and the temple, that God would welcome people into the Holiest Place without their assistance? Or maybe it could mean that God is on the loose – that God is through with being contained in a stone structure and behind a thick curtain and wants to run free through the world like the wind. That's a nice sentiment, but not likely from today's vantage point. Today it best symbolises that no place is holy any more. If a murder like this can take place in the so-called Holy City, supported by the so-called holy priesthood, then holiness is nothing but a sham. It's a torn curtain, and behind it only emptiness lies.

On top of it all, we have to come to terms with the fact that Jesus seemed to know all this was coming. True, at the last minute, just before the betrayal and arrest, he prayed that the cup might pass from him. But he had been telling us that something terrible was coming – telling us since back in Caesarea Philippi, when Peter confessed him as the liberating King and the true Leader, telling us in many ways, even in his parables.

He loved life. Yet he did not cling to it. He loved life. Yet he was not controlled by the fear of death. In the garden on

Thursday night it seemed as if, to him, the fear of death was more dangerous than death itself, so he needed to deal with the fear once and for all. But look where that got him. Maybe it would have been better for him to flee back to Galilee. Lots of other people are living in communes out in the desert, waiting for Jerusalem and all it represents to crumble under its own weight. Maybe that was what we should have done. But it's too late now.

That one Roman soldier was impressed by him, but the others – all they cared about was seeing who would win a dead man's garment with a roll of the dice. True to form – playing games and obsessed with clothes and money to the very end!

Then came that moment when one of the rebels who was being crucified with Jesus started mocking him. When the other rebel spoke up to defend Jesus, Jesus said those kind words to him about being with him in paradise. Even then he had compassion for someone else. Even in death he was kind to a neighbour. And finally there was that haunting moment when he spoke of forgiveness . . . for those who were crucifying him, and for us all.

Normal, sane people would have said, 'God, damn them to hell for ever for what they have done!' But not Jesus. 'They don't understand what they're doing,' he said.

What did our leaders think they were doing? Protecting law and order? Preserving the status quo? Conserving what little peace and security we have left? Silencing a heretic or blasphemer? Shutting down a rabble-rouser and his burgeoning movement?

Right up to the last minute we dared hope that God would send in some angels, stop the whole charade and let everyone see how wrong they were and how right Jesus was. But no last-minute rescue came. Only death came. Bloody, sweaty, filthy, ugly death. Just before he died, it seemed that even he had lost faith. 'My God, my God, why have you forsaken me?' he cried. Maybe some shred of hope remained, though, because his last words were, 'Father, into your hands I commend my spirit.'

Now. Now, he is dead. Does that mean this uprising is dead too? We feel a chill as we realise that possibility. What do we do now? Do we leave, go back home, pick up our lives where we left them before all this started for us? Do we try to carry on the teaching of a . . . dead, defeated, failed and discredited leader? Do we turn cynical, disillusioned, dark, bitter? Fishing and tax collecting will seem meaningless compared to the memories of these last three years. But that's all we have left . . . fishing, tax collecting, and memories. The adventure of Jesus is dead and done.

Maybe we have all been fools. Maybe Pontius Pilate was right when he told Jesus that truth didn't matter, only power matters – the power of swords and spears, chariots and crosses, whips and nails. Or maybe the Sadducees and their rich friends in Jerusalem are right: life is short, and then you die, so amass all the money you can, by any means you can. And while you can, eat the best food and drink the best wine, because that's all there is.

Wine. That brings us back to Thursday night, there around the table. 'Remember me. Remember me. I will not eat of this until . . .' Until?

Did Jesus really believe that death wasn't the last word? Did he really believe that there was any hope of . . .

That's too much to believe today. Today we sink in our doubt. Today we drown in our despair. Today we are pulled down, down, down in our pain and disappointment. Today we allow ourselves to question everything about the story we have been told.

Creation? Maybe God made this world, or maybe it's all a cruel, meaningless joke.

Crisis? Maybe violence and hate are just the way of the world.

Maybe they're not an intrusion or anomaly; maybe they're the way things are and will always, always be.

Calling? Forget about being blessed to be a blessing. Today we lie low and nurse our wounds. It is a dangerous world out there. We would be wise to stay inside and lock all doors.

Captivity? Who cares if Moses succeeded in getting our ancestors out of slavery in Egypt? Jesus failed, and there's no Moses for us now. We're still captives, worse off than we were before that crazy Galilean came and raised our hopes.

Conquest? If the most violent win and the non-violent are killed, what kind of world is it?

Conversation? Today it seems that the sceptics and doubters were right. There's nothing to say except, 'Vanity of vanities. All is vanity!' Today's lament feels like the only sure truth in all the sacred Scriptures!

Christ? What Christ? He lies in a grave, cold and dead, and with him all our hopes for a better way to be alive. Let the women prepare to embalm his corpse, if they can find it. Probably the Romans tore it to pieces and fed the fragments to the dogs.

Engage

1. What one thought or idea from today's lesson especially intrigued, provoked, disturbed, challenged, encouraged, warmed, warned, helped or surprised you?

2. Share a story about a time when you felt deep despair or disillusionment.

3. How do you respond to this opportunity to express your doubts so freely and honestly?

4. For children: What was a really sad or scary time in your life?

5. Activate: Today, take some time to allow yourself to feel emptiness, doubt, disappointment and fear, and don't try to explain them away. But keep open to the possibility that God is bigger than your biggest fear, disillusionment or sorrow.

6. Meditate: Hear Jesus crying, 'My God, my God, why have you forsaken me?' And allow the parts of your own heart that feel forsaken to find a voice with Jesus.

CHAPTER 33

The Uprising Begins (Easter Sunday)

Ezekiel 37:1–14

Luke 24:1–32

Were not our hearts burning within us while he was talking to us on the road, while he was opening the scriptures to us?

Colossians 1:9–29

Let's imagine ourselves with the disciples on the first Easter Sunday.

———————

Here's what we heard. At dawn, before the sun has risen, some women who are part of our movement went to the tomb to properly wash Jesus' corpse and prepare it for burial. When they arrived, they had a vision involving angels. One of the women claimed that Jesus appeared to her. The rest of us think it was just the gardener.

The gardener! What a place to be buried – a grave in a garden! A bed of death in a bed of life!

The women came and told the disciples. Peter went running back and found the tomb empty. Empty! And the burial cloths were still there, neatly folded. Who would take a naked corpse and leave the bloody cloths that it was wrapped in? Peter wondered what was going on – but he didn't have any clear theory.

We all speculated, but none of us knew what to think. We

decided to go back home. That's where we are now – walking on the road back home. It's about a seven-mile walk to our little town of Emmaus. It takes a couple of hours. Along the way we've been talking about all this, trying to come up with some kind of interpretation of the events that have transpired. Now we notice this other fellow walking towards us, a stranger. We lower our voices. He comes a little closer.

'What are you folks talking about?' he asks.

One of us replies, 'Are you kidding? Are you the only person in this whole region who doesn't know all that's been happening around Jerusalem recently?'

'Like what?' he asks.

We tell him about Jesus, that he was clearly a prophet who said and did amazing things. We tell him how the religious and political leaders came together to arrest him. We go into some detail about the crucifixion on Friday. 'We had hoped . . .' one of us says, and pauses. 'We had hoped . . . that this Jesus was the one who was going to turn things around for Israel, that he would set us free from the Roman occupation.'

We walk on a few steps, and he adds, 'And this morning was the third day since his death, and some women from our group told us that they had a vision of angels who said he was alive.' It's pretty clear from the tone of his voice that none of us take the report of the women very seriously.

That's when the stranger interrupts. 'You just don't get it, do you?' he says. 'This is exactly what the prophets said would happen. They have been telling us all along that the Liberator would have to suffer and die like this before entering his glory.' As we continue walking, he starts explaining things to us from the Scriptures. He begins with Moses, and step by step he shows us the pattern of God's work in history, culminating in what happened in Jerusalem in recent days. God calls someone to proclaim God's will. Resistance and rejection follow, often culminating in an expulsion or murder to silence the speaker. But this isn't a sign of defeat. This is the only way God's most important messages are ever heard – through someone on the verge of being rejected. God's word doesn't come in dominating, crushing force. It comes only in vulnerability, in weakness, in gentleness . . . just as we have seen over this last week.

At this point, we realise we've reached home already, and as we slow down, the stranger just keeps walking. We plead with him to stay here with us, since it's getting late and will soon be dark. So he comes in and we sit down at our little table for a meal. He reaches to the centre of the table and takes a loaf of bread and gives thanks for it. He breaks it and hands a piece of it to each of us and . . .

It hits us at the same instant. This isn't a stranger . . . this is . . . it couldn't be – yes, this is Jesus! We each look down at the fragment of bread in our hands, and when we look back up to the stranger . . . he is gone!

And we start talking, one interrupting the other.

'When he spoke about Moses and the prophets, did you feel . . . ?'

'. . . Inspired? Yes. It felt like my heart was glowing, hotter and hotter, until it was ready to ignite.'

'Did this really happen, or was it just a vision?'

'*Just* a vision? Maybe a vision means seeing into what's more real than anything else.'

'But it wasn't just me, right? You saw him too, right? You felt it too, right?'

'What do we do now? Shouldn't we . . . tell the others?'

'Yes, let's do it. Let's go back to Jerusalem, even though it's late. I could never sleep after experiencing this!'

So we pack our gear and rush back to the city, excited and breathless. On our earlier journey, we were filled with one kind of perplexity – disappointment, confusion, sadness. Now we feel another kind of perplexity – wonder, awe, amazement, almost-too-good-to-be-true-ness.

'Do you realise what this means?' one of us asks, and then answers his own question: 'Jesus was right after all! Everything he stood for has been vindicated!'

'Yes. And something else. We never have to fear death again.'

'And if that's true,' another answers, 'we never need to fear Caesar and his forces again, either. Their only real weapon is fear, and if we lose our fear, what power do they have left? Ha! Death has lost its sting! That means we can stand tall and speak the truth, just like Jesus did.'

'We never need to fear anyone again.'

'This changes everything.'

'It's not just that Jesus was resurrected. It feels like we have arisen too. We were in a tomb of defeat and despair. But now – look at us! We're truly alive again!'

We talk as fast as we walk. We recall Jesus' words from Thursday night about his body and blood. We remember what happened on Friday when his body and his blood were separated from one another on the cross. That's what crucifixion was, we realise: the slow, excruciating, public separation of body and blood. So, we wonder, could it be that in the holy meal, when we remember Jesus, we are making space for his body and blood to be reunited and reconstituted in us? Could our remembering him actually re-member and resurrect him in our hearts, our bodies, our lives? Could his body and blood be reunited in us, so that we become his new embodiment? Is that why we saw him and then didn't see him – because the place he most wants to be seen is in our bodies, among us, in us?

It's dark when we reach Jerusalem. Between this day's sunrise and today's sunset, our world has been changed for ever. Everything is new. From now on, whenever we break the bread and drink the wine, we will know that we are not alone. The risen Christ is with us, among us, and within us – just as he was today, even though we didn't recognise him. Resurrection has begun. We are part of something rare, something precious, something utterly revolutionary.

It feels like an uprising. An uprising of hope, not hate. An uprising armed with love, not weapons. An uprising that shouts a joyful promise of life and peace, not angry threats of hostility and death. It's an uprising of outstretched hands, not clenched fists. It's the 'one day' we have always dreamed of, emerging in the present, rising up among us and within us. It's so different from what we expected – so much better. This is what it means to be alive, truly alive. This is what it means to be en route, walking the road to a new and better day. Let's tell the others: The Lord is risen! *He is risen, indeed!* Lord is risen! *He is risen, indeed!* Lord is risen! *He is risen, indeed!*

Engage

1. What one thought or idea from today's lesson especially intrigued, provoked, disturbed, challenged, encouraged, warmed, warned, helped or surprised you?

2. Share a story about a time in your life when despair was replaced with hope.

3. How do you respond to the idea that the Eucharist dramatises Jesus' body and blood being reunited in us, transforming us into a community of resurrection?

4. For children: Why do you think Jesus' friends were so happy on Easter morning?

5. Activate: This week, remember the contrast between how life looks on Friday, Saturday and Sunday of Holy Week. Ask God to help you see with Easter eyes.

6. Meditate: Imagine the scene when the risen Christ broke the bread and suddenly disappeared. Hold that moment of disappearance in silence, and open your heart to the possibility of absence becoming fullness.

CHAPTER 34

The Uprising of Fellowship

Psalm 133

John 20

Peace be with you. As the Father has sent me, so I send you.

Acts 8:26–40

Matthew, Mark and Luke tell the story of Jesus in ways similar to one another (which is why they're often called the Synoptic Gospels – with a similar optic, or viewpoint). Many details differ (and the differences are quite fascinating), but it's clear the three compositions share common sources. The Fourth Gospel tells the story quite differently. These differences might disturb people who don't understand that storytelling in the ancient world was driven less by a duty to convey true details accurately and more by a desire to proclaim true meaning powerfully. The ancient editors who put the New Testament together let the differences stand as they were, so each story can convey its intended meanings in its own unique ways.

One place where details differ among the Gospels is in what happened right after the resurrection. Mark's Gospel, which scholars agree was the earliest one to be written down, ends abruptly without any details about the days and weeks after the resurrection. In Luke's Gospel and its sequel, the book of Acts, Jesus explicitly tells the disciples to stay in Jerusalem. In contrast, in Matthew's Gospel, the risen Jesus greets only some female disciples in Jerusalem. He tells these women to instruct the male disciples to go to Galilee, over sixty miles away, where he will appear to them later. In John's Gospel, the risen Christ appears to the disciples in Jerusalem on the evening of resurrection Sunday and then again a week later. And some time after that, the disciples leave Jerusalem and go to Galilee, where he appears to them once more.

For the next two weeks, we'll imagine ourselves with the disciples in the Fourth Gospel, this week in Jerusalem and next week in Galilee.

———————

We were afraid that first Sunday night, just three days after Jesus died. Really afraid. We were afraid to go outside in case someone might recognise us as Jesus' friends and notify the authorities. To them, Jesus was nothing more than a troublemaker and rabble-rouser. The rumours about Jesus rising from the dead, spread by some of the women among us, only made matters worse. The authorities would know by those rumours that dreams of an uprising hadn't completely died. Which meant that we were in danger. Real danger. So we locked ourselves in a room. But even there we were afraid, because at any moment some temple guards or Roman soldiers might bang on the door.

So there we remained, tense, jumpy, simmering with anxiety. What happened on Friday had been ugly, and we didn't want it to happen to the rest of us. Every sound startled us. Suddenly, we all felt something, a presence, familiar yet . . . impossible. How could Jesus be among us?

'Peace be with you,' he said. He showed us his scarred hands and feet. It started to dawn on us: the women's reports were not just wishful thinking – they were true, and we too were experiencing the risen Christ. 'I give you my peace,' he said again. And then he did three things that changed us for ever.

First he said, 'As the Father sent me, so I am sending you.' Here we were, huddled in our little safe house like a bunch of cowards, and he was still interested in sending cowards like us to continue his mission!

Next he came close to us and breathed on us. 'Welcome the Holy Spirit,' he said. Of course, this reminded us all of the story in Genesis when God breathed life into Adam and Eve. It was a new beginning, he was telling us. It was a new Genesis, and we were to be the prototypes of a new kind of human community.

Next came the greatest shock of all. After what happened on Friday, anyone with scars like his would have been expected to say, 'Go and get revenge on those evil beasts who did this to me.' But Jesus said, 'I'm sending you with the power to forgive.'

Peace! Forgiveness! Those aren't the responses you expect from someone who had suffered what Jesus suffered. But in that brief moment when our locked hideout was filled with his presence, that was the message we all received.

All of us except Thomas, that is. Thomas wasn't with us that night. When we saw Thomas later and told him what we had experienced, he was his typical sceptical self. 'I want to touch those scars with my own hands and see for myself, or I won't believe,' he said. A week later, we were all together again, this time with Thomas. We were still nervous about the authorities, so we were careful to keep the doors locked.

Just as before, Jesus' presence suddenly became real among us – visible, palpable. He spoke peace to us, and then he went straight to Thomas, inviting him to see, touch, believe. He did not criticise Thomas for doubting. He wanted to help him believe.

'My Lord and my God,' Thomas replied. We couldn't help

but remember back on Thursday night, when Thomas asked Jesus where he was going and what was the way to get there. Jesus replied, 'I am the way.' Philip then asked Jesus to show us the Father, and Jesus said, 'If you have seen me, you've seen the Father.' Now, ten days later, it seemed as if Thomas was beginning to understand what Jesus had meant. He saw God in a scarred man whose holy aliveness is more powerful than human cruelty.

That's one thing you have to say about Thomas: even though he didn't believe at first, he stayed with us, open to the possibility that his doubt could be transformed into faith. He kept coming back. He kept showing up. If he hadn't wanted to believe, he had a week to leave and go back home. But he didn't. He stayed. Not believing, but wanting to believe.

And from that night, we learned something essential about what this uprising is going to be about.

It isn't just for brave people, but for scared folk like us who are willing to become brave. It isn't just for believers, but for doubting folk like Thomas who want to believe in spite of their scepticism. It isn't just for good people, but for normal, flawed people like you and me and Thomas and Peter.

And I should add that it isn't just for men, either. It's no secret that men in our culture often treat women as inferior. Even on resurrection morning, when Mary Magdalene breathlessly claimed that the Lord was risen, the men among us didn't offer her much in the way of respect. There were all sorts of ignorant comments about 'the way women are'. Now we realise the Lord was telling us something by bypassing all the male disciples and appearing first to a woman. As we look back, we realise he's been treating women with more respect than the rest of us have right from the start.

We have a term for what we began to experience that night: *fellowship*. Fellowship is a kind of belonging that isn't based on status, achievement or gender, but instead is based on a deep belief that everyone matters, everyone is welcome and everyone is loved, no conditions, no exceptions. It's not the kind of belonging you find at the top of the ladder among those who think they are the best, but at the bottom among all the rest, with all the other failures and losers who have either climbed the ladder and fallen, or never got up enough gumption to climb in the first place.

Whatever else this uprising will become, from that night we've known it is an uprising of fellowship, a community where anyone who wants to be part of us will be welcome. Jesus showed us his scars, and we're starting to realise we don't have to hide ours.

So fellowship is for scarred people, and for scared people, and for people who want to believe but aren't sure what or how to believe. When we come together just as we are, we begin to rise again, to believe again, to hope again, to live again. Through fellowship, a little locked room becomes the biggest space in the world. In that space of fellowship, the Holy Spirit fills us like a deep breath of fresh air.

———————

This week and in the weeks to come, a leader can introduce this concluding ritual:

Let us lift a glass [or 'Let us stand and extend our hands'] and say, 'The Lord is risen!' *He is risen, indeed!*
We too are rising up! *We are rising up, indeed!*
Let us arise in fellowship. *In fellowship, indeed!*

Engage

1. What one thought or idea from today's lesson especially intrigued, provoked, disturbed, challenged, encouraged, warmed, warned, helped or surprised you?

2. Share a story about an experience of true fellowship.

3. How do you respond to the idea that Christian fellowship is for scarred and scared people – without regard to gender, status or achievement?

4. For children: Tell us about your best friends and why they're so special to you.

5. Activate: This week, aim to create spaces for an uprising of fellowship where people feel unconditionally welcome and included – whether in your home, in an office, on public transport, in a restaurant, on the street, or wherever.

6. Meditate: Imagine you're Thomas at the moment Jesus shows his scarred hands, feet and side. See where Thomas's experience from that night would resonate with your life today.

CHAPTER 35

The Uprising of Discipleship

Psalm 25
Luke 10:1–11, 17–20
John 21:1–15

Feed my lambs.

Let's imagine ourselves with the disciples, a short time after the resurrection, in Galilee.

———————

There were several of us together that day. We had left the big city of Jerusalem and gone back to Galilee, our home region to the north. Thomas was there, and so were Peter, Nathaniel, James and John, plus a few more. Out of the blue, late in the day, Peter said he wanted to go fishing. Fishing, of all things!

We weren't sure why, but we joined him anyway. We dropped our long gill net time after time through the night, re-enacting an old, familiar ritual. And time after time we hauled it in, hoping for something. But the net never struggled against us, never signalled the weight or life of a catch.

It was dawn when we saw a stranger on the shore about a

hundred yards from us. Unsuccessful fishermen know the hated question: 'Hey boys! Having any luck?'

'Nothing,' we replied glumly.

He yelled, 'Drop your net over on the other side of the boat. You'll find fish there.'

There's nothing like having a stranger on the shore giving you advice after you've been fishing all night. But we did what he said.

And then it happened. We started feeling the net move. Not just a few fish, but a heavy, wriggling, squirming shoal! Most of us were thinking about the fish. But one thought only of that stranger on the shore. 'It's the Lord!' Peter said. He immediately threw on his shirt and swam to shore while the rest of us hauled in the net. It's a wonder it didn't tear with all that weight!

When the rest of us came ashore, the stranger already had some bread laid out, with a charcoal fire glowing and some fish cooking. He invited us to add a few of our own fish to the meal, so Peter went out to pull a few from the net.

'Let's have breakfast,' the stranger said.

We all had this sense of who he was, so nobody asked any questions. He broke the bread and gave it, and then the fish, to us. It seems strange to do something so normal . . . eat breakfast . . . under such extraordinary circumstances. But that was what we did. Later we remembered how Jesus had taken the role of a servant the night before the crucifixion, washing our feet. Now he was in the same role, serving us a meal. He turned to Peter to deal with some unfinished business between them.

That night when Jesus was arrested, Peter had fallen apart. When armed guards arrived, Peter panicked, pulled out his sword and slashed off somebody's ear. In a matter of seconds, he managed to violate half of what Jesus had taught us for the better part of three years. Later, he denied that he even knew Jesus, not once but three times, and he threw in some choice language in doing so. On the morning of the resurrection, he was frantic and confused, and that was just days after he had bragged about how loyal he would be. It wasn't pretty, and we all knew this instability weighed heavy on the mind of the man Jesus had renamed 'the Rock'.

'Simon, son of John, do you love me more than these?' Jesus asked, using Peter's original name rather than 'Peter the Rock'. We weren't sure what Jesus meant by 'more than these'. Did he mean more in comparison to us, his fellow disciples? Did he mean more than the fish, the boat and the net – symbols of his old life before it was interrupted by Jesus? Peter ignored any ambiguity. 'Yes, Lord. You know I love you.'

'Then take care of my lambs,' Jesus replied. Then, as if Peter's first reply didn't count for much, Jesus asked him again: 'Simon, son of John, do you love me?' Peter replied in the same way the second time, and Jesus said, 'Shepherd my sheep.' Then the question came a third time, echoing in all our minds Peter's three denials. Peter replied even more strongly this time. 'Lord, you know everything. Of course you know I love you!' Once again, Jesus told him to shepherd his sheep.

And that was it. It was as if all Peter's failures melted behind us in the past, like a bad night of fishing after a great morning catch. The past and its failures didn't count any more. What counted was love . . . love for Jesus, love for his flock.

Like a lot of us, Peter had a way of getting it right one minute and wrong the next. Sure enough, a few minutes later, Peter had forgotten about love for the flock and was treating one of the other disciples as a rival, a competitor. Jesus responded forcefully. 'Stop worrying about anyone else. You follow me!'

Those words remind us of how this whole adventure began for us, with Jesus issuing that simple, all-or-nothing invitation: *Follow me!* Three years later, it's still about that one essential thing: following him. Of course, that's what the word *disciple* has meant all along – to be a follower, a student, an apprentice, one who learns by imitating a master.

You can imagine the honour, for uneducated fishermen like us, to sit at the feet of the greatest teacher imaginable. And now we feel it is an even greater honour to be sent out to teach others, who will in turn teach and train others in this new way of life. This revolutionary plan of discipleship means that we must first and foremost be examples. We must embody the message and values of our movement. That doesn't mean we are perfect – just look at Peter. But it does mean we are growing and learning, always humble and willing to get up again after we fall, always moving forward on the road we are walking. As Jesus modelled never-ending learning and growth for us, we will model it for others, who will model it for still others. If each new generation of disciples follows this example, centuries from now apprentices will still be learning the way of Jesus from mentors, so they can become mentors for the following generation.

Once, a while back, Jesus sent us out on a kind of training mission, preparing us for this day. He wouldn't let us bring anything – not even a wallet, satchel or sandals. He sent us out in complete vulnerability – like sheep among wolves, he said. In each town we would need to find hospitable people to shelter us and feed us – 'people of peace', Jesus called them. They would become our partners, and with their support we would proclaim the kingdom of God in word and deed to their neighbours. If people didn't respond, he told us to move on and not look back. We were looking for places, like fields that are ready for harvest, where the time was right and people wanted what we had to offer. We returned from that training mission full of confidence and joy.

Once again it is time for us to follow Jesus' example and teaching, even though he will not be physically present. He invited us to be his disciples, so now we will invite others to become disciples too. And they in turn will invite still others. In this way, a worldwide movement of discipleship can begin this morning, here on this beach with this handful of tired but resilient fishermen. Small beginnings with unlikely people, given lots of time and lots of faith and lots of hope and love, can change the world.

Like Peter, if we lose our focus, we will be tempted to turn on each other – comparing, criticising, competing. That's why, like Peter, each of us needs to hear Jesus say, 'Stop worrying about anyone else! *You* follow *me*!'

I think Jesus chose fishermen like us for a good reason. To be part of his uprising, we must be willing to fail a lot, and to keep trying. We will face long, dark nights when nothing happens. But we can never give up hope. He caught us in his net of love, so now we go and spread the net for others. And so, fellow disciples, let's get moving. Let us walk the road with Jesus.

———————

Let us lift a glass and say, 'The Lord is risen!' *He is risen, indeed!*
We too are rising up! *We are rising up, indeed!*
Let us arise in fellowship. *In fellowship, indeed!*
Let us arise in discipleship. *In discipleship, indeed!*

Engage

1. What one thought or idea from today's lesson especially intrigued, provoked, disturbed, challenged, encouraged, warmed, warned, helped or surprised you?

2. Share a story about how you have been drawn towards discipleship through another person.

3. How do you relate to the story of Peter with its dramatic ups and downs?

4. For children: If you could help other children learn one important thing, what would it be, and how would you teach them?

5. Activate: This week, keep your eyes open for hospitable 'people of peace' who can be your allies in the uprising of peace that Jesus started.

6. Meditate: In silence, hold the image of tired fishermen at daybreak, being told to cast their nets one more time. What does this image say to you in your life right now?

CHAPTER 36

The Uprising of Worship

Psalm 103
Acts 2:41–47

They devoted themselves to the apostles' teaching and fellow-ship, to the breaking of bread and the prayers.

1 Corinthians 14:26–31
Colossians 3:12–17

Let us imagine ourselves among the early disciples in Jerusalem, a year or so after Christ's death and resurrection.

———

Many months have passed since the uprising began. For a short time, there were frequent reports of people seeing the risen Christ in a variety of locations. Soon, though, those reports became less frequent until they ceased entirely. A story spread that Jesus had ascended to heaven and was now sitting at God's right hand. That fuelled a lot of speculation and debate about what we should expect. Some think God is going to stage a dramatic intervention any day. Some have even stopped working in anticipation of a massive change. But many of us have inter-preted Jesus' ascension and enthronement to mean it is now time to get to work, living in light of what Jesus already taught us. We're convinced that what matters now is not for Christ to appear *to* us, but for Christ to appear *in* us, *among* us and *through* us. He wants us to be his hands, his feet, his face, his smile, his voice . . . his embodiment on Earth.

We gather frequently as little communities that we call *ecclesia*. We borrowed this term from the Roman Empire, just as we 'borrowed' the cross and reversed its meaning. For the Romans, an ecclesia is an exclusive gathering that brings local citizens together to discuss the affairs of the empire. Our ecclesia brings common people together around the affairs of the kingdom of God. Whenever and wherever the Roman ecclesia gather, they honour and worship the emperor and the pantheon of gods that support him. Whenever and wherever we gather, we honour and worship the living God, revealed to us in Christ, through the power of the Holy Spirit.

Our ecclesia gather for worship wherever we can – in homes, public buildings or outdoor settings. And we gather whenever we can – but mostly at night, since that's when nearly everyone – even the slaves among us – can assemble. We often gather on Sunday, the day Jesus rose and this uprising began, but none of us would argue about which day is best, since every day is a good day to worship God.

For us, worship includes four main functions. We begin with the teaching of the original disciples, whom we now call *apostles*. Just as an apprentice carpenter is called a master carpenter once he has learned the trade, well-trained disciples who are sent out to teach others are called *apostles*. The apostles tell us the stories of Jesus, things they saw and heard as eyewitnesses of his time among us. They read the Law and the Prophets, and explain how our sacred texts prepared the way for Jesus and his good news. The apostles and their assistants also write letters that are shared from one ecclesia to the next. Our leaders read these letters aloud to us, since many of us can't read ourselves. Whether in person or by letter, through the teaching of the apostles we learn the words of Jesus, the stories about Jesus, the parables he told, the character he embodied, so we can walk the road he walked.

Second, our worship includes breaking the bread and drinking the wine, as Jesus taught us. Usually, this is part of a meal that we call our 'love feast' or 'the Lord's table'. It is so unlike anything any of us have ever experienced. Everywhere in our society, we experience constant divisions between rich and poor, slave and free, male and female, Jew and Greek, city-born and country-born, and so on. But at the Lord's table, just as it was when Jesus shared a table with sinners and outcasts, we are all one, all loved, all welcome as equals. We even greet one another with a holy kiss. Nobody would ever see a high-born person greeting a slave as an equal – except at our gatherings, where those social divisions are being forgotten and where we learn new ways of honouring one another as members of one family.

At our love feasts we say the words Jesus said about the bread being his body given for us, and the wine being his blood shed for us and for our sins. Those words 'for us' and 'for our sins' are full of meaning for us. Just as we take medicine 'for' an illness, we understand that Jesus' death is curing us of our old habits and ways. For example, when we ponder how he forgave those who crucified him, we are cured of our desire for revenge. When we see how he trusted God and didn't fear human threats, we are cured of our fear. When we remember how he never stopped loving, even to the point of death, we are cured of our hatred and anger. When we imagine his outstretched arms embracing the whole world, we feel our hearts opening in love for the whole world, too, curing us of our prejudice and favouritism, our grudges and selfishness.

Along with the apostles' teaching and the holy meal, our worship gatherings include fellowship or sharing. We share our experiences, our sense of what God wants to tell us, our insights from the Scriptures. We also share our fears, our tears, our failures and our joys. There is a financial aspect to our sharing as well. At each gathering we take an offering to distribute to those who are most in need among us and around us – especially the widows and the orphans. None of us is rich, but through our sharing none of us is in need either.

Finally, along with gathering for teaching, the holy meal and fellowship, our worship gatherings are for prayer. Some of our prayers are requests. We have learned that it is far better to share our worries with God than to be filled with anxiety about things that are out of our control anyway. We constantly pray for boldness and wisdom so that we can spread the good news of God's love to everyone everywhere. We bring the needs and sorrows of others to God, too, joining our compassion with God's great compassion. We pray for everyone in authority – that they will turn from injustice, violence and corruption to ways of justice, peace and fairness. We pray especially for those who consider themselves our enemies. The more they curse and mistreat us, the more we pray for God's blessing on them, as Jesus taught us to do.

Some of our prayers are confessions. We freely confess our sins to God, because Jesus taught us that God is gracious and forgiving. God's grace frees us from hiding our wrongs or making excuses for them. We don't want to pretend to be better than we really are, and so prayers of confession help us be honest with God, ourselves and one another.

All of our prayers lead us to thanksgiving and praise. We feel such joy to have God's Spirit rising up in our lives that we can't be silent. We sing our deep joy and longing, sometimes through the ancient psalms and also through spiritual songs that spring up in our hearts. The more we praise God, the less we fear or are intimidated by the powers of this world. And so we praise and worship God boldly, joyfully, reverently and freely, and we aren't quiet or shy about it!

When we gather, the Holy Spirit gives each of us different gifts to be used for the common good. Someone may be gifted to teach or lead. Someone may be moved to write and sing a song. Someone may be given an inspired word of comfort or encouragement or warning for our ecclesia. Someone may be given a special message of knowledge, insight or teaching. Someone may speak in an unknown language, and someone may pray with great faith for a healing or miracle to occur. The same Spirit who gives the gifts is teaching us to be guided by love in all we say and do, for love matters most for us. It is even greater than faith and hope!

We don't want to give anyone the impression that everything is perfect with us. We have lots of problems and a lot to learn. But somehow, our problems seem small in comparison to the joy that we feel. This is why, even when we are tired from long days of work, even when we are threatened with persecution, even when life is full of hardships and we feel discouraged or afraid, still we gather to rise up in worship. In the face of Christ, we have come to see the glory of God, the love of God, the wisdom of God, the goodness of God, the power of God, the kindness of God . . . the fullness of God. In light of that vision of God in Christ, how can we not worship?

Let us lift a glass and say, 'The Lord is risen!' *He is risen, indeed!*

We too are rising up! *We are rising up, indeed!*

Let us arise in fellowship. *In fellowship, indeed!*

Let us arise in discipleship. *In discipleship, indeed!*

Let us arise in worship. *In worship, indeed!*

Engage

1. What one thought or idea from today's lesson especially intrigued, provoked, disturbed, challenged, encouraged, warmed, warned, helped or surprised you?

2. Share a story of a time when your heart was full of worship.

3. How do you respond to the four functions of gathered worship – teaching, bread and wine, fellowship, and prayer?

4. For children: What do you like most and least about gathering for worship?

5. Activate: This week, look for opportunities to share with others what you gain from being part of an ecclesia – a gathered community of fellowship, discipleship and worship.

6. Meditate: Choose one word that points to an attribute of God – *glory*, *wisdom*, *justice*, *kindness*, *power*, etc. Hold that word in your heart and mind, and in silence worship God. Then choose another word and hold it together with the first in silent worship. Then add a third, and so on.

CHAPTER 37

The Uprising of Partnership

Psalm 146

Matthew 10:16–20; 11:28–30; 28:16–20

Go therefore and make disciples of all nations.

Acts 16:11–40

Let's imagine it is about AD 51 and we are with a group of disciples in Philippi, about halfway between Jerusalem and Rome.

———————

For almost twenty years now the uprising has been spreading. We still remember Jesus' words about scattering seed and seeing it grow, or kneading yeast into dough so the bread will rise, or extending like fruitful branches from a central vine. We dare to believe that through tiny little seeds like us, through the yeast of our little ecclesia, through the spreading branches of this expanding movement, the world is beginning to change. Nobody knows exactly how many disciples there are, but every day, it seems, more are being added.

We've already seen uprisings of justice, peace and joy spread across Judea and Samaria, and now, Paul, Timothy, Luke, Silas, Priscilla, Aquila and many others travel across the empire, developing ecclesia in all its major cities. We have been invited to join them in Philippi.

Philippi is famous because, as a Roman colony, it's like a little outpost of Rome. The people of Philippi are loyal Romans – the citizens, that is. The slaves here, just like everywhere in the empire, are not so happy with the *Pax Romana*. They do disproportionately large amounts of work and enjoy disproportionately small amounts of 'pax'. The same could be said for women in the empire. It was a group of women we first met here several days ago, down by the river where they gather for prayer. A businesswoman named Lydia welcomed us – and our message. She and her household were baptised, and she gave us a place to stay at her large home. It's not at all surprising that women were the first to welcome us. Luke keeps reminding us that ever since Mary, they've been leaders in the uprising.

If slaves and women are the worst-off people in the empire, young female slaves are the most vulnerable by far. It was a slave girl who next demanded our attention in Philippi. She made a lot of money for her owners by going into a trance and telling fortunes. Whenever we walked by her on the way to the riverside, she would start shouting about us: 'These men are slaves of the Highest God of All. They proclaim to you the way of liberation!' You can imagine how slave-owners feel when slaves shout about liberation. And you can imagine how believers in the Greek and Roman gods feel when people talk about 'the Highest God of All'. It sounds very threatening to their economy and their religion – their whole Roman way of life.

This went on for a couple of days until finally, yesterday, Paul got annoyed. We were not sure why, exactly. He may have been frustrated that the girl was drawing attention to us in such an inflammatory way. He may have been embarrassed that a fortune-teller was speaking up for us. Or he may have been frustrated that this outspoken girl with so much energy, intelligence and courage was reduced to slavery. Paul constantly reminds us that all people have equal dignity in Christ, male or female, slave or free, Jew, Greek, Roman or foreigner. Anyway, for whatever reason, yesterday he had enough. He turned to her and commanded the spirit of fortune-telling to come out of her in the name of Jesus Christ. And from that moment, no more trances. No more fortune-telling. And no more money for the men who exploited her!

The situation deteriorated rapidly. The furious slave-owners grabbed Paul and another member of our group, Silas, and dragged them into the central plaza of the city where all the markets were. They told the city officials that Paul and Silas were Jewish revolutionaries, advocating a lifestyle that good Romans could never accept. The words *Jew* and *lifestyle* were code words that the city officials picked up. We Jews, after all, derive our basic identity from the story of God liberating us from slavery in Egypt. Of all people in the empire, we Jews are considered most resistant to Roman domination. So the slave-owners quickly whipped the people of the market into a frenzy. Soon, by order of the city officials, Paul and Silas were stripped naked, severely beaten and dragged off to prison, where they were put in chains in the innermost cell.

Late last night, Paul and Silas were singing praises to God. It was as if they were saying, 'You can lock us up, but you can't shut us up!' Their songs of praise demonstrated that they feared neither the whole Roman system of slavery, domination and intimidation, nor the petty gods that upheld it. The other prisoners, as you could imagine, were quite impressed by their courage, if not their singing voices. Suddenly, around midnight, there was an earthquake. Now earthquakes aren't terribly rare in Philippi, but this kind of earthquake was completely unprecedented. It didn't cause the jail to crash in a heap of rubble. It produced no casualties. It simply shook the jail gates and chains so they came unfastened! It was an earthquake of liberation, not destruction. Imagine that!

When the jailer rushed in to check on his prisoners, he was terrified. He knew that if they escaped, he would be put into prison himself, and perhaps tortured too. So he pulled out his sword and decided that suicide was better than being thrown into the miserable prison system that he managed. Paul shouted out to him, 'Don't do it, man! We're all here!'

At this point, the poor jailer was even more shocked. Here his prisoners were concerned about his welfare! They were choosing to stay in prison voluntarily to keep him from suffering for their escape! He brought them outside the prison and fell down on his knees in front of them, trembling with emotion. 'Gentlemen, what must I do to experience the liberation you have?' he asked. There was that word *liberation* again – the same word the slave girl had used.

'Have confidence in the Lord Jesus, and you will be liberated, and so will your whole household,' Paul said. The jailer must have understood those words 'Lord Jesus' to be in contrast to the emperor's title, 'Lord Caesar'. He realised that Paul was telling him to stop being intimidated by Caesar's system of threats, whips, swords, chains, locks and prisons. He heard Paul's words as an invitation to live under a different lord or supreme leader, in a different system, a different empire, a different kingdom – the one Jesus leads, one characterised by true freedom, true grace and true peace.

The jailer took them to his own house, washed their wounds and gave them a good meal. He had already been transformed – from a jailer to a gracious host! And when Paul and Silas told the man, his family and his slaves more about Jesus and the uprising, they were all baptised.

Early this morning, the city officials realised that they had violated legal protocols by giving in to the wealthy businessmen's demands. So they sent police to the jail with orders to get Paul and Silas out of town as soon as possible. But Paul refused to leave. 'They made a mockery of justice by publicly humiliating, beating and imprisoning two Roman citizens without a trial, and now they want us to participate in a cover-up? No way! If they want us to leave, they need to come in person, apologise, and personally escort us from the city.' When the police returned with news that the two prisoners were actually Roman citizens, the city officials were as scared as the jailer had been after the earthquake. Like him, all they could think of was how much trouble they would be in with the higher-ups! So they complied with Paul's demands and politely requested that Paul and Silas leave the city immediately.

Paul wasn't in any rush. He decided to stop and spend some time here at Lydia's house, where the rest of us have been waiting. We quickly gathered the newly forming ecclesia. Paul and Silas shared the story you just heard. Everyone is brimming with excitement, overflowing with joy. We are partners in an earthquake of liberation! As we move forward together in this partnership in mission for peace and freedom, injustice at every level of society will be confronted, and people at every level of society will be set free!

Let us lift a glass and say, 'The Lord is risen!' *He is risen, indeed!*

We too are rising up! *We are rising up, indeed!*

Let us arise in fellowship. *In fellowship, indeed!*

Let us arise in discipleship. *In discipleship, indeed!*

Let us arise in worship. *In worship, indeed!*

Let us arise in partnership. *In partnership, indeed!*

Engage

1. What one thought or idea from today's lesson especially intrigued, provoked, disturbed, challenged, encouraged, warmed, warned, helped or surprised you?

2. Share a story about a time when you felt like one character in this story.

3. How do you respond to the idea that Paul and Silas were engaged in protest and civil disobedience in Philippi? Under what circumstances would you risk arrest, imprisonment or death?

4. For children: Have you ever been part of a really good team? Tell us about it.

5. Activate: This week, look for counterparts to the slave girl in your world. Do what you can to stand with them and stand up for them and show them you respect their dignity.

6. Meditate: Hold in your imagination the picture of jail doors shaking open. What could this image mean for your life? Listen in your deepest heart for an answer.

CHAPTER 38

The Uprising of Stewardship

Deuteronomy 15:1–11

1 Timothy 6:3–19

. . . we brought nothing into the world, so that we can take nothing out of it; but if we have food and clothing, we will be content with these.

2 Corinthians 8:1–15

Let us imagine we are with Paul and his team of disciples in the city of Corinth in AD 51.

———————

We'll never forget Philippi and what we learned there about the uprising. Since leaving the Roman colony, we've visited several other cities including Thessalonica and Berea. Now we have come to a city called Corinth. It's a city with a dirty reputation, well deserved in many ways. The people here are tough. Mean. Selfish. There are all kinds of religions, lots of temple prostitution, all the worst of big-city life. But even here, an ecclesia of discipleship, fellowship, worship and partnership is forming. It looks like Paul, Silas and Timothy plan to settle here for a year or more. They have joined with a local couple, Priscilla and Aquila, to start a small business making tents. Together, we can produce and sell tents to make enough money that we won't be a burden on the ecclesia here.

Speaking of money, you don't have to live very long to know that money rules this world. People with money have power, and to them what matters most is getting more of both. We see that here in Corinth, and it's obvious around the whole empire.

Paul is very suspicious of money. To him, loving money is at the root of all kinds of evil. What really counts isn't gold, but the contentment that comes from desiring God above all else.

Again and again he teaches us that the drive to accumulate money wastes our lives. Our real ambition should be to build a big account of good works – acts of generosity and kindness on behalf of those considered the last, the least and the lost. Paul loves to quote Jesus' words that it is better to give than to receive. That's why he's got us making tents: he wants us to have enough money to provide for our own needs, plus more to share with others.

When the uprising first began in Jerusalem, people started bringing all their possessions to the apostles. Since they knew it wasn't God's will for some of us to have luxuries while others lacked necessities, those with surplus began to share freely with those in need. We held all things in common. As you might expect, that created some problems. Some old prejudices sprang up between Jews and Greeks, and some people began playing games, pretending to be more generous than they really were. In spite of the problems, holding all things in common was a beautiful thing. Some of us still practise the 'all things in common' rule as they did at the beginning, and some have modified that rule.

But what hasn't changed, and what must never change, is this: we realise that the systems of this world run on one economy, and we in the commonwealth of God run on another. In our alternate economy, those who have a lot don't hoard it; they share it. Those who have been given much in terms of money and power feel not a sense of privilege and superiority, but a sense of greater responsibility for their neighbours who are vulnerable and in need. We measure our well-being and holiness by the condition of the weakest and neediest among us.

Across the Roman Empire, and especially here in Corinth, people exhaust themselves to get rich, and in so doing they cause much harm. Some exploit the land. You might say they are thieves who take more from the bank of creation than they put back, and in that way they steal from unborn generations. Others exploit people of this generation. They are thieves who make big profits through the sweat of their poorly paid neighbours, reducing them, if not to slavery, then to something almost the same. They are often very subtle in the ways they do this, using banks, investments and loans to enrich themselves as they impoverish others. It's a dirty economy, and those who profit by it gain the world and lose their souls.

'What's yours is mine,' some people say, 'and I want to steal it!' 'What's mine is mine,' some people say, 'and I want to keep it!' 'What's mine is God's,' we are learning to say, 'and I want to use it for the common good.' We call that attitude *stewardship*.

Stewardship applies to all areas of our lives – how we use time, potential, possessions, privilege and power. Whatever we do, we try to give it our very best, because we work for Christ and not just for money. We want no part of dishonest or harmful employment, so if necessary we change jobs, or we work for reform so we can stay in our current jobs with a clear conscience. As we are being transformed personally, we seek to transform our economic systems from corrupt to ethical, from destructive to regenerative, from cruel and dehumanising to kind and humane. We believe this pleases God.

When it comes to how we spend our earnings, stewardship means living below our means. We do so by dividing our income into three parts. First, we determine a percentage that we will use to provide for our needs and the needs of our families. That's just basic decency. Second, we determine a percentage to save, since wisdom requires foresight. Even ants know to save some of their summer's work to get them through the winter. Third, we set aside the largest portion we can for God's work of compassion, justice, restoration and peace.

Some of this third portion goes to people like Paul, Silas and Timothy, who lead and serve the ecclesia springing up around the world. Some of it goes to members of the ecclesia who are in need – the sick, the widows, the orphans, the elderly and those who have lost their homes, their land and their work. Some of it goes to meet the needs of others near or far – as an expression of God's love and ours. That's what stewardship is, really: love in action.

Paul always reminds us that nothing has any value without love. That explains why money is so deceptive. It deceives people about what has true value. You cannot serve two masters, Jesus taught. If you love God, you will hate money, because it always gets in the way of loving God. If you love money, you will hate God, because God always gets in the way of loving money.

It is foolishness to live above your means. It is selfishness to spend all your money on yourself. It is godliness to give – to produce a surplus that is used for the commonwealth of God, which is an uprising not of greed but of joyful generosity and creative stewardship.

––––––––––

Let us lift a glass and say, 'The Lord is risen!' *He is risen, indeed!*
We too are rising up! *We are rising up, indeed!*
Let us arise in fellowship. *In fellowship, indeed!*
Let us arise in discipleship. *In discipleship, indeed!*
Let us arise in worship. *In worship, indeed!*
Let us arise in partnership. *In partnership, indeed!*
Let us arise in stewardship. *In stewardship, indeed!*

Engage

1. What one thought or idea from today's lesson especially intrigued, provoked, disturbed, challenged, encouraged, warmed, warned, helped or surprised you?

2. Share a story about a time when you got mixed up about what really has value.

3. How do you respond to the idea of dividing your earnings into three parts – to spend, save and give?

4. For children: If someone gave you a whole lot of money, what would you do with it?

5. Activate: If you've never developed a budget where you specify what percentage of your income you will spend, save and give, do so this week. And if you have such a budget, reassess and see if you can raise your standard of giving by a percentage or two. If possible, meet with a close friend from your learning circle to speak openly of your financial lives and priorities. If you don't already do so, consider pooling your giving power through this learning circle.

6. Meditate: Quietly ponder the tension between loving God and loving money. See if any insights come to you. Ask God to help you be a wise steward or manager of the resources that are entrusted to you.

CHAPTER 39

Whatever the Hardship, Keep Rising Up!

Isaiah 40:27–31

. . . they shall mount up with wings like eagles, they shall run and not be weary, they shall walk and not faint.

Acts 9:1–25
2 Corinthians 6:1–10; 11:22–33

Let us imagine ourselves in Rome, in about AD 64.

———

Over thirty years have passed since Jesus launched this uprising of faith, hope and love in our world. Over a dozen years have passed since we travelled with Paul around the Mediterranean. Since then, the uprising has continued to spread. New leaders have arisen. People around the empire have joined us. We know the movement is gaining strength.

It is gaining strength largely because of the hardships we have faced. There have been persecutions from outsiders, betrayals by insiders and stupid arguments that wasted time and drained our energy. There have been divisions, moral scandals, financial improprieties, all kinds of crazy teachings that confuse and distract, power struggles, sad things that in many ways show how easy it is to forget what this whole movement is supposed to be about. As we've offended each other and forgiven each other, as we've experienced rifts and then reconciliations, we've learned that God doesn't give us shortcuts around hardships, but strengthens us through them.

Speaking of hardships, we recently heard that Paul was under house arrest in Rome. Timothy told us Paul was feeling lonely and cold in the winter chill, and a little bored, too. So we joined Timothy and came to Rome to be with him. We brought him a warm coat and things to read, among other things. Since we arrived, a steady stream of visitors comes every day to talk with Paul about Jesus and the commonwealth of God, the great abiding passions of his life.

In the evenings, Paul often tells us stories about his many adventures. To our great surprise, the stories he likes to tell most are those of struggle. 'If I'm going to brag like a fool,' he says, 'it will be about my weaknesses, limitations, sufferings and scars.'

Sometimes Paul shows us those scars – from whippings he received on five occasions, and beatings with rods that he received three times, including that unforgettable day in Philippi. He reminds us that even Jesus could only lead the way to God's new commonwealth through suffering. 'Through many hardships you enter the commonwealth of God,' he says. He loves to tell the story – and we love to hear it – of how he first experienced the risen Christ over a three-day period, and how from the start he knew that his path would involve suffering.

The uprising had only been underway for about three years. Saul – the name by which Paul was known back then – had been its most passionate enemy. He hated the Way, as it was called back then. He became obsessed with stamping it out. He travelled around the region arresting, imprisoning and executing women as well as men in the name of God and the Scriptures. When he was on his way to Damascus to continue his bloody and hateful work, he was struck to the ground by a blinding

light. He heard a voice saying, 'Saul, Saul, why do you perse-
cute me?' He asked who was speaking to him, and the voice
said, 'I am Jesus, the one you are persecuting. Now get up and
go into the city and you will be shown what to do next.' This
shattering experience of spiritual insight left him unable to see
physically. So he had to be led into Damascus by the hand. For
three days he sat in darkness, unable to see. Obviously, he had
a lot to think about.

A complete stranger named Ananias came to visit him.
Ananias was a disciple, a follower of Jesus and the Way – exactly
the kind of person Paul had come to Damascus to arrest, torture
and kill. Ananias could have killed his blind and defenceless
enemy. But instead he spoke words of kindness to him. 'Brother
Saul,' he said, 'the Lord Jesus who appeared to you sent me to
you so your sight could be restored and so you could be filled
with the Holy Spirit.' Ananias laid his hands on him and prayed
for his vision to be restored.

When Paul opened his eyes, the first face he saw was that of
Ananias. Ananias warned him that the road ahead would be full
of hardship, and that has been the case – for Paul, and for all of
us on the Way.

Of course, as followers of the Way, we face the normal hardships of life – sickness, setbacks, delays, conflict, struggle. Paul
has had his share of those. Once he survived a shipwreck, only
to get bitten by a snake. How he laughs when he tells us that
one! And there was the time he preached for so long that a
young man got drowsy, dropped off to sleep and fell out of a
second-storey window. Paul laughs even more when he tells
that one. Thankfully, it turned out OK in the end. In fact, after
healing the victim of his long sermon, Paul went back and
preached for several more hours!

Paul is getting older now. He is constantly plagued by eye
troubles and other aches and pains. Being under house arrest

means poor food, cold, restricted movement and uncertainty about what the future holds, especially now, with Nero as emperor. Enough said about that. On a deeper level, Paul often speaks with deep regret about a break with two of his former friends, Barnabas and John Mark. He still dreams of reconciliation. And he carries constant concern for the ecclesia spread out across the empire, the way a mother carries her children in her heart even after they're grown.

In the face of all this hardship, Paul admits getting depressed at times. But he tells us that it is only through hardship, through discouragement, through exhaustion, that we learn to draw on the power of God's Spirit within us. It is only when we come to the end of our own strength, and even then refuse to give up, that we discover God's strength. 'When we are weak, then we are strong,' he says.

Hardships make us bitter . . . or better. They lead us to breakdown . . . or to breakthrough. If we don't give up at that breaking point when we feel we've reached the end of our own resources, we find a new aliveness, the life of the risen Christ rising within us. Paul often says it like this: 'I have been crucified with Christ. So it is no longer my prideful self who lives. Now it is Christ, alive in me.'

Hardships not only teach us to live in dependence upon God, but they also teach us interdependence with others. So through hardship, we move from 'me' to 'we'. Paul reminds us that he discovered Christ not only in his vision, but also in Ananias. And after Ananias, he met Christ in the ecclesia in Damascus, the ecclesia in Antioch, and in so many individuals too – in women like Lydia, Prisca and Julia, in men like Timothy and Titus . . . and yes, even dear Barnabas and John Mark too.

Paul isn't the least bit shy about speaking of his tenuous future. 'The only thing ahead for me is imprisonment and persecution,' he says. 'But I don't count my life of any value to myself.

My only ambition is to finish my course and fulfil the ministry the Lord Jesus has given me: to tell everyone everywhere about the good news of God's grace.'

These days there's a lot of unrest. The Zealots are stirring up rebellion in Jerusalem, and if that happens the Roman military will crush it and reduce Jerusalem to ashes and rubble. Here in Rome, Nero is utterly powerful and utterly insane. He takes sick pleasure in executing people on a whim, and any day Paul could be his next entertainment. But Paul refuses to complain – he can't stand complaining. He just keeps rejoicing and singing and being grateful for each day, each breath, each heartbeat – just as he did that night with Silas in the jail in Philippi. 'For me to live is Christ,' he says. 'But to die will be gain.' Paul has followed Jesus' example, and in so doing he has set an example for us . . . an example of enduring hardship and seeing joy beyond it.

We've been enduring hardship and experiencing joy for thirty years now. Paul will soon be gone. And then it will be up to us to carry on – leading with joy through whatever hardships we will face. Who knows where the road will lead? God will be with us, and we will make the road by walking, together.

———————

Let us lift a glass and say, 'The Lord is risen!' *He is risen, indeed!*

We too are rising up! *We are rising up, indeed!*

Let us arise in fellowship. *In fellowship, indeed!*

Let us arise in discipleship. *In discipleship, indeed!*

Let us arise in worship. *In worship, indeed!*

Let us arise in partnership. *In partnership, indeed!*

Let us arise in stewardship. *In stewardship, indeed!*

And whatever the hardship, we will keep rising up. *Through hardship, indeed!*

Engage

1. What one thought or idea from today's lesson especially intrigued, provoked, disturbed, challenged, encouraged, warmed, warned, helped or surprised you?

2. Share a story about one of your greatest hardships.

3. How do you respond to the idea that we discover God's strength only through our weakness?

4. For children: What's something that you really don't like doing, but you make yourself do it anyway?

5. Activate: This week, when you're tempted to complain, look for a blessing that could come from enduring hardship well.

6. Meditate: In silence, ponder Paul's words, 'For me to live is Christ' and 'Christ lives in me.' How does your heart respond?

Third Quarter Queries

If possible, compose prayerful, honest and heartfelt replies to these queries in private, and then gather to share what you have written. The Five Guidelines for Learning Circles in Appendix II may be helpful to guide your sharing. You may also find it helpful to invite a trusted spiritual leader to serve as 'catechist' and ask him or her for additional guidance, feedback and instruction. Make it safe for one another to speak freely, and let your conversation build conviction in each of you as individuals, and among you as a community.

1. Summarise the message of the Sermon on the Mount and what it means to you.
2. Recount the events of Palm Sunday, Holy Thursday, Good Friday and Holy Saturday, and their meaning for you today.
3. What does it mean to you to make the Easter affirmation that Christ is risen indeed?

4. What does it mean to you to be part of an uprising of fellowship and discipleship?
5. What does it mean to you to be part of an uprising of worship and partnership?
6. What does it mean to you to be part of an uprising of stewardship and hardship?
7. How has your understanding of God and yourself changed through your participation in this learning circle?

PART 4

ALIVE IN THE SPIRIT OF GOD

In the previous three sections of this book, we have placed ourselves in the story of creation, the adventure of Jesus and God's peaceful uprising against the forces of fear, oppression, hostility and violence. Jesus promised that the Holy Spirit would take the work he began and extend it across space and time, creating a global spiritual community to keep welcoming and embodying what he called the reign or kingdom or commonwealth of God.

In this final section, beginning with the season traditionally known as Pentecost, we ask this key question: How can we participate with the Spirit in this ongoing spiritual movement? That word *spiritual* means a lot of things, but for us it will mean any experience of or response to the moving of the Spirit of God in our lives and in our world.

CHAPTER 40

The Spirit Is Moving! (Pentecost Sunday)

John 3:1–21

Acts 2:1–41

. . . I will pour out my Spirit upon all flesh, and your sons and your daughters shall prophesy, and your young men shall see visions, and your old men shall dream dreams.

Romans 6:1–14

Following Jesus today has much in common with the original disciples' experience. We are welcomed as disciples by God's grace, not by earning or status. We learn and practise Christ's teaching in the company of fellow learners. We seek to understand and imitate his example, and we commune with him around a table. But there is an obvious and major difference between our experience and theirs: they could see Jesus and we can't. Surprisingly, according to John's Gospel, that gives us an advantage. 'It's better that I go away so the Spirit can come,' Jesus said. If he were physically present and visible, our focus would be on Christ *over there, right there, out there* . . . but because of his absence, we discover the Spirit of Christ *right here, in here, within.*

Jesus describes the Spirit as *another* comforter, *another* teacher, *another* guide – just like him, but available to everyone, everywhere, always. The same Spirit who had descended like a dove upon him will descend upon us, he promises. The same Spirit who filled him will fill all who open their hearts.

Take Paul, for example. He never saw Jesus in the flesh, but he did experience the Spirit of Christ. That was enough to transform him from a proud and violent agitator of hostility to a tireless activist for reconciliation. Through this experience of the Spirit, he seemed to live inside Christ and look out through Christ's eyes upon the world. And the opposite was equally true: through the Spirit, Christ lived inside Paul and looked through Paul's eyes upon the world. 'I in Christ' and 'Christ in me' – that captures so much of Paul's vision of life.

For Paul, life in the Spirit means a threefold sharing in the death, burial and resurrection of Jesus. First, as we turn from old habits and patterns, our 'old self' with all its pride, greed, lust, anger, prejudice and hostility dies with Christ. That former identity with all its hostilities is nailed to the cross and left behind. In this way, life in the Spirit involves a profound experience of *letting go* of what has been so far.

Then, Paul says, we join Jesus in the powerlessness and defeat of burial, symbolised by baptism. We experience that burial as a surrender to silence, stillness, powerlessness, emptiness and rest, *a letting be.*

Then we join Jesus in the dynamic, surprising uprising of resurrection. The surrender, silence, emptiness and rest of *letting go* and *letting be* make us receptive to something new. Like a vacuum, that receptivity welcomes infilling and activation . . . and so we experience a *letting come* of the Spirit of God.

The Bible describes the Spirit with beautiful and vivid imagery: Wind. Breath. Fire. Cloud. Water. Wine. A dove. These dynamic word pictures contrast starkly with the heavy, fixed imagery provided by, say, stone idols, imposing temples or thick theological tomes. Through this vivid imagery, the biblical writers tell us that the Spirit invigorates, animates, purifies, holds mystery, moves and flows, foments joy and spreads peace.

For example, in the first chapter of Genesis, God's Spirit hovers over the primal waters like *wind*, creating beauty and novelty out of chaos. The Spirit then animates living creatures like *breath*. Then, in Exodus, God's Spirit appears as *fire* in the burning bush, beckoning Moses, and then as a pillar of *cloud and fire* moving across the wilderness, cooling by day and warming by night, and leading the way to freedom. Centuries later, when John the Baptist comes on the scene, he says that just as he immerses and marks people with *water*, his successor will immerse and mark people with the *Spirit*. When John baptises Jesus, bystanders see the Spirit descending like a *dove* upon him. At the beginning of his ministry, Jesus dramatises his mission by turning water, which is kept in stone containers used for religious ceremonies, into a huge quantity of *wine* to infuse joy at a wedding banquet. Later, he promises people that if they trust him, they will experience rivers of living *water* springing up from within.

At the core of Jesus' life and message, then, was this good news: the Spirit of God, the Spirit of aliveness, the Wind-breath-fire-cloud-water-wine-dove Spirit who filled Jesus is on the move in our world. And that gives us a choice: do we dig in our heels, clench our fists and live for our own agenda, or do we let go, let be and let come . . . and so be taken up into the Spirit's movement?

That was what the disciples experienced on the day of Pentecost, according to Luke, when the Spirit manifested as wind and fire. Suddenly the Spirit-filled disciples began speaking in languages they had never learned. This strange sign is full of significance. The Spirit of God, it tells us, is multilingual. The Spirit isn't restricted to one elite language or one superior culture, as almost everyone had assumed. Instead, the Spirit speaks to everyone everywhere in his or her native tongue.

What happened at Pentecost reverses the ancient story of the

Tower of Babel, when ambitious Babylonians grasped at god-like power by unifying everyone under one imperial language and culture. At Babel, God opposed that imperial uniformity and voted for diversity by multiplying languages. Now, in the Pentecost story, we discover a third option: not unity without diversity, and not diversity without unity, but unity and diversity in harmony.

In the millennia since Christ walked with us on this Earth, we've often tried to box up the 'wind' in manageable doctrines. We've exchanged the fire of the Spirit for the ice of religious pride. We've turned the wine back into water, and then let the water go stagnant and lukewarm. We've traded the gentle dove of peace for the predatory hawk or eagle of empire. When we have done so, we have ended up with just another religious system, as problematic as any other: too often petty, argumentative, judgemental, cold, hostile, bureaucratic, self-seeking, an enemy of aliveness.

In a world full of big challenges, in a time like ours, we can't settle for a heavy and fixed religion. We can't try to contain the Spirit in a box. We need to experience the mighty rushing wind of Pentecost. We need our hearts to be made incandescent by the Spirit's fire. We need the living water and new wine Jesus promised, so our hearts can become the home of dove-like peace.

Wind. Breath. Fire. Cloud. Water. Wine. A dove. When we open up space for the Spirit and let the Spirit fill that space within us, we begin to change, and we become agents of change. That's why we pause in our journey to gather together around a table of fellowship and communion. Like the disciples in the upper room at Pentecost, we present ourselves to God. We become receptive for the fullness of the Spirit to fall upon us and well up within us, to blow like wind, glow like fire, flow like a river, fill like a cloud and descend like a dove in and among us. So let us open our hearts. Let us dare to believe that the Spirit we read about in the Scriptures can move among us today, empowering us in our times so we can become agents in a global spiritual movement of justice, peace and joy.

So, are we ready? Are we willing to die with Christ? Are we willing to *let go*?

And are we willing to be buried with Christ? Are we willing to *let be*?

And are we willing to rise with Christ? Can we inhale, open our emptiness, unlock that inner vacuum, for the Spirit to enter and fill – like wind, breath, fire, cloud, water, wine and a dove? Are we willing to *let come*?

Let it be so. Let it be now. Amen.

Engage

1. What one thought or idea from today's lesson especially intrigued, provoked, disturbed, challenged, encouraged, warmed, warned, helped or surprised you?

2. Share a story about a time when you experienced the Holy Spirit in a special way.

3. How do you respond to the imagery of death, burial and resurrection with Christ?

4. For children: What do you think it means for a person to be filled with God?

5. Activate: Make it a habit in the coming days to take a deep breath and then exhale to express *letting go*. Then remain breathless for a moment – to express *letting be*. Then inhale to express *letting the Spirit come* to fill you.

6. Meditate: In silence, hold the word *open* in God's presence. Let images of openness come to you. Direct this openness to God's Spirit as a desire to be filled.

CHAPTER 41

Moving with the Spirit

John 15:1–8

Galatians 3:19 – 4:7; 5:1, 13–26

. . . the fruit of the Spirit is love, joy, peace, patience, kindness, generosity, faithfulness, gentleness, and self-control. There is no law against such things.

Colossians 2:6–7; 3:1–17

The wind can be blowing, but if your sail isn't raised, you won't go far. You can be surrounded by oxygen, but if you don't breathe, it won't do you any good. The sap can be flowing, but if a branch isn't connected to the vine, it will wither. If you don't have kindling and wood in your hearth, a lit match won't burn long. It's the same with the Spirit. We are surrounded with the aliveness of the Spirit. All that remains is for us to learn how to let the Spirit fill, flow and glow within us.

We start in the heart – the wellspring of our desires. That's where our problems begin, and that's where our healing begins too. When we desire to be filled with the Spirit, the Spirit begins to transform our desires so that God's desires become our own. Instead of doing the right thing because we *have* to, we do the right thing because we *want* to – because we are learning to truly desire goodness. Once our desires are being changed, a revolution is set in motion.

The New Testament gives us a simple image for how desire translates into action: *walking*. When we were newborn, we couldn't even roll over, much less crawl, much less walk and run. Eventually a desire for movement stirred within us, and we gradually and clumsily translated that desire into action – first rolling over, then crawling, then standing and toddling, and eventually walking. Step by step, with lots of stumbles and falls, we eventually mastered the art of translating our desire into movement. And so now, with hardly a thought, we walk, we run, we jump, we dance.

This image of walking is everywhere in the Scriptures. Walk in the Spirit, we are told. Walk in the light. Walk in love. Walk in newness of life. Walk by faith. Walk in good works. Walk in truth. To be a disciple is to follow a mentor, which means walking in the mentor's footsteps. The image is simple . . . one step at a time, drawn by desire, leaning forward, doing the next right thing, keeping our focus on our goal, leaving the past behind. If you stumble, regain your balance and keep walking. If you fall, get up again and keep walking. If you're distracted or wander off the path, reorient yourself towards your goal and keep walking.

Jesus used another vivid image to convey the same reality: a branch abiding in a vine. If the branch were to separate itself from the vine, it would wither and die. But if it simply stays connected, the vine's aliveness flows into the branch and bears fruit through it. So if we abide or remain in vital connection to Christ, the Spirit will flow with God's aliveness in and through us, making us both beautiful and fruitful.

Paul employed several similar images. Stir up the fire in you, he said to his young protégé, Timothy. Just as fires need to be tended, our inner life needs to be tended too. In his letter to the Colossians, he used the image of welcoming a guest, making room in our hearts so the Spirit of Christ can 'dwell in us richly'. In Ephesians, he made an analogy to drinking wine. Just as drinking your fill of alcoholic spirits can change your behaviour for the worse, being filled with the Holy Spirit will change your behaviour for the better.

If you want to gain practice walking in the Spirit or abiding in Christ or tending the inner flame, you can start when you wake up tomorrow morning. Before your feet hit the floor, open your heart to the Spirit. Ask God to help you walk in the Spirit, step by step through the day. Ask God to help you abide in the Vine so good fruit will naturally develop in your life. Ask God to keep the fire burning within you. Just starting the day this way will make a difference.

As you build that habit of yielding yourself to the Spirit morning by morning, you can build the habit of checking in with the Spirit hour by hour throughout the day. At each mealtime, you can offer a prayer of thanksgiving and you can reconnect with the Spirit. As you travel from place to place, as you wait for someone, whenever you have a free moment, you can offer yourself to God: 'Here I am, Lord. Please move in and through me to bless others.' Whenever an emergency or challenge arises, you can lean on the Spirit: 'Give me wisdom, Spirit of God. Give me strength. Give me patience.' When you sense that you've let something other than God's Spirit fill you and direct you – anger, fear, prejudice, lust, greed, anxiety, pride, inferiority or rivalry, for example – you can stop, acknowledge your misstep, and re-surrender to the Spirit. It's like breathing – exhaling an acknowledgement of your misstep and inhaling forgiveness and strength to start walking in the Spirit again.

At the end of the day, you can look back with gratitude, resting in the Spirit until a new day begins and you continue walking the journey of faith.

As we walk in the Spirit, we pass through different kinds of terrain. We walk through beautiful valleys where life is full of joy and we feel like dancing. We walk on long uphill climbs where we seem to slide back two steps for every three steps of ascent. We walk along slippery trails where it's easy to fall, and through swampy patches where we can get bogged down. We walk through dark passages where we can easily lose our way, and across flat terrain where nothing seems to change mile after mile. We walk through dangerous territory where bullets fly and it's easy to get wounded, and in peaceful places where we can breathe freely. Through it all, we need patience, endurance and perseverance so that no matter what happens, we'll keep putting one foot ahead of the other.

If we don't give up, as mile adds to mile, each of us will have some stories to tell . . . stories of how the Spirit guided, empowered, inspired, restrained, sustained and trained us in the fine art of aliveness. And that's another great blessing of being part of a community of faith. Along the way, we gather around a table or campfire and share our stories about the journey so far. We share our joys and sorrows. We share mistakes we've made and falls we've taken and lessons we've learned. We share ways in which we've experienced the Spirit moving in us, among us and through us. Through this sharing, we encourage each other. And then we get back on the road.

Sadly, lots of people get distracted and lose their way. Instead of continuing to walk in the Spirit, they slow down to look back proudly on how far they've come. They become highly impressed by all they've learned – theological concepts, Bible lore, religious history and so on. Pretty soon, they come to a standstill and brag among themselves, comparing themselves to others who haven't walked as far or fast or cleverly as they have. They form little encampments, sitting around day after day, quarrelling about this or that fine point of walking theory. Pretty soon they're so out of shape they give up walking altogether and specialise in talking about the way others walk.

That's their choice. But for us . . . let's keep walking. Let's keep on the road. However far we've come, there's far more ahead to explore. The Spirit is on the move, so let's keep moving too.

Engage

1. What one thought or idea from today's lesson especially intrigued, provoked, disturbed, challenged, encouraged, warmed, warned, helped or surprised you?

2. Share a story about how the Spirit has encouraged you through others at this table.

3. How do you respond to the warning about losing your way and becoming a critical bystander rather than a humble walker?

4. For children: Have you ever taken a hike in the woods? Tell us about it. Did you learn anything on the way?

5. Activate: This week, aim to 'check in' with the Spirit each morning and evening, and several times throughout the day. And look for opportunities to share stories of what the Spirit is doing in your life.

6. Meditate: Hold the image of a ship raising its sail to the wind. Ponder what it would mean for you to raise your sail to the Holy Spirit. Let a prayer arise within you.

CHAPTER 42

Spirit of Love: Loving God

Psalm 116
Romans 8:1–17
Ephesians 3:14–21

I pray that . . . you may be strengthened in your inner being with power through his Spirit . . . . so that you may be filled with all the fullness of God.

Wherever God's Spirit is at work in the world, people are drawn more deeply to love . . . beginning with loving God.

Of course, we must acknowledge that the word *God* has become a big problem for a lot of people. How can they love a God who is an angry old white man with a beard, oppressing women and minorities, promoting discrimination and war, and blessing the destruction of the planet? How can they love the curator of a religious museum who seems to have a taste for all that is outdated, archaic, dour and dusty? How can they love the host of an unending religious broadcast where everyone is always artificially smiling and excessively, unrealistically happy, desperate for you to send in your next generous financial contribution? How can they love a testy border guard who won't let new arrivals through heaven's passport control office unless they correctly answer a lot of technical doctrinal questions with a score of 100 per cent?

Hot-headed religious extremists, lukewarm religious bureaucrats and cold-hearted religious critics alike have turned the word *God* into a name for something ugly, small, boring, elitist, wacky, corrupt or violent – the very opposite of what it should mean. Maybe God is more turned off to the word *God* than anyone else! And maybe the distaste of many for the word *God* as it is commonly used actually reveals a corresponding love that longs for what God truly is.

Whatever ember of love for goodness flickers within us, however feeble or small . . . that's what the Spirit works with, until that spark glows warmer and brighter. From the tiniest beginning, our whole lives – our whole hearts, minds, souls and strength – can be set aflame with love for God.

Even those of us who have always believed in God's existence and never had any big problems with the word *God* . . . when it comes to actually loving God, we can feel a little intimidated. We don't know where to begin.

But really, it's not so different from loving another human being.

When we speak of loving another human being, we naturally move towards that person in a special way. We appreciate the qualities of the beloved. We respect and honour the beloved's dignity. We enjoy the beloved's company and feel curious about the beloved's personhood. We want to support the beloved's dreams and desires. And we make ourselves available for the beloved to respect, honour, enjoy, know and support us too, because to be 'in love' is to be in a mutual relationship.

Similarly, when we learn to love God, we appreciate God's qualities. We honour and respect God's dignity. We enjoy God's presence and are curious to know more and more of God's heart. We support God's dreams coming true. And we want to be appreciated, honoured, enjoyed, known and supported as well – to surrender ourselves to God in mutuality.

It all begins with moving towards God, taking a first step by simply showing up, becoming aware of God's presence and presenting ourselves to God. It's as simple as saying, 'God, here I am,' or 'God, here you are,' or even better, 'God, here we are, together.'

A second step is appreciation. Sometimes we take a spouse, child, parent or friend for granted. Then some shock or threat occurs – an accident, a disease or an argument through which they are nearly taken from us. Suddenly, we appreciate afresh this precious person we've been taking for granted. If we don't want to take God for granted, we can express gratitude and appreciation for what it means to have God in our lives. That's why many of us try to begin each day and each meal with a prayer of thankful appreciation – it's a way of being sure we don't take God and God's blessings for granted. If the simple word *here* helps us show up, the simple word *thanks* can help us with appreciation.

A third step is to cultivate honour and respect for God – not just gratitude for what God does for us or gives us, but respect for God's dignity, honour for God's character. That's why many of us try to begin each week with a time of gathered worship and to begin and end each day with a few moments of praise. A single simple word like *Hallelujah* might help us, or even *Wow!* or *O!*

We all know that we do the opposite of loving God some-times. We remain aloof or preoccupied, we complain instead of appreciate, and we ignore or disrespect rather than honour God. That's where a fourth step comes in: learning to say we're sorry and to express to God our regrets. When we say and mean a simple sentence like 'I'm sorry' or 'Lord, have mercy', we move towards God again, receiving forgiveness and renewing our loving connection.

If love means supporting the beloved's dreams and plans, we

love God by expressing our support for what God desires. We express this support whenever we pray, 'May your kingdom come. May your will be done on Earth as it is in heaven.' We do so whenever we come to God in empathetic concern for others, joining our compassion with God's compassion for those in need, sorrow or pain. By refusing to allow numbness or hardness of heart to gain a foothold in our lives, we keep our hearts aligned with God's heart, and in this way express love for God. Sometimes, holding up the name or face of a person in God's presence, simply breathing the words 'Please help him' or 'Please bless her', can be a way of loving God by loving those God loves.

If love is about mutuality, love also means opening ourselves for God to support our dreams and desires. In that way, every time we cry out, 'Help me, Lord!' we are expressing love for God. Why that is the case becomes obvious when we consider the opposite. Imagine shutting out a friend, parent or spouse from our need, sorrow or pain. Imagine never asking for help. That would be a sign of indifference and distrust, not love. So opening ourselves to God when we're in need says that we trust God and want God to accompany us, support us and befriend us in every way.

We trust those we love most with our deepest fears, doubts, emptiness and disillusionment. So we love God when we share those vulnerable aspects of our lives with God. Just as a little child in the middle of a temper tantrum can shout, 'I hate you, Mummy!' only because he knows his outburst will not end their relationship, we can express to God our deep doubts, anger or frustrations only because we possess an even deeper trust in God's love. At times, then, our hearts cry out, 'When, Lord? How long, Lord?' or 'Why?' or even 'No!' But the fact that we share this pain with God rather than withhold it turns out to be an expression of love.

Imagine an elderly couple who have loved one another through a long lifetime, or an adult child sitting at the bedside of a dying parent. Often their love is expressed most powerfully by presence and touch, not by words. Simply being together, holding hands, smiling, sitting close in mutual enjoyment – these are profound expressions of love, beyond words. Something like this develops over time in our relationship with God.

Like one tuning fork that resonates effortlessly with another, we release our whole being to resonate with the love, grace and joy of God. We feel a habitual attentiveness to God that spontaneously smiles or reaches out in an affectionate touch – without obligation, without trying, without even thinking. No words are necessary as we simply and deeply enjoy being together here and now. We are not alone. We are loved. We love.

Remembering our true identity in the family of creation, being rooted and grounded in love, we experience the multidimensional love of Christ that surpasses all knowledge, and we are filled with the very fullness of God. In that fullness, we simply breathe, be and let be. This is life in the Spirit, being in love, with God – true aliveness, indeed.

Engage

1. What one thought or idea from today's lesson especially intrigued, provoked, disturbed, challenged, encouraged, warmed, warned, helped or surprised you?

2. Share a story about a time when you felt most 'in love' with God.

3. How do you respond to the comparison between human love and loving God?

4. For children: The Bible says, 'God is love.' What do you think that means?

5. Activate: Use some of the simple words from this chapter – *here*, *thanks*, *O*, *sorry*, and so on – to practise postures of love for God.

6. Meditate: Invest a few minutes to practise simply being with God, in silence, in love. When your mind distracts you and wanders off, simply acknowledge that this has happened and turn your attention back to God, being aware of God's constant loving attention towards you.

CHAPTER 43

Spirit of Love: Loving Neighbour

Acts 10

1 Corinthians 13

Love is patient; love is kind; love is not envious or boastful or arrogant or rude. It does not insist on its own way; it is not irritable or resentful . . .

Where the Spirit is moving, love for God always, always, always overflows in love for neighbour. And according to Jesus, our neighbour isn't just the person who is like us, the person who likes us, or the person we like. Our neighbour is anyone and everyone – like us or different from us, friend or stranger – even enemy. As Peter learned in his encounter with Cornelius, the Spirit wants to break down walls of prejudice and hostility so that we stop judging *us* as clean and *them* as unclean, opening the way for strangers and enemies to become neighbours, friends, family.

That comes as a shock to many of us who were taught that *same is safe* and *different is dangerous*. That belief probably served our ancestors well at certain points in our history. Their survival often depended on maintaining trust in 'our' tribe and fear of other tribes. That's why they used paint, feathers, clothing, language and even religion as markers, so everyone would know who was same and safe and *us*, and who was different and dangerous and *them*.

Driven by that belief, our ancestors spread out across the world, each tribe staking out its own territory, each guarding its borders from an invasion by others, each trying to expand its territory whenever possible, each driving others further and further away. No wonder our history is written in blood: wars, conquests, invasions, occupations, revolutions and counter-revolutions. The winners take all, and the losers, if they aren't killed or enslaved, escape to begin again somewhere else.

Eventually, because the Earth is a sphere, our dispersing tribes had to come full circle and encounter one another again. That is our challenge today. We must find a way to live together on a crowded planet. We have to graduate from thinking in terms of 'our kind versus their kind' to thinking in terms of 'humankind'. We must turn from the ways of our ancestors and stop trying to kill off, subjugate or fend off everyone we judge different and dangerous. We must find a new approach, make a new road, pioneer a new way of living as neighbours in one human community, as brothers and sisters in one family of creation.

That's why the apostle Paul repeatedly describes how in Christ we see humanity as one body and our differences as gifts, not threats, to one another. In Christ, Paul came to realise that people aren't different because they're trying to be difficult or evil – they're different because the Spirit has given them differing gifts. Just as a foot needs an eye to tell it where to step, and just as a nose needs a hand to grasp the food it smells, and just as feet, eyes, noses and hands all need kidneys and bones and skin . . . we humans need other humans who are different from ourselves. The Spirit of God, we learn, is a team spirit, and in the holy team Spirit, we experience a unity that is energised by diversity.

That doesn't mean all our tribes need to wear the same paint and feathers, speak the same language, cook with the same spices and celebrate the same religious holidays. But it means all our human tribes – nations, religions, cultures, parties – need to convert from what we might call dirty energy to clean energy to fuel our tribal life. True, the dirty energy of fear, prejudice, supremacy, inferiority, resentment, isolation and hostility is cheap, abundant and familiar. That's why our societies run on it, even though it's destroying us. More than ever before in our history, we need a new kind of personal and social fuel. Not fear, but love. Not prejudice, but openness. Not supremacy, but service. Not inferiority, but equality. Not resentment, but reconciliation. Not isolation, but connection. Not the spirit of hostility, but the holy Spirit of hospitality.

So the 'most excellent way', Paul said, is the way of love. Old markers of gender, religion, culture and class must recede: 'There is neither Jew nor Gentile, slave nor free, male nor female, for you are all one in Christ Jesus.' Old tribal indicators, he says, count for nothing: 'the only thing that counts is faith working through love.' Where the Spirit is, love is. Where the Spirit teaches, people learn love. Faith communities at their best are Spirit-schools of love, engaging everyone, from little children to great-grandparents, in lifelong learning. In the school of the Spirit, everyone majors in love.

Of course, if love remains a generality, it's just a word. That's why the New Testament is serious about translating love into practical, specific, concrete, down-to-Earth action. Because each of us has something to give and much to receive, the term *one another* keeps popping up on page after page of the New Testament. These 'one anothers' tell us what the prime directive – *love one another* – looks like in action:

1. **Love one another.** (John 13:34; 15:12, 17; Rom. 13:8; 1 Thess. 4:9; Heb. 13:1; 1 Pet. 1:22; 3:8; 4:8; 1 John 3:11, 23; 4:7, 11; 2 John 1:5).

2. **Serve one another; wash one another's feet.** (John 13:14; Gal. 5:13).

3. **Be at peace with one another.** (Mark 9:50; 1 Thess. 5:13.

4. **Be devoted to one another.** (Rom. 12:10).

5. **Honour one another.** (Rom. 12:10).

6. **Live in harmony with one another.** (Rom. 12:16).

7. **Stop judging one another.** (Rom. 14:13).

8. **Accept one another.** (Rom. 15:7).

9. **Greet one another warmly.** (Rom. 16:16; 1 Cor. 16:20; 2 Cor. 13:12; 1 Pet. 5:14).

10. **Agree with one another.** (1 Cor. 1:10).

11. **Wait for one another.** (1 Cor. 11:33).

12. **Have equal concern for one another.** (1 Cor. 12:24–25).

13. **Do not provoke or envy one another.** (Gal. 5:26).

14. **Carry one another's burdens.** (Gal. 6:2).

15. **Bear with one another in love.** (Eph. 4:2; Col. 3:13).

16. **Be kind, compassionate and forgiving to one another.** (Eph. 4:32; Col. 3:13; 1 Thess. 5:15).

17. **Submit to one another.** (Eph. 5:21).

18. **Do not lie to one another.** (Col. 3:9).

19. **Teach and admonish one another.** (Eph. 5:19; Col. 3:16).

20. **Encourage and edify one another.** (1 Thess. 5:11; Heb. 3:13).

21. **Spur one another on to love and good deeds**. (Heb. 10:24–25).

22. **Do not slander one another**. (Jas 4:11).

23. **Do not grumble against one another**. (Jas 5:9).

24. **Confess your sins to one another and pray for one another**. (Jas 5:16).

25. **Offer hospitality to one another**. (1 Pet. 4:9).

26. **Be humble toward one another**. (1 Pet. 5:5).

For all of us who want to be part of the movement of God's Spirit in our world, there is no more important and essential pursuit than love. That's why we walk this road. That's why we seek to improve our fluency and grace in 'one-anothering' – especially with people who seem very different from us. For in the story of creation, in the adventure and uprising of Jesus, and in the movement of the Spirit, to love is to live.

Engage

1. What one thought or idea from today's lesson especially intrigued, provoked, disturbed, challenged, encouraged, warmed, warned, helped or surprised you?

2. Share a story about a time when someone affirmed one of your unique gifts or abilities, and when you appreciated the unique gifts or abilities of someone else.

3. How do you respond to the list of one another's?

4. For children: What's something you're really good at, and something you're not so good at?

5. Activate: Take a few minutes with each person around your table to identify and affirm some gifts or virtues you see in them. Have someone place a hand on that person's head or

shoulder and pray for the Spirit to fill and empower that person in love.

6. Meditate: In silence, simply hold the term 'one another' before God. Open yourself to the depths of meaning in this beautiful term.

CHAPTER 44

Spirit of Love: Loving Self

Proverbs 4

Romans 12:3–21

We have gifts that differ according to the grace given to us . . .

James 1:2–8; 3:13–18

If love for God is always linked with love for others, and if we are to love others *as we love ourselves*, what does it mean to love ourselves? Could the Spirit of God teach us a holy and healthy kind of self-love?

Of course, advertisers and politicians often tempt us to become more *selfish* or *self-centred* – our doing so is often in their *self-interest*. But the Spirit teaches us a profoundly different way of loving ourselves – a way of maturity that involves self-examination, self-control, self-development and self-giving. These practices of mature self-care enable us to love God and others more fully and joyfully.

Now our struggles with self are often struggles with pleasure, for the self is, among other things, a pleasure-seeking entity. When it comes to pleasure, if you listen to some people, you might conclude that God is a divine killjoy, sitting in heaven with a sourpuss glare, eyes roaming to and fro across the Earth to find anyone who is having fun – especially sexual fun – and *stop it immediately*! If the pleasures of life were compared to the awe of looking into the Grand Canyon, these anxious people worry so much about someone falling over the edge that they erect fences further and further back … so far, in fact, that you can no longer enjoy the view!

Pleasure, of course, was originally the Creator's idea. By giving us taste, smell, sound, sight and touch, God was making possible an amazing array of pleasures: from eating to sex, from music to sport, from painting to gardening, from dance to travel. Human pleasure is a good and beautiful creation, mirroring, it would seem, a great capacity for enjoyment that exists in God. We are told that God takes pleasure in creation and in us, something all parents, teachers and artists understand in relation to their children, students and works of art. So again and again in the Bible, we are reminded that our Creator has given us all things to enjoy richly, and that in God's presence is fullness of joy. The Creator is definitely pro-pleasure.

If that's the case, why do we find so many warnings and rules about pleasure in the Bible? Those rules make sense when you realise how easily all life's great pleasures – food, drink, sex, owning, winning, resting, playing, working – can become addictive and destructive. When we indulge in pleasures without self-examination or self-control, great pleasure can quickly lead to great pain – for the addicts themselves and for those whose lives are touched by their addiction.

So rules about pleasures have an important place. The desire centre within us that demands 'what I want, when I want it, as much as I want' can all too easily become an addictive dictator. We all need to learn to say 'No, that's not right', or 'No, this isn't the right time', or 'No, that's enough for now'. Without wise rules and that basic level of self-control to follow them, we'll all be stuck in childish, selfish, self-destructive and even suicidal immaturity. But the Spirit never gives rules the final word. Living by rules – 'law' in the Bible – is at most like primary school.

Primary school has its place, but if we're never allowed to graduate to secondary school, it feels like a prison. So when we're ready, the Spirit always leads us to graduate from rule-oriented primary school to secondary school with its new emphasis: wisdom. From basic questions like *Is this right or wrong, legal or illegal?* we graduate to questions of wisdom: *Will this help or hinder me in reaching my highest goals? Where will this lead in the short, medium and long term? What unintended consequences might it entail? Who might be hurt by this? Are there better alternatives? Is now the best time? Should I seek wise counsel before moving forward?*

Wisdom helps us see how a hasty purchase of a desired indulgence can lead to the long-term pressure of debt. Wisdom reminds us that a one-night sexual liaison can lead to lasting tragic consequences for both parties, plus their spouses, children, parents and many others – literally for generations to come. Wisdom knows that a single ill-advised business shortcut to increase profits can ruin a reputation earned over decades – as can one careless sentence spoken in anger or dishonesty. Wisdom remembers that habitual overindulgence in alcohol, drugs, tobacco or even food can greatly shorten your life. And wisdom warns that even one night of drunkenness or one outburst of anger can end your life and the lives of others. Wisdom guides us to see beyond life's immediate pleasures to potential consequences that are less obvious and less pleasant.

Wisdom also helps us see how excessively denying ourselves pleasure can itself become unwise. For example, if a mum and dad are so exhausted from the work of parenting that they forget to keep their romance alive, they can drift apart even though they're sleeping under the same roof. Wisdom guides them to nurture their romance and sexuality so they'll be less vulnerable to infidelity – and so their family will stay in a sustainable, healthy, life-giving balance. The same goes for someone who loves his work and gets great pleasure from it. If he works too much, his life will fall out of balance . . . and soon he will hate his work. So a wise person learns that he must find pleasures outside work so that his work will remain pleasurable rather than addictive. A wise person in this way practises self-care, sometimes stepping on the brakes and sometimes stepping on the accelerator of pleasure.

We all need wisdom to know our limits and keep our balance, to know when to say 'Yes' and when to say 'That's enough' or 'That's unwise' or 'This isn't the right time'. We need wisdom to know when to ask for help – from a friend or professional – when we are in over our heads. We need wisdom to monitor the difference between legitimate desires and dangerous temptations. We even need wisdom to keep different kinds of pleasure in a healthy and sustainable balance. As a wise teacher said, 'Watch over your heart with all diligence, for from it flow the springs of life' (Prov. 4:23, NASB).

After all, nobody is more likely to ruin your life than you. By pursuing wisdom, you get out of your own way. You learn to be a friend to yourself instead of your own worst enemy. You learn self-examination, self-control, self-development and self-care – so you can better practise true self-giving towards God and others. Rules are good, wisdom is better, and love is best of all.

Could this be a central purpose of the universe – to provide an environment in which self-control, wisdom and love can emerge and evolve? Could this be a central purpose in our lives – to mature in self-control, wisdom and love? And could this be a central purpose of religion and spirituality – to multiply contagious examples of maturity, to create communities where the more mature can mentor others, to build a global Spirit movement towards individual and collective maturity?

So. You have this self. What you do with it matters a lot. You can be self-absorbed, self-contained, self-centred, selfish, self-consumed – and your closed-in self will stagnate, spoil and deteriorate over time. Or you can engage in Spirit-guided self-examination, self-control, self-development and self-giving – and your self will open and mature into a person of great beauty and Christ-like maturity.

God, it turns out, isn't a divine killjoy. God wants you to love you the way God loves you, so you can join God in the one self-giving love that upholds you and all creation. If you trust your self to that love, you will become the best self you can be, thriving in aliveness, full of deep joy, part of the beautiful whole. That's the kind of self-care and love of self that is good, right, wise and necessary. And that's one more reason we walk this road together: to journey ever deeper into the beautiful mystery of the Spirit's love. There we find God. There we find our neighbour. And there we find ourselves.

Engage

1. What one thought or idea from today's lesson especially intrigued, provoked, disturbed, challenged, encouraged, warmed, warned, helped or surprised you?

2. Share a story about how a rule, a wise saying and a mentor have helped you.

3. How do you respond to the idea that if we love ourselves, we will practise self-examination, self-control, self-development, self-care and self-giving rather than self-indulgence?

4. For children: What are some things that usually make you feel sad, grouchy, happy and superhappy?

5. Activate: This week, pair up with someone else from this circle and meet privately to talk honestly and confidentially about how you're doing in the areas of self-examination, self-control, self-development, self-care and self-giving.

6. Meditate: Imagine those who love you most – parents, a spouse, friends, children and God. Now imagine standing with them as they see and love you. In silence and in God's presence, hold yourself in that kind of love.

CHAPTER 45

Spirit of Unity and Diversity

Proverbs 8
John 17:1–23
Ephesians 4:1–16

There is one body and one Spirit . . . one hope . . . one Lord, one faith, one baptism, one God and Father of all, who is above all and through all and in all.

In the centuries after Jesus walked this Earth, theologians and mystics who reflected on Jesus' life and teaching were faced with a paradox. They agreed there was only one God as their tradition had taught. But the oneness of the Creator wasn't as flat or static as they had assumed. In Christ and through the Spirit, they came to see that God's unity was so deep and dynamic that it included diversity. And this diversity didn't compromise God's unity but made it more beautiful and wonderful. Over time, they tried to describe this mysterious paradox. After much dialogue and debate, a radically new understanding and teaching about God emerged. They had to create a whole new term to convey it: *Trinity*. There were, naturally, three parts to the teaching.

First, through Jesus and his good news they had come to know and relate to God in a parental way. Like a parent, God was the source of all creation, the giver of all life and existence. God's parental love held all creation in a family relationship. This parental givingness, this reproductive creativity and fertility, this primal motherly and fatherly generosity, they called *God the Father*. There were reasons why they only rarely used *motherhood* to describe God back then. Were they here today, they would probably include both *motherhood* and *fatherhood* and speak of *God's parental love*.

Second, in Jesus they came to see a childness in God, a givenness of the child-life corresponding to the givingness of the parent-life. If God the Father gave of God's self, the self-gift was simultaneously God and an offspring, or self-gift, of God. If God the Creator was self-expressive, the self-expression, or Word, was simultaneously God and the Word, or expression, of God. This primal givenness, self-outpouring or expressivity they called *God the Son*, or *God the Word*.

Through Jesus and his good news, they had also experienced a third reality: the loving, harmonious Spirit that flowed in and between and out from the first and the second. This loving and unifying presence, this primal harmony, this deep, joyful, contagious communion they called *God the Spirit*.

This all sounds highly speculative, but it was a sincere attempt to put into words the radical way they were rethinking and freshly experiencing God in the aftermath of their experience of Jesus. By God's parental love, through Christ's beautiful life, death and resurrection, and through the Holy Spirit, they felt that they had been caught up into this divine communion themselves. God could never again be for them a distant, isolated One to whom they were 'the other'. Now they knew God as a dynamic and hospitable one-another in whom they lived, moved and had their being. The Trinity described how they experienced God 'from the inside'.

Because they had been trained in Greek philosophy as well as in the Bible, of course they used philosophical language in their deliberations. Sometimes they overestimated the capacity of their philosophical terms to capture God's unfathomable depths. When they erred in this way, they grew proud and used the new teaching of the Trinity as a weapon. But at their best, they remained humble and awestruck by the realisation that God was a mystery so big and deep and beautiful that human words could never fully contain it. Like fingers, words could point up and out and in to God, but they could never grasp God like a flipped coin caught in a clenched fist. When they spoke from this humility and awe, the teaching of the Trinity brought healing – reminding us that the word *doctrine* and the word *doctor* share a common root.

This healing teaching began unleashing a revolution that is still unfolding today in at least five distinct but related ways.

First, the teaching of the Trinity leads us beyond *violent* understandings of God. The many Greek and Roman gods of ancient tradition were, truth be told, a gang of overgrown adolescents who had more power than moral maturity. They were competitive and egotistical projections of human nature, glorious and gracious one minute, vindictive and cruel the next. But now, imagine the shift when we understand our source and destiny not as a rivalrous gang but as a loving, non-violent community.

This insight was revolutionary, because even the Supreme Being of monotheism was often seen as the violent patron of one nation, religion and culture. Such a Supreme Being typically ruled by instilling fear, making threats and crushing the non-compliant. But again, imagine the change when our vision of God shifts from a violent dictator to a kind and caring father who loves all and wants the best for all. And imagine how in the Son, or Word, we see God as one who identifies, serves and suffers with creation as Christ did, who would rather be tortured and killed than torture or kill. And then, imagine how the image of a violent commander sending us into the world to wage war is eclipsed by the image of a gentle, healing, reconciling, purifying, empowering Spirit who descends upon us like a dove. A healing teaching, indeed!

Similarly, this healing teaching leads us beyond *fixed* or *frozen* understandings of God. After all, if God in Christ surprised us once, showing us we had a lot left to learn, shouldn't we expect more surprises? And if Jesus told us the Spirit would guide us into more truth when we were ready to bear it, shouldn't we expect to learn more whenever we can bear more? And so the old image fades of God as a removed and unmoved mover, static, fixed and frozen. In its place, we see God as a whirling, intimate, glorious dance of eternal, creative, joyful movement. What a revolution!

Third, through the Trinity we transcend *us-them, in-out* thinking. Imprisoned in our old familiar dualistic thinking, we were always dividing the world into *mine* and *yours*, *one* and *other*, *same* and *different*, *better* and *worse*. In the Trinity, we move beyond that dualism so that *mine* and *yours* are reconciled into *ours*. *One* and *other* are transformed into *one another*. *Same* and *different* are harmonised without being homogenised or colonised. *Us* and *them* are united without loss of identity and without dividing walls of hostility. To put it in philosophical terms, dualism doesn't regress to monism. It is transcended.

The healing teaching of Trinity also helps us transcend *top-down* or *hierarchical* understandings of God. If God's Father-ness elevates and includes Son-ness in full equality, do you see what that means? If God's Son-ness doesn't grasp at equality, but rather mirrors the Father's self-giving and self-emptying love, do you see what that means? If the Spirit is not subordinated as inferior but is honoured and welcomed as equal, do you see what that means? God is characterised by equality, empathy and generosity rather than subordination, patriarchy and hierarchy.

These four shifts in our understanding predictably lead to a fifth. Our ancestors assumed that God's holiness would be polluted by any contact with imperfection. So in their minds, God was *exclusive* and unwilling to associate with any imperfection. But Jesus, in his habit of eating with 'sinners', gave us a new vision of God. God's holiness is drawn to unholiness the way a doctor is drawn to disease. Rather than catching disease, God's holiness 'infects' the sick with a chronic case of regenerating health. Rather than being polluted by association with imperfection, God's holiness perfects imperfection. In this way, the healing teaching of Trinity undermines *exclusivist* understandings of God, presenting us with a God who doesn't reject imperfection but embraces it, and in so doing perfects it and makes it holy.

Sadly, too often our forebears wielded a warped and jagged understanding of the Trinity as a weapon. In so doing, they reinforced violent, static, dualist, hierarchical and exclusive understandings of God. But it's still not too late. If we open our hearts, we can feel the Spirit guiding us now to let the healing teaching of the Trinity continue its joyful revolution. Perhaps we are now ready to bear it . . . and to dare to practise it. Because if God is not violent, static, dualist, hierarchical or exclusive, neither should we be.

To join the movement of the Spirit is to let our trinitarian tradition continue to live, learn and grow . . . so the hostile one-versus-otherness of Earth can become more like the hospitable one-anotherness of heaven. From beginning to end, the Spirit leads us into vibrant diversity and joyful unity in beautiful harmony.

Engage

1. What one thought or idea from today's lesson especially intrigued, provoked, disturbed, challenged, encouraged, warmed, warned, helped or surprised you?

2. Share a story about how your understanding of God changed – suddenly or gradually – at some point in your life.

3. How do you respond to the proposal that a deep appreciation of the Trinity can move us beyond violent, static, dualist, hierarchical and exclusive understandings of God?

4. For children: What do you like about music? What makes music so special?

5. Activate: If the Trinity isn't just a concept to be believed but is a way of life to be practised, this week try moving towards the other whenever you can – seeking to show others the honour, love and respect that are shared among Father, Son and Spirit.

6. Meditate: Ponder these words from John 17:21: 'As you, Father, are in me and I am in you, may they also be in us.' Then simply hold the word *us* in reverence before God.

CHAPTER 46

Spirit of Service

Matthew 23:1–12

The greatest among you will be your servant. All who exalt themselves will be humbled, and all who humble themselves will be exalted.

John 13:1–15
Philippians 2:1–11

The Spirit leads us downwards.

That may come as a surprise to people who are raised in a culture that is obsessed with upward mobility. We climb social ladders. We rise to a higher standard of living. We reach for a higher position. We want to be on top. Some use drugs so that whatever their actual circumstances, they will at least feel high. Even our religious communities often have an 'up, up and away' mentality – flying away to heaven, leaving this old Earth below and behind.

But the Spirit leads us downwards. To the bottom, to the place of humility, to the position and posture of service . . . that's where the Spirit, like water, flows.

Jesus modelled this for us. Before Jesus, and even after him, most people assumed that God was at a great distance above us. To approach God meant to leave this world. But Jesus modelled a profoundly different vision. God comes down. God meets us where we are, in our neighbourhood, on our level, where we need

God most. God descends to the pit of need, suffering and abandonment. God is not distant from us, aloof, across a chasm, far above looking down. No, God is with us. Here. Now. In reach.

While we race to get to the head of the table, Jesus shocks everyone and takes the role of a servant, washing their feet. While we push and squeeze into the inner circle, Jesus shocks everyone and walks out to the margins to hang out with the outcasts and outsiders. While we struggle to make ourselves rich – often at the expense of others – Jesus shocks everyone. He pours out everything he is and has. While we fight to seize power over others, Jesus empowers others by standing with them in solidarity, by listening to them with respect, by seeking to make them successful, even at great cost to himself.

If you listen to the Spirit, here is what will happen to you. You'll be at a party and you'll notice on one side of the room all the beautiful people laughing and having fun together. In a far corner, you'll notice a person who is alone, feeling awkward, not knowing anyone. The Spirit will draw you to the person in need. You may become the bridge that connects the outsider to the insiders – and in that connection, both will be better off.

If you listen to the Spirit, here is what will happen to you. You'll be in a voting booth or in a position of power. People more powerful than you will appeal to you for your vote, your support, your co-operation. They will have a lot to offer you if you comply. But the Spirit will draw you to use your vote and your power for those who aren't at the table of privilege – the homeless, the sick or infirm in body or mind, the poor, the unemployed, those with special needs, the refugee, the immigrant, the alien, the minority, the different, the odd, the last, the least, the lonely and the lost. The Spirit will invite you to hear their concerns, take them to heart and join your heart with theirs.

Here's what will happen to you if you listen to the Spirit. You will realise that someone is angry at you or resentful towards you. You will hear that someone has spread false information about you or worked behind your back to do you harm. Everything in you will want you to write them off or get them back. But the Spirit will draw you towards them in humility. 'I have a problem and need your help,' you will say. 'I feel there may be some tension or distance between us. I want to close the gap and be sure things between us are good.' Your opponent may be too angry or insecure to respond well, but whatever happens, know this: the Spirit is at work in you.

Here's what will happen if you listen to the Spirit. You will make a mistake and you will be tempted to cover it up, minimise it, make an excuse for it, hide it from view. But the Spirit will draw you to admit it, first to yourself and to God, and then to those who deserve to know. You will say, 'Here's what I did . . . I was wrong. Will you forgive me?' In that acknowledgement, God will be real. In your humility, God will be present. For the Spirit moves downwards.

Here's what will happen if you listen to the Spirit. You will see a person or a group being vilified or scapegoated. Everyone is blaming them, shaming them, gossiping about them, feeling superior to them, venting their anxieties on them. If you join in, you'll feel part of the group. If you're silent, they'll assume you're with them. But the Spirit will draw you to differ courageously and graciously. 'I'm sorry,' you'll say, 'but I see things very differently. I know this person. He is my friend. She is a good person. They are human beings just like us.' You will risk your reputation in defending the person or people being scapegoated. And in that risk, both you and they will know that God's Spirit is alive and at work in your midst.

If you listen to the Spirit, here's what will happen to you. It will be late. You will be tired. There will be dishes to do or clothes to pick up or rubbish bins to empty. *Someone else should have done this*, you will think with anger. You will rehearse in your mind the speech you will give them. And then you will think, *But I guess they're just as tired and overworked as I am. So maybe I can help.* You won't do this as a manipulative ploy, but as a simple act of service. Or maybe, if their negligence is habitual, you won't step in, but you will find a way to gently, kindly, wisely speak to them and help them better fulfil their responsibilities. Either way, as you serve, you will know that God is real, for God is alive in you.

Here's what will happen to you if you listen to the Spirit. You will be in a public place. You will see a person who, by their dress or language or mannerisms, is clearly from another religion, another culture, another social class. That person will be uncomfortable or in need. And you will feel the Spirit inspiring a question within you. 'If I were in their shoes – in an unfamiliar or uncomfortable environment, what would I want someone to do for me?' And you will move towards them. You will overcome differences in language or culture. Your kind eyes and warm smile and gentle presence will speak a universal language of neighbourliness. And in that moment, they will feel that God is real, for God's Spirit is alive in you.

There is a prison near you. A hospital. A park or a bridge or an alley where homeless people sleep. A playground or shopping centre where teenagers hang out and get into trouble. Or there's a country in great need or a social problem that few people notice. If you listen to the Spirit, you will be drawn towards an opportunity to serve. At first, the thought will frighten or repel you. But when you let the Spirit guide you, it will be a source of great joy – one of the richest blessings of your life.

One more thing. There will be times in your life when you will need to be served – not to be the one serving. But even then, you will have the opportunity to appreciate, bless and thank those who serve you, and in so doing, you and they will experience mutual service, one of life's greatest joys.

The Spirit of God leads downwards. Downwards in humility. Downwards in service. Downwards in solidarity. Downwards in risk and grace. You used to strive to be cool, but the Spirit makes you warm. You used to strive to climb over others, but the Spirit leads you to wash their feet. You used to strive to fit in among the inner circle, but the Spirit dares you to be different on behalf of the outcasts and outsiders. You don't find God at the top of the ladder. No, you find God through descent. There is a trapdoor at the bottom, and when you fall through it, you fall into God.

It happened to Jesus. It will happen to you too, if you follow the Spirit's lead.

Engage

1. What one thought or idea from today's lesson especially intrigued, provoked, disturbed, challenged, encouraged, warmed, warned, helped or surprised you?

2. Share a story about a time when you served someone else, and about a time when you were served.

3. How do you respond to the specific scenarios presented in the lesson, including the last one about being served?

4. For children: Some people think getting your own way is the greatest thing in life. Other people think helping others is the greatest thing in life. Some people think both are true. What do you think?

5. Activate: This week, be open to the Spirit leading you downwards. Come to the next learning circle ready to share your experiences.

6. Meditate: Imagine yourself among the original learning circle of disciples. Jesus comes to wash your feet. Simply let that experience play out in your imagination in silence.

CHAPTER 47

The Spirit Conspiracy

Ephesians 5:15 – 6:9
Philemon 1:8–19
Hebrews 13:1–8

Let mutual love continue. Do not neglect to show hospitality to strangers . . .

James 5:1–6

There are circles of people that the Spirit of God wants to touch and bless, and you are the person through whom the Spirit wants to work. Your mission, should you choose to accept it, is to conspire with the Spirit to bring blessing to others.

Let's start with your family. Nobody is better positioned to wound and harm your spouse than you, and nobody better to love and enhance your spouse's thriving than you. The same goes for your parents, your children, your siblings. The Spirit wants to conspire with you in making their lives rich, full, free, good and fruitful.

When Jesus wanted to confront religious hypocrisy in his day, he pointed out the way hypocrites served their religion at the expense of their families. Paul picked up this theme in his letters to the early churches, calling such behaviour worse than unbelief. So Paul urged husbands and wives to submit to one another and show one another true love and respect. Although his writings may strike us as chauvinistic by today's standards, they were progressive by the standards of his time, because they promoted mutual responsibility, not merely top-down privilege. Similarly, he told children to obey and honour their parents, and parents to nurture their children and raise them without frustrating them – presumably by excessively high or unclear demands. And Paul repeatedly showed special consideration for widows – which today might mean an elderly aunt, uncle or grandparent, or any family member who is alone and vulnerable.

Paul quickly moved out from the circle of family to what we would call the circle of work. In his day, slavery was a social norm. Where he had the opportunity – as he did with a church leader named Philemon – he urged slave-owners to release their slaves and accept them as equals. Where that couldn't be done, he urged slave-owners to transcend the normal master-slave relationship and dare to treat their slaves with kindness – to mirror the kindness of God.

Similarly, he urged slaves to transcend social norms by doing their work with pride and dignity. Before, they might have given the least required by a human master. But now in the Spirit, they would work for and with God. They would do whatever was required and even more, giving their best.

James took Paul's concern for a Spirit-led work ethic to the level of business management and economic policy. In strong language, he warned rich employers not to underpay their workers. What employers might call 'keeping labour costs low', James called wage theft, and he reminded employers that God hears the cries of every underpaid labourer.

Our economic behaviour will change greatly when we stop asking typical questions like 'How little will the market or the law allow me to pay this person?' Instead, the Spirit leads people to conspire around new questions like 'What would God consider fair and generous pay to this person? How can we expand the bottom line from economic profit to something deeper and broader – economic, social and ecological benefit? How could our business and economic systems and policies become less harmful and more beneficial to aliveness on planet Earth – for us and for future generations? Could we measure success not by how much we consume and how fast we consume it, but by how well we live, care and serve?' Just imagine how the business world would change if more and more of us went to work conspiring goodness in the Spirit.

In the next circle out beyond family and work relationships, the Spirit activates our concern for people in our neighbourhoods, including strangers we meet on the street. Whatever their race, class, religion, political party or sexual identity, they too are our neighbours, and the Spirit will constantly awaken us to opportunities to serve and care. Biblical writers constantly emphasise the importance of hospitality – especially to strangers. 'As you have done for the least of these, you have done for me,' Jesus said. So the Spirit is looking for conspirators who are interested in plotting goodness in their communities. 'What would our community look like if God's dreams for it were coming true?' we ask. The answer gives us a vision to work towards.

From the circles of family, work and neighbourhood, the Spirit moves us to another sphere of concern: vulnerable people who would normally be forgotten. According to James, our religion is nothing but hot air if we don't translate our faith into action in regard to the vulnerable and easily forgotten around us. So the Spirit invites us to conspire for the well-being of orphans, widows, undocumented aliens, refugees, prisoners, people with special needs, the sick, the poor, the homeless, the uneducated, the unskilled, the unemployed and the underpaid.

Then there's the still larger circle of our civic and community life. We're told in the New Testament to pray for and show due respect for our political leaders. We're told to avoid debt – except the perpetual debt of love that we owe to every human being. In today's world, that means everyone on the planet, because as never before our world is bound together in one global ecology, one global economy and one global military-industrial complex. To be in tune with the Spirit is to transcend all smaller boundaries and to conspire in terms of the planetary whole.

There's another circle that we can't dare forget: the circle that includes our critics, opponents and enemies – the people who annoy us and those we annoy, the people who don't understand us and those we don't understand, the people who try our patience and those whose patience we try. Rather than write them off as unimportant and unwanted, we need to rediscover them as some of the most important people we know. If we ignore them, our growth in the Spirit will be stunted. If we let the Spirit guide us in what we say to their faces and behind their backs, we will become more Christ-like.

Speaking of our words, one of the most important ways the Spirit moves us to care for people in all these circles is by training us to control the tongue. Words can wound, sometimes deeply: careless words, critical words, condemning words, harsh words, insulting words, dehumanising words, words of gossip or deception. If your life were a ship, your words would be its rudder, James implies (3:1–12). So if you want to be a mature agent in the movement of the Spirit in our world, conspire with the Spirit in your choice of every single word.

You'll never regret forgoing an unkind word. And you'll never regret uttering a kind and encouraging word. An overworked person doing customer service, a housekeeper in a hotel, a landscaper or caretaker, a harried mother on a plane with a cranky child, the cashier at a busy fast-food outlet, your child's third-year teacher, the nurse in the emergency room – how much could they be encouraged today by a kind word from you, not to mention by a card, a gift, a large tip, a written note? If you're a part of the Spirit's conspiracy, you can be God's secret agent of blessing to anyone in any of these circles.

There's one other circle we haven't mentioned: the circle of your community of faith. It's the learning circle that forms whenever we encourage each other to let the Spirit keep flowing and moving in one another's lives. It's important to keep showing up and to show up with a good attitude. It's especially important to be a channel of blessing to those who lead in your community of faith . . . being sure they don't have to worry about money, for example, and being sure they feel truly appreciated. Their work is so important and surprisingly hard. Your encouragement could make the difference in whether they give up or keep giving their best.

The largest circle of all extends beyond humans and includes all living things and the physical structures on which we all depend: air, rain, soil, wind, climate. You can't claim to love your neighbour and pollute the environment on which he depends. You can't claim to love the Creator and abuse the climate of this beautiful, beloved planet. The Spirit that moves among us is the same Spirit that moves in and through all creation. If we are attuned to the Spirit, we will see all creatures as our companions . . . even as our relatives in the family of God, for in the Spirit we are all related.

In all these circles, you can be part of the Spirit conspiracy that is spreading quietly across our world. Your mission, should you choose to accept it, is to be a secret agent of God's commonwealth, conspiring with others behind the scenes to plot goodness and foment kindness wherever you may be.

Engage

1. What one thought or idea from today's lesson especially intrigued, provoked, disturbed, challenged, encouraged, warmed, warned, helped or surprised you?

2. Share a story about a time when you felt the Spirit guided you to go above and beyond your normal way of responding to a situation.

3. How do you respond to the idea that our words are a rudder that steers our lives?

4. For children: Could you share a story about a time when someone used words that hurt your feelings? And could you share a story about a time when someone used words that made you feel wonderful?

5. Activate: Choose one of the circles from this lesson and make it your focus in the week ahead.

6. Meditate: In your imagination, walk through a typical day, from waking up to going to bed at night. Imagine yourself as a portal of blessing in each circle of influence. Simply pray, 'Let it be so.'

CHAPTER 48

Spirit of Power

Acts 4:1–31

1 Thessalonians 5:1–11

2 Timothy 1:1–14

. . . God did not give us a spirit of cowardice, but rather a spirit of power and of love and of self-discipline.

Ephesians 6:10–20

Sooner or later, everyone should be arrested and imprisoned for a good cause. Or if not arrested and imprisoned, put in a position of suffering and sacrifice. Or if not that, at least be criticised or inconvenienced a little. Because if we're co-conspirators with the Spirit of God to bring blessing to our world, sooner or later it's going to cost us something and get us into trouble.

Jesus told his followers to 'count the cost'. He promised that those who walk his road would experience push-back, even persecution. And he often described that push-back as demonic or satanic in nature. Some people today believe Satan and demons to be literal, objective realities. Others believe they are outmoded superstitions. Still others interpret Satan and demons as powerful and insightful images by which our ancestors sought to describe shadowy realities that are still at work today. In today's terminology, we might call them social, political, structural, ideological and psychological forces. These forces take control of individuals, groups and even whole civilisations, driving them towards destruction.

Think of it like this: you can have a crowd of normal, happy people dancing in a popular nightclub. Suddenly someone shouts, 'Fire!' and people panic. Within seconds, everyone stampedes towards the exits. Soon, some people are being trampled – even killed – in the chaos, which means that others are doing the trampling and killing. None of the happy dancers in that club would have been seen as heartless killers before the scare. But we might say 'the spirit of panic' possessed them and drove them to violence. That spirit had a will of its own, as it were, turning peaceful, decent individuals into a ruthless, dangerous mob that became every bit as dangerous as the threat it feared.

Now, imagine a similar spirit of racism, revenge, religious supremacy, nationalism, political partisanship, greed or fear getting a foothold in a community. You can imagine previously decent people being possessed, controlled and driven by these forces, mindsets or ideologies. Soon, individuals aren't thinking or feeling for themselves any more. They gradually allow the spirit of the group to possess them. If nobody can break out of this frenzy, it's easy to imagine tragic outcomes: vandalism, riots, beatings, lynchings, gang rapes, house demolitions, plundered land, exploited or enslaved workers, terrorism, dictatorship, genocide. Bullets can fly, bombs explode and death tolls soar – among people who seemed so decent, normal and peace loving just minutes or months before.

You don't need to believe in literal demons and devils to agree with Jesus and the apostles: there are real and mysterious forces in our world that must be confronted. But how? If we respond to violence with violence, anger with anger, hate with hate, or fear with fear, we'll soon be driven by the same unhealthy and unholy forces that we detest and are trying to resist. To make matters worse, we'll be the last to know what's driving us, because we'll feel so pure and justified in our opposition. 'We must be good and holy,' we will say to ourselves, 'because what we're fighting against is so evil!'

We can see in this light why ancient people described Satan as a deceiver, an accuser and a liar. When we allow ourselves to come under the spell of an ideology or a similar force, we feel utterly convinced that evil is over there among *them*, and only moral rightness is here among *us*. In this accusatory state of mind, focused so exclusively on the faults of our counterparts, we become utterly blind to our own deteriorating innocence and disintegrating morality. Even when we begin to inflict harm on those we accuse, we are unable to see our actions as harmful. Self-deceived in this way, we lie to ourselves and live in denial about what we have become.

That's why Paul had so much to say about 'spiritual warfare' against 'the principalities and powers' that rule the world. He kept reminding the disciples that they weren't struggling against flesh-and-blood people. They were struggling against invisible systems and structures of evil that possess and control flesh-and-blood people. The real enemies back then and now are invisible realities like racism, greed, fear, ambition, nationalism, religious supremacy and the like – forces that capture decent people and pull their strings as if they were puppets to make them do terrible things.

In that light, being filled with and guided by the Holy Spirit takes on profound meaning – and practical importance. Where unholy, unhealthy spirits or value systems judge and accuse, the Holy Spirit inspires compassion and understanding. Where unholy, unhealthy spirits or movements drive people towards harming others, the Holy Spirit leads us to stand up boldly and compassionately for those being harmed. Where unholy, unhealthy spirits or ideologies spread propaganda and misinformation, the Holy Spirit boldly speaks the simple truth. Where unholy, unhealthy spirits or mindsets spread theft, death and destruction, God's Holy Spirit spreads true aliveness.

How do we resist being 'possessed' by the unholy, unhealthy systems that are so prevalent and powerful in today's world? Sometimes it's as simple – and difficult – as responding to harsh words with a kind, disarming spirit. When a website vilifies a group, for example, you might add a gentle, vulnerable comment: 'You're talking about people I count among my closest friends.' When a religious group, overly confident in its own purity or rightness, condemns others, you might humbly and unargumen-tatively quote a relevant Scripture: 'Whoever thinks he stands should take care, lest he fall,' or 'Knowledge puffs up, but love builds up.' When powerful forces organise to do harm, you may need to form or join some sort of collective, non-violent action – a march, a boycott or buy-cott, a protest, even non-violent civil disobedience. Whether in small, quiet ways or big, dramatic ones, if we join the Spirit in the ongoing mission of Jesus, we won't be overcome by evil; we will overcome evil with good.

But don't expect overcoming evil with good to be popular, easy, convenient or safe, as Paul's words to his young protégé, Timothy, make clear: 'God has not given us a spirit of cowardice but of power, love, and a sound mind.' When people are threat-ening you, hating you and calling you a heretic, an infidel, or worse – a bold and courageous spirit of empowerment, love and a sound mind is exactly what you need!

Paul, of course, spoke from personal experience. He had once been a confident, accusatory, violent persecutor of those he considered evil – utterly sure of himself, utterly convinced of his moral rightness in all he did. When he encountered Jesus and was filled with the Holy Spirit, he soon became the one being persecuted. The Spirit gave him non-violent boldness to face repeated arrests, beatings, imprisonments and ultimately, according to tradition, beheading by Nero in Rome. Clearly, for Paul, being a leader in the Spirit's movement wasn't a boring desk job!

No wonder one of the most oft-repeated themes in the New Testament is to *suffer graciously*, echoing Jesus' words about turning the other cheek. In 1 Peter 2:21 and 23 (CEB), for example, we read, 'Christ . . . left you an example so that you might follow in his footsteps . . . When he was insulted, he did not reply with insults. When he suffered, he did not threaten revenge. Instead, he entrusted himself to the one who judges justly.' To do that takes courage and power. It takes love. And it takes a sound – or non-reactive – mind. In other words, it takes the Holy Spirit.

As we walk this road together, we are being prepared and strengthened for struggle. We're learning to cut the strings of 'unholy spirits' that have been our puppet-masters in the past. We're learning to be filled, led and guided not by a spirit of fear, but by the Holy Spirit instead . . . a spirit of power, love and a sound mind to face with courage whatever crises may come.

When a crisis hits, unprepared people may be paralysed with fear, but we'll set an example of confidence and peace. Unprepared people may not know where to turn, but we'll have this circle of peace in which to welcome them. Unprepared people may turn on one another and pull apart, but we'll turn towards one another and pull together. Unprepared people may withdraw into survival mode, but we'll have strength enough to survive and more to share. Through the Spirit, we will have unintimidated power, unfailing love and a sound, non-reactive mind. When necessary, we will suffer graciously. For we will know that for us, whatever happens, even the end of the world . . . isn't really the end of the world.

Engage

1. What one thought or idea from today's lesson especially intrigued, provoked, disturbed, challenged, encouraged, warmed, warned, helped or surprised you?

2. Share a story about a time when you suffered in some way for standing up for what was right, or when someone else paid a price for standing up for you.

3. How do you respond to the idea that racism, revenge, religious supremacy, tribalism, political partisanship, fear or economic greed can 'possess' people?

4. For children: What would you do to help a child who is being bothered by a bully?

5. Activate: All of us can't do everything or fight every injustice everywhere. But we all should have 'some skin in the game' (some real involvement) on a handful of issues about which we feel a special call to action. Identify some of your issues and look for ways to stand up for them this week.

6. Meditate: Imagine your life as a tree in a storm. Imagine deep roots, a strong trunk and flexible branches. After holding this image for a few moments, ask God for the strength to stand bold and strong against whatever adversity may come.

CHAPTER 49

Spirit of Holiness

Psalm 98
John 14:15–18, 25–27; 15:26–27; 16:33
1 Corinthians 3:9–15; 15:20–28

. . . so that God may be all in all.

Jesus promised his followers three things. First, their lives would not be easy. Second, they would never be alone. Third, in the end, all will be well.

But all is not well now, and that raises the question of how . . . how does God get us from here to there? How does God put things right?

The word in the Bible for putting things right is *judgement*. Unfortunately, many today, drawing from the concept of a judge in today's court system, understand *judgement* to mean nothing more than condemnation and punishment. In contrast, in biblical times, good judges did more than condemn or punish. They worked to set things right, to restore balance, harmony and wellbeing. Their justice was restorative, not just punitive. The final goal of judgement was to curtail or convert all that was evil so that good would be free to run wild.

It's obvious to everyone that this kind of justice doesn't always happen in a satisfying way in this life. So people of faith have trusted that God can continue to set things right on the other side of the threshold of death. Through the idea of final judgement, we have dared to hope that somehow, beyond what we see in history, restorative justice could have the last word.

Final judgement, or final restoration, means that God's universe arcs towards universal repentance, universal reconciliation, universal purification, universal 'putting wrong things right'. That means more than saying that everything that can be punished will be punished: it means that everything that can be restored will be restored. It means the disease will be treated and healed, not just diagnosed. It means everything will, in God's ultimate justice, not only be evaluated: it will be given new value.

So when we say, with the writer of Hebrews (Heb. 9:27), that 'it is appointed for mortals to die once, and after that the judgement', we are not saying 'and after this, the condemnation'. We are saying 'after this, the setting right'. With John, we dare to believe that to 'see God as God is', to be in God's unspeakable light, will purge us of all darkness:

> See what love the Father has given us, that we should be called children of God; and that is what we are. The reason the world does not know us is that it did not know him. Beloved, we are God's children now; what we will be has not yet been revealed. What we do know is this: when he is revealed, we will be like him, for we will see him as he is. And all who have this hope in him purify themselves, just as he is pure. (1 John 3:1-3)

Since 'what we will be has not yet been made known', it is hard to say anything more, except this: in the end, God will be all in all, and all will be well.

Does that mean there will be no cost, no loss, no regret, no mourning? This is where the so-often misused image of fire

301

comes in. Many a hellfire-and-brimstone preacher has depicted fire as an instrument of torture, but it is far better understood as an instrument of purification. Paul describes it this way: God's purifying fire can't consume 'gold, silver and precious stones', because in so doing God would be destroying something good, which would render God evil. The cleansing or refining fire of God must destroy only the 'wood, hay and stubble' of hypocrisy, evil and sin.

So if some of us have constructed our lives like a shoddy builder, using worthless building materials, there won't be much of our life's story left. We will experience the purification of judgement as loss, regret, remorse. We thought we were pretty smart, powerful, superior or successful, but the purifying fire will surprise us with the bitter truth. In contrast, others of us who thought ourselves nothing special will be surprised in a positive way. Thousands of deeds of kindness that we had long forgotten will have been remembered by God, and we will feel the reward of God saying, 'Welcome into my joy!'

This understanding of God's restorative judgement changes the way you live before death. It makes you eager to use your wealth to make others rich, not to hoard it. It inspires you to use your power to empower others, not to advance yourself. It liberates you to give and give so that you will finish this life having given more than you received. It encourages you to try to be secretive about your good deeds because you would rather defer the return on your investment to the future. In fact, this hope makes you willing to give up this life, if necessary, for things that matter more than survival.

And this hope also changes the way we see trials and difficulties in this life. If we see trials and difficulties not as a punishment for our wrongs, but as a refining fire to strengthen and purify us, trials become our friends, not our enemies. So, in this light, delay is like a fire that burns away our impatience.

Annoyances are like flames that burn away our selfishness. The demands of duty are like degrees of heat that burn away our laziness. The unkind words and deeds of others are like a furnace in which our character is tempered, until we learn to bless, not curse, in response. It's not even worth comparing our short-term trials, Paul said, to the long-term glory that comes from enduring them. Whatever we face – ease or struggle, life or death, Paul's encouragement is the same: 'Therefore, my beloved, be steadfast, immovable, always excelling in the work of the Lord, because you know that in the Lord your labour is not in vain.'

If we believe in judgement – in God's great 'setting things right', we won't live in fear. We'll keep standing strong with a steadfast, immovable determination, and we'll keep excelling in God's good work in our world. If we believe the universe moves towards purification, justice and peace, we'll keep seeking to be pure, just and peaceable now. If we believe God is pure light and goodness, we'll keep moving towards the light each day in this life. Then, one day, when our time comes to close our eyes in death, we will trust ourselves to the loving Light in which we will awaken, purified, beloved, for ever.

Until then, the Spirit leads us along in that arc towards restoration and healing. Like a mother in childbirth, groaning with pain and anticipation, the Spirit groans within us. She will not rest until all is made whole, and all is made holy, and all is made well.

Life will not be easy. We will never be alone. In the end all will be well. That is all we know, and all we need to know. Amen.

Engage

1. What one thought or idea from today's lesson especially intrigued, provoked, disturbed, challenged, encouraged, warmed, warned, helped or surprised you?

2. Share a story about a time when what seemed impossible became possible and then actual for you.

3. How do you respond to the idea that life's troubles are like a refining or purifying fire?

4. For children: What are some of the places where you feel most peaceful and safe? What makes those places so special?

5. Activate: This week, hold on to the hope that God is setting things right. Notice what effect this hope has in your inner life and outer behaviour.

6. Meditate: Imagine a refiner's fire. As you picture that image of heat and purification, ask yourself what areas of your life are being purified these days. Hold those areas up to God.

CHAPTER 50

Spirit of Life

Psalm 90
Luke 20:27–38
Philippians 1:20–30

For to me, living is Christ and dying is gain.

We all will die one day. Mortality rates remain at 100 per cent, and nobody among us is getting any younger. Among the Spirit's many essential movements in our lives is this: to prepare us for the end of our lives, without fear.

So many us are afraid to even think about death, much less speak of it. That fear can enslave us and can rob us of so much aliveness. The Spirit moves within us to help us face death with hope, not fear . . . with quiet confidence, not anxiety. 'The law of the Spirit of life in Christ Jesus,' Paul said (Rom. 8:2), 'has set you free from the law of sin and of death.'

Here's a way to think about death. We often speak of God as the one who was, who is, and who is to come. The God who *was* holds all our past. The God who *is* surrounds us now. And the God who *is to come* will be there for us beyond this life as we know it. With that realisation in mind, death could never mean leaving God, because there is nowhere we can escape from God's presence, as the psalmist said (139:7). Instead, death simply means leaving the presence of God in this little neighbourhood of history called the present. Through death, we join God in the vast, forever-expanding future, into which both past and present are forever taken up.

Some religious scholars tried to trap Jesus once by bringing up a conflict between moral sense and belief in the afterlife. If there is life after death, they asked, does that mean that a woman who was widowed seven times in this life will have seven husbands in the next? You can almost see them smirking, thinking themselves very clever for stumping the rabbi. In response, Jesus said that to God, all who ever lived are alive (Luke 20:38). In that light, death is merely a doorway, a passage from one way of living in God's presence in the present to another way of living in God's presence – in the open space of unseized possibility we call the future.

We've all heard the cliché about someone being 'so heavenly minded he's no earthly good', and maybe we've met people on whom the cliché fits like an old bedroom slipper. But there is also a way of being so earthly minded that you're no earthly good. And there's a way of being heavenly minded so that you are more earthly good than you ever could have been any other way. To be liberated from the fear of death – think of how that would change your values, perspectives and actions. To believe that no good thing is lost, but that all goodness will be taken up and consummated in God – think of how that frees you to do good without reservation. To participate in a network of relationships that isn't limited by death in the slightest degree – think of how that would make every person matter and how it would free you to live with boundless, loving aliveness.

So what might we expect to happen when we die? Nobody knows for sure, but in light of Jesus' death and resurrection, we can expect to experience death as a passage, like birth, the end of one life stage and the beginning of another. We don't know how that passing will come ... like a slow slipping away in disease, like a sudden jolt or shock in an accident. However it happens, we can expect to discover that we're not falling out of life, but deeper into it.

On the other side, we can expect to experience as never before the unimaginable light or energy of God's presence. We will enter into a goodness so good, a richness so rich, a holiness so holy, a mercy and love so strong and true that all of our evil, pride, lust, greed, resentment and fear will be instantly melted out of us. We will at that moment more fully understand how much we have been forgiven, and so we will more than ever be filled with love ... love for God who forgives, and with God, love for everyone and everything that has like us been forgiven.

We can expect to feel a sense of reunion – yes, with loved ones who have died, but also with our great-great-great-great-grand-parents and our thirty-second cousins a thousand times removed whose names we've never known but to whom we are in fact related. That sense of relatedness that we now feel with closest of kin will somehow be expanded to every person who has ever lived. And that sense of relatedness won't stop with human beings, but will expand infinitely outwards to all of God's crea-tion. We can expect to feel the fullest, most exquisite sense of oneness and inter-relatedness and harmony – a sense of belong-ing and connection that we approached only vaguely or clumsily in our most ecstatic moments in this life.

We can expect to feel differently about our sufferings. We will see not the short-term pain that so preoccupied us on the past side of death, but instead the enduring virtue, courage and compassion that have been forged in us through each fall of the hammer on the anvil of pain. So we will bless our sufferings and feel about them as we feel about our pleasures now. What has been suffered or lost will feel weightless compared to the substance that has been gained.

We can expect to feel a limitless sense of 'Ah yes, now I see'. What we longed for, reached for, touched but couldn't grasp, and knew in part will then be so clear. And all our unfulfilled longing on this side of death will, we can expect, enrich and fulfil the having on that side of death. We can expect to feel as if we're waking up from being half asleep, waking into an explosion of pure, utter gratitude as we suddenly and fully realise all we've had and taken for granted all along.

You may imagine that dying will be like diving or falling or stepping into a big wave at the beach. You will feel yourself lifted off your feet and taken up into a swirl and curl and spin more powerful than you can now imagine. But there will be no fear, because the motion and flow will be the dance of Father, Son and Holy Spirit. The rising tide will be life and joy. The undertow will be love, and you will be drawn deeper and deeper in.

We normally don't look forward to the process of dying, and most of us would be happy if the dying process is as short and painless as possible. But if we allow the Spirit to prepare us for dying by contemplating it in these ways, we can begin to understand the dual pull that Paul wrote about: 'For me to live is Christ but to die is gain.' On the one hand, we feel a pull to stay here in this life, enjoying the light and love and goodness of God with so many people who are dear to us, with so much good work left to be done. On the other hand, we feel an equal and opposite pull towards the light and love and goodness of God experienced more directly beyond this life.

Many of us remember the experience as children of 'waiting your turn'. Maybe it was waiting your turn to ride a pony at the county fair, or waiting your turn to play a game, or waiting your turn to ride a sled down a hill in winter snow. Imagine the feeling of having had your turn on this Earth and having enjoyed it thoroughly. Now you are ready to step aside to let someone else have their turn. In that way, even dying can be an act of love and generosity: vacating space to make room for others, especially generations as yet unborn, just as others vacated their space so you could have your turn in this life. Perhaps the act of letting others have their turn will be one of our most mature and generous actions, a fitting end to our adventure in this life. At that moment, it will be our turn to graduate into a new adventure, beyond all imagining.

As we walk this road, we not only remember the past, we also anticipate the future, which is described as a great banquet around God's table of joy. When you pass from this life, do not be afraid. You will not pass into death. You will pass through death into a greater aliveness still – the banquet of God. Trust God, and live.

Engage

1. What one thought or idea from today's lesson especially intrigued, provoked, disturbed, challenged, encouraged, warmed, warned, helped or surprised you?

2. Share a story about one of your significant encounters with death.

3. How do you respond to the idea that people are enslaved by the fear of death?

4. For children: Tell us about someone in your family who died. What do you remember about them, or what have you learned about them from people who knew them?

5. Activate: Set a time this week to meet with another member of your learning circle in private. Create space to listen to one another talk freely about your own deaths, in light of this lesson.

6. Meditate: Take one of the images of death from this lesson – being caught up in a wave, falling through this life into deeper life, waking up, birth, passing through a doorway – and hold it in God's presence until you feel death can be your friend, not your enemy.

CHAPTER 51

Spirit of Hope

Psalm 126
Revelation 1:9–19; 19:11–16; 21:1–8; 22:16–21

The Spirit and the bride say, 'Come.' And let everyone who hears say, 'Come.' And let everyone who is thirsty come.

The last book in the Bible is the book of Revelation, also known as the Apocalypse (or unveiling). Some people ignore it, wondering why such an odd composition was even included in the biblical library. Other people seem obsessed by it. They are certain that it is a coded 'history of the future', telling us how the world will one day end.

That way of reading Revelation is based on a lot of assumptions that deserve to be questioned. For example, did God create a closed and predetermined universe, or a free and participatory one? Is the future a film that has already been shot, so to speak, and we are just watching it play? Or is the future open, inviting us not simply to resign ourselves and adapt, but to be protagonists who invent, improvise and help create the outcome as God's co-workers and fellow actors?

Having left behind the 'road map of the future' way of reading Revelation, more and more of us are rediscovering it in a fresh way. The first step in this fresh approach is to put the text back in its historical context. Our best scholars agree it was composed during the bloody reign of either Nero in the AD 60s or Domitian in the AD 90s. Life was always hard in the Roman Empire for poor people, as it was for most of the followers of Jesus. But life was extremely precarious when the man at the helm of the empire was vicious, paranoid and insane, as both Nero and Domitian were. Life got even tougher when the madman on the throne demanded to be worshipped as a god, something followers of Jesus would never do.

Under these circumstances, you can imagine the followers of Christ thinking something like this: *Jesus has been gone now for decades. The world doesn't seem to be getting better. If anything, with a mad dictator in Rome, it's getting worse. Maybe Jesus was wrong . . . maybe it's time for us to forget about this 'turn the other cheek and love your enemies' business. Maybe we need to take matters into our own hands and strap on a sword to fight for our future. Or maybe we should just eat, drink, make money and be merry, because tomorrow we might all be dead.*

In this light, Revelation was the very opposite of a codebook that mapped out the end of the world in the distant future. It addressed the crisis at hand. Even if the emperor is mad, Revelation claimed, it's not the end of the world. Even if wars rage, it's not the end of the world. Even if peace-loving disciples face martyrdom, it's not the end of the world. Even if the world as we know it comes to an end, that ending is also a new beginning. Whatever happens, God will be faithful and the way of Christ – a way of love, non-violence, compassion and sustained fervency – will triumph.

Along with its historical context, we would be wise to understand the literary context for Revelation, which is *literature of the oppressed*. Literature of the oppressed arises among people living under dictatorships who have no freedom of speech. If they dare to criticise the dictator, they'll be 'disappeared' and never seen again. Before being executed, they may be brutally tortured so their oppressors can extract names of others they should arrest, torture and elicit still more names from. No wonder people learn to be silent in a dictatorship.

But being silent in the presence of injustice feels like a way of co-operating with it.

As literature of the oppressed, the book of Revelation provided early disciples with a clever way of giving voice to the truth – when freedom of speech was dangerous in one way, and remaining silent was dangerous in another. Instead of saying, 'The Emperor is a fraud and his violent regime cannot stand,' which would get them arrested, Revelation tells a strange story about a monster who comes out of the sea and is defeated. Instead of saying, 'The religious establishment is corrupt,' it tells a story about a whore. Instead of naming today's Roman Empire as being doomed, they talk about a past empire – Babylon – that collapsed in failure.

If we keep reading Revelation as a road map of a predetermined future, the consequences can be disastrous. For example, we may read the vision of Jesus coming on a white horse (Rev. 19:11ff.) and think that's about a Jesus completely different from the one we met in the Gospels. This Jesus won't be a peace-and-love guy any more, but a violence-and-revenge guy. What might happen if we leave the peace-and-love Jesus in the past and follow a violence-and-revenge Jesus into the future?

We may read about people being thrown into a lake of fire at the end of Revelation (20:7ff.), and if we take it literally we may see God as some kind of a sadistic torturer. If God tortures for eternity, might it be OK for us to do the same in our next war or political upheaval? Or if we interpret literally the passage in Revelation (21:1) that makes it sound like the Earth will be destroyed, might we think, *Hey, why worry about overconsumption, environmental destruction or climate change? God is going to destroy the world soon anyway, so we might as well pitch in!* There is a high cost to reading Revelation outside its historical and literary context.

People who read Revelation without understanding that context tend to miss some telling details. For example, when Jesus rides in on the white horse, his robes are bloodstained and he carries a sword. Many have interpreted this scene as a repudiation of Jesus' non-violence in the Gospels. But they miss the fact that he carries his sword in his mouth, not his hand. Instead of predicting the return of a killer Messiah in the future, Revelation recalls the day in the past when Jesus rode into Jerusalem on a donkey. His humble words of peace, love and justice will, Revelation promises, prove more powerful than the bloody swords of violent emperors. In addition, we notice his robe is bloodstained before the battle begins, suggesting that the blood on his robe is not the blood of his enemies, but is his own, shed in self-giving love. In that light, Revelation reinforces rather than overturns the picture we have of Jesus in Matthew, Mark, Luke and John.

There's a beautiful visionary scene at the end of the book of Revelation that is as relevant today as it was in the first century. It doesn't picture us being evacuated from Earth to heaven as many assume. It pictures a New Jerusalem descending from heaven to Earth. This new city doesn't need a temple because God's presence is felt everywhere. It doesn't need sun or moon because the light of Christ illuminates it from within. Its gates are never shut, and it welcomes people from around the world to receive the treasures it offers and bring the treasures they can offer. From the centre of the city, from God's own throne, a river flows – a river of life or aliveness. Along its banks grows the Tree of Life. All of this, of course, evokes the original creation story and echoes God's own words in Revelation: 'Behold! I'm making all things new!'

Rather than giving its original readers and hearers a coded blueprint of the future, Revelation gave them visionary insight into their present situation. It told them that the story of God's work in history has never been about escaping Earth and going up to heaven. It has always been about God descending to dwell among us. Faithfulness wasn't waiting passively for a future that had already been determined. Faithfulness meant participating with God in God's unfolding story. God wasn't a distant, terrifying monster waiting for vengeance at the end of the universe. God was descending among us here and now, making the tree of true aliveness available for all.

What was true for Revelation's original audience is true for us today. Whatever madman is in power, whatever chaos is breaking out, whatever danger threatens, the river of life is flowing now. The Tree of Life is bearing fruit now. True aliveness is available now. That's why Revelation ends with the sound of a single word echoing through the universe. That word is not *Wait!* Nor is it *Not Yet!* or *One day!* It is a word of invitation, welcome, reception, hospitality and possibility. It is a word not of ending, but of new beginning. That one word is *Come!* The Spirit says it to us. We echo it back. Together with the Spirit, we say it to everyone who is willing. *Come!*

Engage

1. What one thought or idea from today's lesson especially intrigued, provoked, disturbed, challenged, encouraged, warmed, warned, helped or surprised you?

2. Share a story about an invitation that changed your life.

3. How do you respond to the idea of Revelation being literature of the oppressed?

4. For children: What is something you are looking forward to, and why?

5. Activate: Whenever you think of the future this week, listen

for the Spirit's invitation to enter the future with hope: *Come!*

6. Meditate: Imagine creation inviting God, and God inviting creation, through that powerful word *Come!* Hold that mutual invitation in your heart.

CHAPTER 52

God in the End

Luke 15:11–32
Romans 8:31–39
1 Corinthians 15:50–58

Therefore, my beloved, be steadfast, immovable, always excelling
in the work of the Lord, because you know that in the Lord your
labour is not in vain.

Astronomers tell us that in a little less than 8 billion years, our sun
will turn into a red dwarf and Earth will be incinerated. Before that
time, they offer a number of other scenarios that could wipe out
human civilisation on our planet – a massive comet or asteroid, a
black hole or a hypernova elsewhere in our galaxy, not to mention
likely fruits of human stupidity in the form of nuclear or biological
warfare, climate catastrophe and environmental collapse.

Somewhere between science and science fiction is the possibility of escaping Earth and populating other planets elsewhere in
the universe if we ruin this one. But even if we manage a 'Plan B',
scientists suspect that the entire universe is winding down. It will
eventually end either in a Big Freeze or a Big Crunch, after which
there will be nobody left to remember that any of this ever
existed. If this prediction is the whole truth, our unremembered
lives and their illusory meaning will be reduced to nothing, gone
for ever – utterly, absolutely, infinitely gone.

In the biblical library, in contrast, neither Big Freeze nor Big Crunch gets the last annihilating word. Instead, we are given an ultimate vision of a Big Celebration. From Genesis to Revelation we find the story of an infant universe into which is born an infant humanity that grows, comes of age, makes mistakes, learns lessons and finally reaches maturity. Like most coming-of-age stories, this one ends with a wedding, as humanity welcomes God into its heart.

What could such a story mean? What could it mean to us right now? Jesus gave us a clue in one of his best-known but least-understood parables. In it, human history can be seen as the story of a family, a father and two sons. The family experiences conflict. The rebellious younger son runs away and for a while forgets his true identity. The dutiful older son stays at home but also forgets his true identity. The younger son reaches a crisis and comes home. He is welcomed by the father, which then creates a crisis for the older son. Of course, the story isn't only about the identity crises of the sons. It also reveals the true identity of the father, whose heart goes out to both brothers, who graciously loves them even when they don't know it, and even when they don't love each other. The story ends with a celebration – a welcome-home party, a reunion party.

Like many of our best stories, it doesn't have to be factual to tell the truth, and its ending is left unresolved. Will the older brother remain outside, nursing his petty resentments? Or will he come inside to join the Big Celebration and rediscover his true identity in the family? We find ourselves cheering for him: 'Come inside, man! Come on! Don't hold back! Come in!' That word *come*, interestingly, is the same word we find echoing at the end of the last book in the biblical library.

If we enter this story and let it do its work on us, we can look out from within it and see ourselves and all creation held in the parental love of God. We can empathise with God, who wants all to come, all to enjoy the feast, all to discover or rediscover their true identity in God's family, in God's love.

This short parable is one of the best mirrors of humanity ever composed. In it, both the rebellious and the religious can see themselves. But more important, it is one of the best windows into God ever composed, because it shows a gracious and spacious heart that welcomes all to the table.

Can you see why it is so good and right for us to pause as we walk this road to gather around a table to celebrate God's love? At this table, we look *back* to Jesus, remembering all he said and did to help us see and enter God's great feast. And at this table, we look *around* at one another, seeing one another – and being seen – with God's eyes of love, as sisters and brothers, part of one human family.

And no less important, at this table we look *forward* to a festive celebration that beckons us from the future. The story began in God's creative love, and it ends in God's creative love, too . . . if such an ending can even be called an ending. Perhaps it is most true to say that any story with God in it is a story that never, ever ends.

The 'Big Freeze or Big Crunch' predictions of the astronomers may be accurate on some limited level, but they don't have the right instruments to detect the widest, deepest dimensions of reality. It takes stories like the ones we have been exploring to help us imagine those deeper and bigger dimensions.

Imagine a moment before the Big Bang banged. Imagine a creativity, brilliance, fertility, delight, energy, power, glory, wisdom, wonder, greatness and goodness sufficient to express itself in what we know as the universe. Try to imagine it, even though you know you cannot: a creative imagination and energy so great that it would produce light, gravity, time and space . . . galaxies, stars, planets and oceans . . . mountains, valleys, deserts and forests . . . salmon, bison, dragonflies and skylarks . . . gorillas, dolphins, golden retrievers, and us.

And then dare to imagine that this is the great, big, beautiful, mysterious goodness, wholeness and aliveness that surrounds us and upholds us even now.

Finally, try to imagine that this is also the great, big, beautiful, mysterious goodness, wholeness and aliveness into which all of us and all creation will be taken up – in a marriage, in a home-coming, in a reunion, in a celebration.

We inherited various words to name this ultimate mystery. In English, *God*. In Spanish, *Dios*. In French, *Dieu*. In Russian, *Bog*. In Mandarin, *Thianzhu*. *Mungu* in Swahili. *Allah* in Arabic. *Edoda* in Cherokee. *Elohim* and *Adonai* and many others in Hebrew. *Wakan Tanka* in Sioux, and so on. So many books have been written to describe and define this mystery. And sadly, so many arguments and inquisitions have been launched and wars waged over it, too. But here in Jesus' parable, as in the closing chapters of Revelation, we get a window into its true heart, its intention, its flow. The whole story flows towards reconciliation, not in human creeds or constitutions, but in love, the love of the One who gave us being and life. We can boast of knowing the 'right' name and still have the wrong understanding. But if we have eyes to see and ears to hear, the great, big, beautiful, wonderful, holy, mysterious, reconciling heart of God waits to be discovered and experienced.

So our journey in the story of creation, the adventure of Jesus and the global uprising of the Spirit has come full circle. It all came from God in the beginning, and now it all comes back to God in the end.

Big Bang to Big Death? Or Big Bang to Big Celebration? If the biblical story is true, it is the latter. In the end as Paul envisioned it, death is swallowed up in a great big victory, as if death were a tiny drop in comparison to God's huge ocean of aliveness. A contemporary writer put the same insight like this: 'All the death that ever was, set next to life, would scarcely fill a cup.'

Human speculation – whether religious or scientific – does the best it can, like a little boat that ventures out on the surface of a deep, deep ocean, under the dome of a fathomless sky. Our eyes cannot see beyond the rim. Our ears cannot hear the music beneath the silence. Our hearts cannot imagine the meaning above us, below us, around us, within us. But the Spirit blows like wind. And so this mystery humbles us even as it dignifies us. This mystery impresses us with our smallness even as it inspires us with our ultimate value. This mystery dislodges us from lesser attachments so we sail on in hope. This mystery dares us to believe that the big love of God is big enough to swallow all death and overflow with aliveness for us all.

'Do not fear,' the Spirit whispers. 'All shall be well.' That is why we walk this road, from the known into the unknown, deeper into mystery, deeper into light, deeper into love, deeper into joy.

Engage

1. What one thought or idea from today's lesson especially intrigued, provoked, disturbed, challenged, encouraged, warmed, warned, helped or surprised you?

2. Share a story about a moment in your life when everything came together and, for at least a moment, 'all was well'.

3. How do you respond to the image of the end as a great homecoming celebration, or a great marriage banquet?

4. For children: If someone said, 'Tell me the five best things about being part of your family,' what would you say?

5. Activate: This week, keep the words 'this mystery' with you . . . and contrast the deep ocean of 'this mystery' with the little boats of human speculation.

6. Meditate: Imagine being on a small boat, buoyed up by depths that you cannot fathom. Feel what it means to be upheld by mystery. Let the peace of God uphold you.

Fourth Quarter Queries

If possible, compose prayerful, honest and heartfelt replies to these queries in private, and then gather to share what you have written. The Five Guidelines for Learning Circles in Appendix II may be helpful to guide your sharing. You may also find it helpful to invite a trusted spiritual leader to serve as 'catechist' and ask him or her for additional guidance, feedback and instruction. Make it safe for one another to speak freely, and let your conversation build conviction in each of you as individuals, and among you as a community.

1. How have you experienced the Spirit through letting go, letting be and letting come?
2. Recount a history of your experience with the Holy Spirit. What are some of your most significant spiritual experiences?
3. How would you explain to sincere spiritual seekers ways to

increase their experience of the Spirit's transforming power in their lives?

4. How are you learning to love God, self, neighbour and enemy?

5. Share your understanding of how the mystery of the Trinity can be a healing (rather than harmful) teaching.

6. How have you experienced the Spirit working through you to serve and bless others, and to confront evil forces in our world?

7. How does the Holy Spirit help you face the future, including your own death?

8. How do you feel about forming and leading a new group to teach others what you have learned through *We Make the Road by Walking*?

Dedication and Acknowledgements

I recently received an e-mail from a young man whom I admire a lot. He started a wonderful organisation that does immense good for children in some of the world's most dangerous places. His Christian faith played a formative role in his development, yet he feels pain about his religious heritage:

> There are a number of my friends, including myself, who feel like we had to let almost everything go to follow Jesus or at least truth and what made sense to us . . . Because things are shifting so much in the world and in our thinking, this process can feel like we are 'on the way out' of the faith. The disorientation creates confusion and leaves us asking what to still believe in. When we let so many things go, what do we know we need to hold on to? We believe deeply in truth but feel like the milieus we grew up with were strategically designed to make us feel like we were losing our souls when we opened our minds.

But even though we have realized that is not the case and have begun to find freedom, we are still left wondering exactly what our convictions actually are . . . I keep feeling like you would be a good person to talk to about it, perhaps even in a room with a few other of these people from my generation . . . **the believers who still want to believe but aren't sure what is left to believe in.**

This book is dedicated to people like this gifted young man and his friends. It is my hope that it will help them find something worth believing in again . . . something to sustain them in their good and meaningful work, something better than what they've left behind.

This book is also dedicated to the memory of Richard Twiss, a friend, colleague and mentor. He died of a heart attack while I was writing this book. A Lakota Sioux who spent many years in more traditional Christian company, in recent years he pioneered a new way of following the path of Jesus in an indigenous way – in bare feet, so to speak, leaving the heavy, steel-toed boots of industrial-era, Euro-American Christianity behind. This beloved *ikce wicasa* was a true trail-blazer who made the road by walking. I and thousands of others feel a deep hole in our hearts since he left. I pray that this book will contribute to the fulfilment of his dreams.

Finally, this book is dedicated to the churches and fellowship groups that have nourished my faith through the years. I learned so much about worship and the Bible at New Hampshire Avenue Gospel Chapel where I grew up, a Plymouth Brethren congregation in Silver Spring, Maryland. That learning continued at the Fellowship in Rockville in its various forms in my high school and college years, along with the Cornerstone community in College Park. Then I learned so much about discipleship, evangelism, fellowship and leadership at Cedar Ridge Community

Church, now in Spencerville, Maryland, the interdenominational congregation in which I had the privilege of serving as a pastor for over twenty years.

For the last five years, I have been a quiet but grateful participant in the life of St Mark's Episcopal in Marco Island, Florida, led by Kyle Bennett, John Ineson, Sue Price and their colleagues, where I have experienced needed rest and recuperation. I have also been blessed, in my travels and speaking, through literally thousands of other churches of many denominations, from Southern Baptist to Greek Orthodox, from Pentecostal to Presbyterian, from Quaker to Roman Catholic to Adventist to Unitarian. I thank God for them all.

As always, I'm grateful to my agent and friend, Kathryn Helmers; along with my publisher, Wendy Grisham; along with Chelsea Apple, Katherine Venn and all the good people of Jericho Books in the US and Hodder & Stoughton in the UK. Rachel Held Evans, Tony Jones, Joel Costa and Charles Toy also deserve great thanks for reading the manuscript and offering needed feedback, as do Sarah Thomas, Bryan and Christy Berghoef and Wendy Tobias, who field-tested the book in groups they lead.

Liturgical Resources

Liturgy means 'an order, plan or format for gathering'. Not every learning circle that works with *We Make the Road by Walking* will want to use the following liturgical resources, but many will find them helpful. They have been kept simple enough that participants can easily learn the responses by heart. Ideally, only the leader or leaders will need print or digital versions in front of them, since the goal is for the liturgy to be a shared social and spiritual experience rather than a script that is read. (A downloadable version is available at www.brianmclaren.net.)

The prayers and other resources in this liturgy are derived from traditional sources, but they are simplified here and adapted for use by a wide range of people from a wide range of religious backgrounds. If you wish that more traditional material were included, of course you can add it. If you wish things were stated differently, of course you can revise them, in keeping with your convictions and commitments. These resources avoid masculine or feminine pronouns for God. They frequently use the direct address *Living God,* but you may wish to substitute other direct addresses as well, such as *Holy One, Living Creator, Spirit of Life,* and so on.

Many groups won't be able to make a one-year commitment. For them, one quarter will be more doable. Church membership classes will find chapters 34–39 on church life especially helpful. At www.brianmclaren.net, you'll find suggestions for using the lessons in a weekend retreat setting, and it's easy to imagine groups using a chapter a day to complete the book in less than two months.

Whenever possible, leadership should be shared widely among group participants so all can develop leadership skills. Whenever school-aged children are present, encourage them to participate to the degree they are able and willing; show them uncommon respect as fellow learners. The group convener or host can assign responsibilities in advance or spontaneously.

For churches using this liturgy for public worship, appropriate music – vocal or instrumental – can be added before, during or after any of the elements. Care should be taken to avoid songs that are contrary to the spirit or content of the lessons. At www.brian-mclaren.net, you will find links to suggested musical resources.

For many groups, a shorter liturgy is recommended: Opening (5 minutes), Scripture Readings (5–7 minutes), Lesson (10–12 minutes), Engagement (20–40 minutes), Benediction (5 minutes). If a group tries the shorter format and is hungry for more, they can experiment with the longer liturgy: Opening, Prayer (5–10 minutes), Scripture Readings, Lesson, Engagement, Offering (2–3 minutes), Eucharist (15 minutes), Benediction.

The context for these liturgical resources may be a meal, worship service, class, home group, choir rehearsal, hike (where the hikers pause periodically along the journey), sports event, drum circle, yoga session, vespers, or some other shared activity. Whatever the context, the tone should be joyful, reverent, energetic and personal.

During a meal or informal gathering time, people can use queries like these to invite one another into meaningful conversation:

How is your life? How is your work? How is your soul?

How have you experienced God at work in you or through you this week?

What was your experience in applying last week's Activate prompt (No. 5 in the 'Engage' section)?

What have been some of your joys and sorrows (or high points and low points) since we last met?

At the beginning of a meal, the following prayer of thanksgiving can be used. The response (in italics) can be signalled by a pause or gesture.

Let us give thanks for this meal, saying, *We thank you, Living God.*

For this breath, for this heartbeat, for the gift of these companions, *we thank you, Living God.*

For this nourishment and flavour, for soil and sunlight, air and rainfall, *we thank you, Living God.*

For all to whom this food connects us, from field to farm and shop to table, *we thank you, Living God.*

As we share this meal together, may our thirst for peace be strengthened and our hunger for justice deepened, until all are fed, and safe, and well.

We thank you, Living God. Amen.

Opening

Whenever it is time to move from the meal or other activity to the lesson and conversation, the convener or host can begin with these words, spoken with joy and energy, never in a dull or mechanical monotone:

One: The Living God is with us!

All: *And with all creation!*

Then, each line of an invocation like the following can be preceded by a bell, a singing bowl, the lighting of a candle, or another simple action that helps participants focus their attention and open their hearts. (Responses are in italics.)

Let us awaken our hearts to the presence of God, saying: *We praise you for your glory.*
God before us, behind us, above us, upholding us . . . *We praise you for your glory.*
God with us, among us, beside us, befriending us . . . *We praise you for your glory.*
God within us, flowing through us, animating, harmonising . . . *We praise you for your glory. Amen.*

The following invocation may be read – again, with sincerity and joy (adapted from the *Book of Common Prayer*, 355):

Almighty God, to you all hearts are open, all desires known, and from you no secrets are hid. Purify and unify the thoughts of our hearts by the inspiration of your Holy Spirit, that we may more perfectly love you and more worthily magnify your holy Name, through Christ our Lord. *Amen.*

Prayer

If one of the following forms of prayer is used each week, over the course of a month, groups can move from thanksgiving (perhaps with hands raised high, palms up) to intercession (perhaps with hands raised shoulder height, palms out in blessing) to confession (perhaps with hands placed over the heart or chest) to contemplation (with hands lowered, palms open). Responses should be spoken with energy and sincerity.

Week 1. A prayer of thanksgiving *(adapted from the* Book of Common Prayer, 836–837*)*

Let us give thanks to the Living God for all the gifts that we enjoy, saying, *We thank you, Living God.*

For the beauty and wonder of your creation, in earth and sky and sea: *We thank you, Living God.*

For all that is gracious in the lives of men and women, revealing the image of Christ: *We thank you, Living God.*

For our daily food and drink, our homes and families, and our friends: *We thank you, Living God.*

For minds to think, hearts to love, and hands to serve: *We thank you, Living God.*

For health and strength to work, and leisure to rest and play: *We thank you, Living God.*

For challenges which call forth new strength, for failures which teach greater humility, and for encouragement to persevere when life is hard: *We thank you, Living God.*

For all who have gone before us, for all who walk beside us, and for all children, who are precious to us and to you: *We thank you, Living God.*

And for the great wisdom and hope that you reveal to us through Jesus, our leader, example, teacher, liberator, and friend: *We thank you, Living God.*

Week 2. A prayer of intercession: *After each request, pause for a moment of silent prayer*

With all our heart and with all our mind and with all our strength, let us pray to the Living God, saying, *Lord, hear our prayer.*

For this good earth, this holy creation, and for the wisdom and will to cherish, understand, reverence, rightly use and conserve it, we pray to the Living God: *Lord, hear our prayer.*

For all in danger, hunger, or sorrow, for the aged and infirm, the widowed and orphaned, the sick and suffering in body or mind, for prisoners and refugees, the poor and oppressed, the unemployed and destitute, the bereaved and alone, the war-torn and wounded, and for all who care for them, we pray to the Living God: *Lord, hear our prayer.*

For all who hold positions of trust in the worlds of religion, education, government, business, community, culture and family, that they may promote the well-being of all creation, we pray to the Living God: *Lord, hear our prayer.*

For any who have caused us pain, for those we struggle to understand and strain to love, for all who do not love us or who consider themselves our enemies, that they may be truly blessed and that we may be fully reconciled, we pray to the Living God: *Lord, hear our prayer.*

For ourselves and our circles of family and friends, for the grace to learn, desire and do your will humbly in our daily life and work, we pray to the Living God. *Lord, hear our prayer.*

Week 3. A prayer of confession: One of the following can be used, read line by line by a leader and repeated by the group, followed by a few moments of silence

Gracious God, we have hurt others, and we have been hurt./ We have presumed upon others, and we have been presumed upon./ We have taken others for granted, and we have been taken for granted./ We have dishonoured others, and we have been dishonoured./ As we receive Your forgiveness for our wrongs,/ we extend forgiveness to others who have wronged us./ Have mercy upon us all. Amen.

Gracious God, our sins are too heavy to carry,/ too real to hide,/ and too deep to undo./ Forgive what our lips tremble to name/ and what our hearts can no longer bear./ Set us free from a past that we cannot change;/ open to us a future in which we can be changed;/ and grant us grace to grow more and more in your likeness and image,/ through Jesus Christ, the light of the world. Amen. (Adapted from the *PCUSA Book of Common Worship*)

Most merciful God,/ we confess that we have sinned against you/ in thought, word, and deed,/ by what we have done, and by what we have left undone./ We have not loved you with our whole heart;/ we have not loved our neighbours as ourselves./ We are truly sorry and we humbly repent./ For the sake of your Son Jesus Christ,/ have mercy on us and forgive us;/ that we may delight in your will,/ and walk in your ways,/ to the glory of your Name. Amen. (From the *Episcopal Book of Common Prayer*)

Week 4. Contemplative prayer can be introduced with words like these

Let us in stillness hold our hearts open to God. When thoughts and worries come, let us release them and return to restful openness, enjoying the companionship of God, who is closer to us than we are to ourselves. We trust that in quietness and surrender, as we breathe out trust and breathe in grace, the deepest part of us will find our home more deeply in the gracious heart of God.

Scripture readings

Most of the Bible was an oral composition before it was a written text, and most of the written texts were meant to be heard aloud and 'live'. In that spirit, whenever possible, participants can learn passages by heart and share them as a form of performance art.[19] Where that isn't possible, each passage should be read by a child or adult who has had time to become familiar with it in advance so it can be read naturally and with feeling. Or

---

19 For training to appreciate and present the biblical text in this way, see the Network of Biblical Storytellers website (www.nbsint.org).

participants can take turns reading the passages aloud around the circle. Your group should agree on which Bible translation(s) you will use in your gatherings, such as the New Revised Standard Version, or the Contemporary English Bible. The passages may be introduced like this:

One: The Living God is with us!

All: *And with all creation!*

One: A passage from [the first passage is presented]. May we be equipped by these words to walk in love for God, ourselves, our neighbours, all people and all God's creation.

All: *Thanks be to God.*

One: A passage from [additional passages are presented]. May we be enlivened by these words to do justice, love kindness and walk humbly with God. [Or:] Through these words, may we see God more clearly, love God more dearly and follow God more nearly, day by day.

All: *Thanks be to God.*

Lesson/Engagement

The chapter can be presented aloud by one person as a short sermon or homily. Or it may be presented by several people reading a few paragraphs each. It should be read with feeling and energy, not in a wooden or mechanical way. If there are Scripture references in parentheses (e.g., John 3:16), don't read them aloud. After the chapter is presented, a facilitator should introduce the 'Engage' time. For large groups, it will be best to break into smaller groups of four people to engage with the questions. (In a church service, people can easily stand and form groups of two or three.) Depending on available time, the leader may need to select which questions will be used and how much time can be allotted to each question.

Engagement should initially be introduced with the Five

Guidelines for Learning Circles (Appendix II).[20] After a few weeks, when everyone is familiar with these five guidelines, the leader can simply use a reminder like this to begin the interaction time: 'Let's recall our five guidelines as we begin: mutual participation, honour, silence, understanding and brevity.' When new people join the group, the five guidelines can be reviewed.

Whenever possible, children should be included in the Engage time, and when that's the case, adults should avoid language that would be inappropriate for children. Some groups may find it helpful to use a talking stick or some other physical object for a person to hold as he or she responds to a question. The speaker then hands the talking stick on to the next person who will share. Anyone is free to pass the stick on to someone else if they would rather not speak.

The Engage questions follow this pattern:

1. *What one thought or idea from today's lesson especially intrigued, provoked, disturbed, challenged, encouraged, warmed, warned, helped or surprised you?* This question invites simple self-reporting and gives a lot of freedom – including the freedom to question, disagree with, or object to anything in the Scripture reading or reflection/sermon. The response should begin like this: 'I was intrigued [or disturbed, etc.] by . . .' followed by an explanation of why the person felt this response.

2. *Share a story about* . . . This question invites the sharing of personal experience. Not everyone will have a response to every question, but often, after a few moments of silence, stories will come to mind and begin to flow.

3. *How do you respond to* . . . These questions invite personal response to an idea, an image or a proposal from the lesson.

20 Some groups may prefer to replace the Engage time with a Create time, in which they respond creatively to the lesson through poetry, drawing, painting, music or other artistic media.

When people respond in different ways to the same prompt, it's an excellent opportunity for learning and growth. There's no need to validate or invalidate any response as long as it is expressed in line with the five guidelines for learning circles.

4. *For children . . .* These questions are fine for adults, too, but they're intended to invite school-aged children to have a voice in the group as equals. It's important for adults not to respond to children's sharing in ways that they will experience as dismissive or demeaning. The goal should be for adults and children alike to be taken seriously, to be drawn into honest thinking and free speech, and to learn together.

5. *Activate . . .* These questions invite participants to move from reflection to action.

6. *Meditate . . .* These prompts create space for participants to open deeper parts of themselves to God.

Offering

This is a good time to include a financial offering as an expression of worship, discipleship and stewardship. Someone can lead in a prayer like this to introduce the offering:

Our gracious and generous Creator,/ you have blessed us with abundance:/ This beautiful earth and all we enjoy,/ health and strength, family and friends;/ work and rest; home and belongings./ We are blessed indeed./ To support this community and provide for those who serve us,/ To help those in need and extend our mission,/ In proportion to what we have earned and saved,/ In gratitude we now joyfully give./ Amen.

A basket may be passed or people may come forward to give, accompanied by joyful music, if possible, to demonstrate that it is indeed more blessed to give than receive. Be sure to handle finances transparently and ethically.

Eucharist

If your tradition and convictions allow you to do so, you may use or adapt the words below to celebrate the Eucharist. Many faith communities require an authorised person to preside in the blessing or consecration of bread and wine. In that case, you may invite that authorised person to join your group and serve in this way. Some traditions allow for previously consecrated bread and wine to be brought to the homebound, prisoners, and so on. A representative from your group may be able to arrange for your group to receive in this way.

For the first few weeks of a gathering, these words may be shared on paper or digitally, or, better, the leader can coach people in the responses. After even a few weeks, the responses are easy enough that they will flow from memory.

The Living God is with us!
And with all creation!
Lift up your hearts!
We lift them to the Living God.
Let us give thanks to the Creator of all.
It is right to give our thanks and praise.
It is right, and a good and joyful thing, always and everywhere to give thanks to you, Living God, who loves us with the faithful care of a father and mother. For this reason, we join with all creation to proclaim your glory:

Holy, Holy, Holy One, God of power, God of love.
Earth, sea and sky are full of your glory.
With joy we praise you! With joy we praise you! Amen!

We praise you and we bless you, holy and gracious Creator, source of life. Your Spirit has always been with creation, guiding its development, calling forth life, infusing beauty, inspiring joy and love. In your infinite love you created us in your image and allowed us to share in the precious gift of life. You gave us a home in this beautiful world to live in harmony with you, with one another, and with all your creatures.

But we have so often turned from your love and wisdom. We have chosen our own way and broken faith with you, our neighbours and our fellow creatures. Now all around us we see the tragic harvest of the bitter seed we have sown.

Yet through it all, you have remained faithful to us. You graciously called us to turn from our destructive ways and return to you. You sent us prophets, priests, sages, storytellers and poets to lead us to repentance and wisdom. In the fullness of time, through Mary, a humble woman full of faith, you sent Jesus into the world.

Living among us, Jesus loved us. In word and deed, he proclaimed the good news of your reign. He broke bread with outcasts and sinners, and in imitation of your perfect love, he taught us to love neighbour, stranger, outsider and enemy. He redirected us from violence to peace, from fear to faith, from rivalry to mutual service, and from worry and greed to generosity and joy. He taught us to pray:

A version of the Lord's Prayer may be said or sung here. For groups unfamiliar with the version that is being used, it can be read by the leader and echoed by the group line by line. Eventually it can be spoken by heart.

The following version of the prayer can be chanted to a scale of five ascending and descending notes (see www.brianmclaren. net for a sample):

1. O God, whose love makes us one family,
2. May your unspeakable name be revered.
3. Now, here on earth, may your commonwealth come,
4. On earth as in heaven, may your dreams come true.

5. Give us today our bread for today.

4. Forgive us our wrongs as we forgive.

3. Lead us away from the perilous trial.

2. Liberate us from the evil.

1. For the kingdom is yours and yours alone.

2. The power is yours and yours alone.

3. The glory is yours and yours alone.

4. Now and for ever, amen.

5. Alleluia . . . 4. Alleluia . . . 3. Alleluia . . . 2. Alleluia . . . 1. Amen.

On the night before he showed us the full extent of his love, Jesus took a loaf of bread, gave thanks, broke it, gave it to his friends and said, 'Take, eat. This is my body which is given for you. Do this in remembrance of me.' As supper was ending, he took a cup of wine. Again he gave thanks and gave it to his friends, saying, 'Drink from this, all of you, for this is my blood of the New Covenant, which is poured out for you and for many for the forgiveness of sins. Whenever you drink this cup, remember me.'

Now, gathered as one family around this table of joyful reconciliation and fellowship, united in your Spirit, we receive these gifts and we gratefully offer you our lives as a living sacrifice. As Christ stretched out his arms upon the cross to welcome the whole world into your gracious embrace, we rejoice to enter that embrace and with you, extend it to all. Through Christ and with Christ and in Christ, in the unity of the Holy Spirit, to the living God be honour, glory and praise, for ever and ever. Amen.

The group should decide in advance how the Eucharist will be observed. If the group is small, the elements can easily be shared around a table. In larger groups, people can come forward and be served. Intinction (where the bread is dipped into the wine) is often advisable for larger groups. Those serving others can say words like these:

The body of Christ, broken for you. *Amen* (or *Hallelujah*, or *Thanks be to God*, etc.).

The cup of liberation, poured out for you. *Amen* (or *Hallelujah*, or *Thanks be to God*, etc.).

Or these:

Take this bread in remembrance of Christ's great love for you, and for all.

Drink this cup in remembrance of Christ's great love for you, and for all.

When everyone has participated, the leader may close with words like these:

As Christ's body and blood were separated on the cross, so now they have been rejoined in us. Let us, then, by faith, now arise, filled with the Spirit, to be the embodiment of Christ in our world.

[Or:] As we have been fed around God's table of grace, let us go forth in grace and hospitality to others.

Some people may be prohibited by conscience or tradition from including the Eucharist in their gathering. In that case, the following words may be used at some point during a shared meal – not as a formal Eucharist, but as a spontaneous 'toast to Jesus and the kingdom* of God'.

One: Let us celebrate Jesus and the kingdom* of God: we lift our bread in memory of Jesus.

All: *To Jesus and the kingdom* of God.*

(A moment of reverent silence is observed before and after eating.)

One: We lift our glasses in honour of Jesus.

All: *To Jesus and the kingdom* of God.*

(A moment of reverent silence is observed before and after drinking.)

One: Amen.

(*Amen, Hallelujah*, or other joyful expressions follow.)

*You may substitute *commonwealth*, *reign*, *dream* or another suitable word for *kingdom*.

Benediction

There are many ways to conclude the gathering. The Lord's Prayer may be recited, if it hasn't been already. A special theme song may be sung, such as the doxology, an amen or hallelujah, or a benediction song. Each member of the group may be asked to share a single word that describes their response to the time together, or a single sentence of gratitude to God or the group. An individual could recite a benediction (see www.brianmclaren. net for links), or your group could compose its own benediction to learn and say by heart in unison as a special way of concluding your time together. The following can be spoken by a leader and echoed by all:

We are a circle/ Of learners and seekers/ Alive in God's story of creation.

We are disciples/ Who follow our leader/ Alive in the adventure of Jesus.

We are uprising/ In a new way of living/ Transformed by the Spirit of God.

Let us go forth in joy and peace/ To love and serve God and our neighbours./ Amen.

Five Guidelines for Learning Circles

A learning circle that gathers to use *We Make the Road by Walking* is on a quest for spiritual formation, reorientation and activation. We aren't seeking to impress each other, to convince each other to agree with us, or to fix each other. We desire everyone to gain deeper understanding from and with one another, and to practise gracious ways of relating to one another. To keep our space safe and open for deeper understanding and growth to occur, we will observe these five guidelines:

1. *The guideline of participation*: Our goal is for all to share and all to learn, so all should feel encouraged but not pressured to participate. Before and after you have made a contribution, welcome others to contribute by listening from the heart with uncommon interest and kindness. In so doing, you will 'listen one another into free speech'. Avoid dominating, and gently seek to draw out those who may be less confident than you. Be sure to express appreciation when others share honestly and from the heart.

2. *The guideline of honour*: We honour one another for having the courage to share honestly and from the heart. It is important to

express your own views freely without insulting the views of others. Advising, silencing, fixing, upstaging, correcting or interrupting others often leaves them feeling dishonoured, so these responses are not appropriate among the learners in this circle. Often, using 'I' language helps in this regard – for example, 'I see that differently' instead of 'You are wrong'. Trust that a safe, honouring environment will make space for their 'inner teacher', God's Spirit, to guide others better than you can.

3. *The guideline of silence*: Silence is an important part of every good conversation. Don't rush to fill silence. Expect that important insights will arise through silence. Often, right after a silence has become a little uncomfortable, it becomes generative and holy.

4. *The guideline of understanding*: Each question or prompt is designed to promote something more important than agreement or argument: understanding – of ourselves and one another. So see differing views as a gift and an opportunity for greater understanding, not argument. Our full acceptance of one another does not infer full agreement with every opinion that is expressed. Assured of mutual honour, in the presence of differing views, we will all experience greater understanding.

5. *The guideline of brevity*: It's important to feel free to think out loud and speak at some length at times. But in general, err on the side of being too brief and having people ask to hear more, rather than on the side of taking more than your share of the group's time.

Each participant should verbally agree to these guidelines, or another set of guidelines the group prefers. Leaders can help the learning circle address problems as they arise, always keeping the goals of spiritual formation, reorientation and activation in mind.